Called to Community

Called to Community

The Life Jesus Wants for His People

Compiled and edited by Charles E. Moore
Foreword by Stanley Hauerwas

Plough

Published by Plough Publishing House
Walden, New York
Robertsbridge, England
Elsmore, Australia
www.plough.com

Plough produces books, a quarterly magazine, and Plough.com to encourage people and help them put their faith into action. We believe Jesus can transform the world and that his teachings and example apply to all aspects of life. At the same time, we seek common ground with all people regardless of their creed.

Plough is the publishing house of the Bruderhof, an international Christian community. The Bruderhof is a fellowship of families and singles practicing radical discipleship in the spirit of the first church in Jerusalem (Acts 2 and 4). Members devote their entire lives to serving God, one another, and their neighbors, renouncing private property and sharing everything. To learn more about the Bruderhof's faith, history, and daily life, see Bruderhof.com. (Views expressed by Plough authors are their own and do not necessarily reflect the position of the Bruderhof.)

ISBN: 978-0-63608-093-2

27 26 25 24   7 8 9 10

Front cover image © plainpicture/whatapicture. Image on cover flaps and pages 1 and 149 courtesy of unsplash. Image on spine courtesy of Brigitte Bouquet. Image on page 69 courtesy of Jill/flickr. Image on page 271 courtesy of Sisqu Tena Juncosa/flickr. Image on page 325 courtesy of Chris Blakeley/creative commons.

A catalog record for this book is available from the British Library.
Library of Congress Cataloging-in-Publication Data

Names: Moore, Charles E., 1956- editor. | Hauerwas, Stanley, 1940- writer of foreword.
Title: Called to community : the life Jesus wants for his people / compiled and edited by Charles E. Moore ; foreword by Stanley Hauerwas.
Description: Second edition. | Walden, New York : Plough Publishing House, 2024. | Summary: "Fifty-two readings on living in intentional Christian community to spark group discussion"-- Provided by publisher.
Identifiers: LCCN 2023035430 (print) | LCCN 2023035431 (ebook) | ISBN 9781636080932 (paperback) | ISBN 9781636080864 (epub)
Subjects: LCSH: Communities--Religious aspects--Christianity.
Classification: LCC BV4517.5 .C35 2024 (print) | LCC BV4517.5 (ebook) | DDC 248.4--dc23/eng/20230829
LC record available at https://lccn.loc.gov/2023035430
LC ebook record available at https://lccn.loc.gov/2023035431

Printed in the United States of America

Life in community is no less than a necessity for us – it is an inescapable "must" that determines everything we do and think. Yet it is not our good intentions or efforts that have been decisive in our choosing this way of life. Rather, we have been overwhelmed by a certainty – a certainty that has its origin and power in the Source of everything that exists.

EBERHARD ARNOLD, Why We Live in Community

CONTENTS

PART IV

Beyond the Community

Stanley Hauerwas

COMMUNITY IS DANGEROUS. This is easy to forget at a time when we often hear calls for more community. Of course, it's quite understandable that many people today feel the need for it. After all, we live in a social order that has confused freedom with the isolation of the self. We may think we know one another, but our "knowing" only intensifies our isolation from one another. This is because, although we bump up against one another, we share no common story and no corresponding judgments about what is true, good, and beautiful. As a result, we become strangers to ourselves and to those we call friends. In such a social order, people too often confuse community with being a crowd. And crowds are intrinsically dangerous.

We live in a time when people think they should have no story other than the story they chose for themselves when they had no story. The story they chose is, they think, the story of freedom. The only problem with this belief is that none of us actually did choose this particular story. As a result, lives lived according to this false story are subject to self-deception and self-hate. Lives so constituted are often quite destructive for any attempt to sustain community life across time.

I began observing that the loneliness created by such an understanding of freedom and autonomy produces a hunger that can be dangerous – and hunger is the right word, indicating as it does the physical character of the desire and need to touch another human being. That is why Alasdair MacIntyre, the great moral philosopher, resists being called a communitarian. MacIntyre resists calls for community because he fears that in this place and time such calls are bound to lead to nationalistic movements. Those who hunger for community should never forget Nuremberg. I share MacIntyre's worry that the label "communitarian" does little to help us understand what kind of community we ought to desire.

All the more, how fortunate we are to have this book! This is not a book that celebrates community as an end in itself. It is written by veterans of community living who know full well the pathologies of community life. I suspect these reflections will make many readers question their assumption that they are called to community. The stark realism of these essays makes clear that when we are dealing with people we must be ready to confront one another with truths about ourselves that we seldom want to acknowledge.

But interestingly enough, the very fact that such confrontation is required is why we cannot live without community. Therefore this book is a treasure of wisdom gained by those who have discovered the necessity of community for our being human.

I can only hope that it will be widely read, because I am certain that contained in this book is the future of being Christian. ◆

Charles E. Moore

H OW WOULD YOU go about destroying community, isolating people from one another and from
a life shared with others? Almost forty years ago
Howard Snyder asked this question and offered the following
strategies: fragment family life, move people away from the
neighborhoods where they grew up, set people farther apart by
giving them bigger houses and yards, and separate the places
people work from where they live.[1] In other words, "partition
off people's lives into as many worlds as possible." To facilitate
the process, get everyone their own car. Replace meaningful
communication with television. And finally, cut down on
family size and fill people's homes with things instead. The
result? A post-familial, disconnected culture where self is king,
relationships are thin, and individuals fend for themselves.

On the whole, this destruction of community has only been
compounded by the advance of digital technology. As Sherry
Turkle observes in her book *Alone Together,* the web's promise
of "bottomless abundance" has left millions inwardly and
relationally famished. We live, Turkle suggests, in a "culture

of simulation," where real, tactile, face-to-face relationships of loyalty and intimacy are all but a memory. Ours is truly an age of isolation, with relationships that may be free but also very shallow and fleeting.[2]

In a culture of connectivity, where we have countless people to text and tweet, millions are under the illusion that a networked life is a rich, meaningful life. But community is more than connectivity. Although it is easier than ever to communicate and stay in touch with one another, we are fast losing the ability to commune with one another. We know how to text, but we don't know how to converse. We exchange vast amounts of information, but find it increasingly difficult to confide in one another. We no longer know how, or think we don't have the time, to give each other our full attention. Though we may not be alone in our virtual worlds, we remain lonely. Our lives lack cohesion: we live in pieces, in fragments, lacking any overall pattern or any steady, identifiable community in which to belong.[3]

Social commentator Michael Frost suggests that our culture has become like an airport departure lounge, "full of people who don't belong where they currently find themselves and whose interactions with others are fleeting, perfunctory, and trivial."[4] Nobody belongs there, nobody is truly present, and nobody wants to be there. We're tourists who graze from one experience to another, nibbling here and sampling there, but with very little commitment to bind us to one another. We exist in an untethered "nowhereness," under the illusion that we are free. And yet, as Robert Wuthnow observes, "community is sputtering to an undignified halt, leaving many people stranded and alone."[5]

The disappearance of community has led to a plethora of human and social problems, which have been exposed and explored in countless books. The question this collection of readings seeks to answer is what we can do about it. Many social commentators have addressed the problem and continue to grapple with it. New structures of belonging have been proposed, many of which hold promise. But as good and viable as these may be, the main thrust behind this book is that the answer lies in the hands of God's people. We need more than new structures. We need spirit-filled ways of living that are capable of combatting the corrosive ideologies of our age that undermine community. Only when the church lives out its original calling, as a contrast community and foretaste of God's coming reign, is there hope for the world. And there is hope. The Bible assures us that through faith in Jesus and by God's spirit a new kind of social existence is possible. Christ has defeated the principalities and powers that keep people apart. In him relationships can be healed and transformed. This is what being the church is all about.

Although many people bemoan the fact that society is so fragmented, a small but growing number of people are daring to step away from the status quo and follow the beat of a different drummer. Committed followers of Christ from every corner of society and from all walks of life are responding to Christ's call to embody an integrated spirituality that encompasses the whole of life and is lived out with others. New intentional communities are emerging that bear witness to Christ's healing power. A radical renaissance is unfolding among disenchanted Christians who are no longer satisfied with either Sunday religion or social activism. These Christians want to actually be the church, to follow Christ *together* and demonstrate in their daily lives the radical, transforming love of God. Of course, in a world in which family life is undermined and faithfulness and loyalty are old-fashioned concepts, living in community will not be easy. The broader culture rarely reinforces values such as fidelity, the common good, and social solidarity. It's everyone out for themselves. We're on our own, whether we like it or not. And yet for growing numbers of Christians this world, with its dominant philosophy of expressive individualism, is not the final adjudicator of what is or is not possible, let alone desirable. The world Christ was born into was also splintered and confused; it was violent, factious, morally corrupt, spiritually bankrupt, full of tensions, and teeming with competing interests. Yet, into this world a brand new social order erupted. It caught everybody's attention, and eventually transformed the entire Roman pagan system.

Throughout the history of the church, movements of renewal have arisen. In each instance, the church's spiritual and corporate life was revitalized. The question before us today is this: Are we ready and eager for a new work of the Spirit in which everything, including our lifestyles and church structures, is turned upside down? If so, this book can help. It is intended to encourage and strengthen the current movement of the Spirit in which people are consciously pledging themselves to live out their faith with others on a radically new basis. Part I presents a vision of community, supplying a theological and biblical ground on which to be God's people together. Many people seek out community to ameliorate such problems as loneliness, economic injustice, racial division, and environmental destruction. This is good, and yet we must step back and first grasp what God's plan is for his people and the way in which we are to build, in the words of Clarence Jordan, a demonstration plot for God's kingdom. Part II tackles the question of what community means and what it takes to nurture it. Forming community is not just a matter of living close to one another. Prisoners do that. Rather, community demands personal sacrifice and personal transformation.

The ideal of togetherness is one thing; becoming a vibrant, united circle of comrades that remain together is another. Part III covers some of the nitty-gritty issues of life in community. New communities of faith often fall to pieces simply because they are not able to navigate the mundane matters of human coexistence. We need to unlearn certain ways of being before we can go the long haul with others. Finally, Part IV addresses the need for every community to see beyond itself. Community is not an end in itself. An inward-looking community will eventually implode. Christ gathered his disciples together to serve a purpose larger than themselves, to pioneer God's coming reign in which all things will be reconciled.

The selections in this volume are, by and large, written by practitioners – people who have lived in community and who have discovered what it takes to fruitfully live a common life with others. The writings of Eberhard Arnold, Dietrich Bonhoeffer, and Henri Nouwen are especially notable. Books such as Arnold's *Why We Live in Community,* Bonhoeffer's *Life Together,* and Nouwen's *Community* should be read in their entirety. Yet there are countless other voices that have wisdom and insight to offer. This collection brings many of these diverse voices together to address some of the most essential issues of community life.

You may be reading this book on your own. However, it is best read and discussed together with others. There is little point in reading a book such as this unless it actually helps you to build community. Whether you have just begun thinking about communal living, have already embarked on this journey, or have been part of an intentional community for many years, the selections in this collection are meant to encourage, challenge, and strengthen you to follow the call to live as brothers and sisters in Christ. Growing together and keeping a community alive takes time and effort. That's why the book has been divided into fifty-two chapters, so you can read one chapter a week and then meet together to discuss what you've read.

It has been said that true community is all or nothing, and that communities which try to get there by degrees just get stuck. This may be true. And yet, much like a healthy marriage, it takes time and wisdom to build a community. It also takes very little to break and destroy a community. Perhaps this is one of the reasons why so few people dare to commit themselves to building a common life. As Henri Nouwen writes, fearful distance is awful, but fearful closeness, if not properly navigated, can turn into a nightmare.[6]

Thomas Merton once noted that living alone does not necessarily isolate people, and that merely living together does not necessarily bring us into communion with one another.[7] So what is the key to communing with one another? Hopefully the selections in this book will help to answer this question. In the meantime, community as Christ intended it demands, if nothing else, a commitment to care for one another right where we are – to be our brother's and sister's keeper despite the limitations of our circumstances. Without simple deeds of love, community is not possible.

Dr. Paul Brand, who devoted himself to eliminating leprosy, was once working alone in an attic when he came across some boxes of skeletons that had been dug up from a monastery. He remembered a lecture he heard given by anthropologist Margaret Mead, who spent much of her life researching prehistoric peoples. She asked her audience, "What is the earliest sign of civilization? A clay pot? Iron? Tools? Agriculture?" No, she claimed, it was a healed leg bone. Brand recalls:

> She explained that such healings were never found in the remains of competitive, savage societies. There, clues of violence abounded: temples pierced by arrows, skulls crushed by clubs. But the healed femur showed that someone must have cared for the injured person – hunted on his behalf, brought him food, and served him at personal sacrifice. Savage societies could not afford such pity. I found similar evidence of healing in the bones from the churchyard. I later learned that an order of monks had worked among the victims: their concern came to light five hundred years later in the thin lines of healing where infected bone had cracked apart or eroded and then grown back together.[8]

Community is all about helping each other – caring enough to invest oneself in the "thin lines of healing." There is no other way to have community. The apostle Paul wrote, "The only thing that counts is faith expressing itself through love" (Gal. 5:6). Words and ideas, forms and structures can take us only so far. In the end, it's a matter of whether we will lay down our lives for one another. For Christ's followers, this is not just a matter of obedience but the distinguishing mark of our witness. Jesus says, "A new command I give you: Love one another. As I have loved you, so you must love one another. By this everyone will know that you are my disciples, if you love one another" (John 13:34–35). ✦

1 Howard A. Snyder, *Liberating the Church: The Ecology of Church and Kingdom* (Downers Grove, IL: InterVarsity Press, 1983), 113–114.

2 Sherry Turkle, *Alone Together: Why We Expect More from Technology and Less from Each Other* (New York: Basic Books, 2011), 6–12.

3 Robert N. Bellah, *Habits of the Heart: Individualism and Commitment in American Life* (New York: Harper and Row, 1985), 177.

4 Michael Frost, *Incarnate: The Body of Christ in an Age of Disengagement* (Downers Grove, IL: IVP Books, 2014), 16.

5 Robert Wuthnow, *Sharing the Journey: Support Groups and America's New Quest for Community* (New York: Simon and Shuster, 1994), 5.

6 Henri J. M. Nouwen, *Lifesigns: Intimacy, Fecundity, and Ecstasy in Christian Perspective* (New York: Doubleday, 2013), 19.

7 Thomas Merton, *New Seeds of Contemplation* (New York: New Directions Books, 1972), 55.

8 Paul Brand and Philip Yancey, *Fearfully and Wonderfully Made* (Grand Rapids, MI: Zondervan, 1980), 68.

PART I

• • • • •

A Call to Community

Everywhere the world is going to pieces. It is crumbling and rotting away. It is going through a process of disintegration. It is dying. And in these fearsome times, through the Holy Spirit Christ places the city-church with its unconditional unity right into the world. The only help for the world is to have a place of gathering, to have people whose will, undivided and free of doubt, is bent on gathering with others in unity.

EBERHARD ARNOLD, God's Revolution

I

The Great Idea

◆ ◆ ◆ ◆ ◆

Fyodor Dostoyevsky

H E H A D L O N G been an official in the town; he was
in a prominent position, respected by all, rich, and
had a reputation for benevolence. He subscribed
considerable sums to the almshouse and the orphan asylum;
he was very charitable, too, in secret, a fact which only became
known after his death. He was a man of about fifty, almost
stern in appearance and not much given to conversation. He
had been married about ten years and his wife, who was still
young, had borne him three children. Well, I was sitting alone
in my room the following evening, when my door suddenly
opened and this gentleman walked in. . . .

And from that time forth he came to see me nearly every
evening. And we should have become greater friends, if only
he had ever talked of himself. But about himself he scarcely
ever said a word, yet continually asked me about myself. In
spite of that I became very fond of him and spoke with perfect

frankness to him about all my feelings; "for," thought I, "what need have I to know his secrets, since I can see without that that he is a good man. Moreover, though he is such a serious man and my senior, he comes to see a youngster like me and treats me as his equal." And I learned a great deal that was profitable from him, for he was a man of lofty mind.

"That life is heaven," he said to me suddenly, "that I have long been thinking about"; and all at once he added, "I think of nothing else indeed." He looked at me and smiled. "I am more convinced of it than you are; I will tell you later why."

I listened to him and thought that he evidently wanted to tell me something.

"Heaven," he went on, "lies hidden within all of us – here it lies hidden in me now, and if I will it, it will be revealed to me tomorrow and for all time."

I looked at him; he was speaking with great emotion and gazing mysteriously at me, as if he were questioning me.

"And that we are all responsible to all for all, apart from our own sins – you were quite right in thinking that, and it is wonderful how you could comprehend it in all its significance at once. And in very truth, so soon as people understand that, the kingdom of heaven will be for them not a dream, but a living reality."

"And when," I cried out to him bitterly, "when will that come to pass? And will it ever come to pass? Is not it simply a dream of ours?"

"What then, you don't believe it," he said. "You preach it and don't believe it yourself. Believe me, this dream, as you call it, will come to pass without doubt; it will come, but not now, for every process has its law. It's a spiritual, psychological process. To transform the world, to recreate it afresh, people must turn into another path psychologically. Until you have become really, in actual fact, a brother to everyone, brotherhood will not come to pass. No sort of scientific teaching, no kind of common interest, will ever teach people to share property and privileges with equal consideration for all. Everyone will think his share too small and they will be always envying, complaining, and attacking one another. You ask when it will come to pass; it will come to pass, but first we have to go through the period of isolation."

"What do you mean by isolation?" I asked him.

"Why, the isolation that prevails everywhere, above all in our age – it has not fully developed, it has not reached its limit yet. For everyone strives to keep his individuality as apart as possible, wishes to secure the greatest possible fullness of life for himself; but meantime all his efforts result not in attaining fullness of life but self-destruction, for instead of self-realization he ends by arriving at complete solitude. All mankind in our age have split up into units; they all keep apart, each in his own groove; each one holds aloof, hides himself and hides what he has, from the rest, and he ends by being repelled by others and repelling them. He heaps up riches by himself and thinks, 'How strong I am now and how secure,' and in his madness he does not understand that the more he heaps up, the more he sinks into self-destructive impotence. For he is accustomed to rely upon himself alone and to cut himself off from the whole; he has trained himself not to believe in the help of others, in people and in humanity, and only trembles for fear he should lose his money and the privileges that he has won for himself. Everywhere in these days people have, in their mockery, ceased to understand that the true security is to be found in social solidarity rather than in isolated individual effort. But this terrible individualism must inevitably have an end, and all will suddenly understand how unnaturally they are separated from one another. It will be the spirit of the time, and people will marvel that they have sat so long in darkness without seeing the light. And then the sign of the Son of Man will be seen in the heavens. . . . But, until then, we must keep the banner flying. Sometimes even if he has to do it alone, and his conduct seems to be crazy, a man must set an example, and so draw people's souls out of their solitude, and spur them to some act of brotherly love, that the great idea may not die." ◆

2

Blessed Community

◆ ◆ ◆ ◆ ◆

Rufus Jones

RELIGION, which is as immemorial as smiling and weeping, does not begin with a Saint Stylites alone on the top of a pillar. If it had so begun the saint would soon have perished without a sympathetic community to see him – or, what is more important, to admire him. It is foolish for us to waste any precious time trying to settle the issue whether religion originates with the individual or the group. It is as absurd as trying to find a stick which has only one end. Individual and group cannot be cut apart and be treated as though either were real as a sundered existence.

The moment an individual has arrived on the scene with a capacity for the mystical, that is, the direct personal apprehension of God and capacity to interpret his experience, there is bound to be behind this individual the long molding processes of history, the accumulations of the experiences and transmissions of many generations. If the given individual runs on

ahead of the group, as a prophet-genius does, it will be along
the lines and in the direction for which the group has long
been preparing the line of march. And the individual does not
possess his insight with a permanent assurance until he has
interpreted it and carried others along with this conviction.
In short, however important the creative insight of the rare
soul may be, religion does not count as a contribution to the
race until a beloved community is formed and the discovery is
interpreted and transmuted into a social movement. As far as
its significance is concerned, religion is essentially social. It is
an affair of a beloved community. . . .

The primary function of a church, if it is to be the continuing
body of Christ in the world, is to raise human life out of its
secular drift and to give reality to the eternal here in the midst
of time. When it ceases to bear witness to the real presence of
an eternal reality operating in and upon our lives, its race is
run; it has missed its mission. But just as certainly the church
is commissioned as the organ of the Spirit to bring health and
healing to our human lives and to the social order in which our
lives are formed and molded.

It may be true, as the higher critics tell us, that the kingdom
of God as presented in the Gospels is not a new social order to
be slowly, painfully, and creatively realized here in the furrows
of our world through the cooperation of God and humankind
together. On the other hand, there is most assuredly a type of
life presented in the Gospels which, when it appears, seems
to be already the kingdom of God – a type of life in which
love is the supreme spring and motive, in which the spirit of
forgiveness has come to ripeness, and which aims to do the will
of God on earth as it is done in heaven. Insofar as the church
carries on and incarnates that commission it becomes the

sower of the seeds of the kingdom of God and the bearer of a
new order for human society.

There is a proverb which says that God empties the nest
not by breaking the eggs, but by hatching them. Not by the
violent method of revolution will the new social order of life
come, not by the legal enforcement of ancient commands, or
by the formal application of texts and sayings, but by the vital
infusion of a new spirit, the propagation of a passion of love
like Christ's, the continuation through the church of the real
presence of eternity in the midst of time, will something come
more like the order of life which we call the kingdom of God.
It is the role of the church, I maintain, to be the fellow laborer
with God for this harvest of life. . . .

Christ calls us to . . . [live] as an organic part of a kingdom, a
fellowship, which expresses in invisible and temporal fashion,
in ever-growing and unfolding degrees, the will of God – the
heart and purpose and spirit of the divine life. Here in this
kingdom God's life differentiates itself and pours itself through
finite lives as the sap of the vine pours itself out into all the
branches and twigs and shoots which go together to make the
vine a vine. It is the vast Yggdrasil tree of a spiritual humanity.
The kingdom, even in its imperfect stage as we now see it – still
a good deal of a mustard seed – is the most impressive revelation of God there is in the world today. It is the only way that
the will and life and love of God can be fully revealed. In this
emergent group life, where love comes more fully into play
than it does anywhere else, we catch some gleams of the Great
Life that works through us now and some prophecies of that
kingdom which shall be when all people see what a few see now.

Life culminates in forms of organism, in which the whole is
always greater than the sum of the parts. The kingdom of God

is the highest form of such organism that has yet emerged – a
corpus spirituale, a "blessed community" – a living whole
in which part contributes to part, and all the parts unitedly
cooperate to express the life of the whole. Each member is both
end and means, an end in itself and a means to the fulfillment
of the life and purpose of the whole. We are as far removed
here as we can be from a scheme of life which focuses upon
rewards or which aims to secure an excess of pleasures over
pains. In fact, we have transcended categories of calculation
and even of causation and have entered into that organic way
of life where each lives for all and where the interpretation of
the life of the whole is the business and, at the same time, the
joy of each member. The formation of such a kingdom, life in
such a kingdom, is the fundamental end of life for Christ, as
set forth in the Gospels. The length of his purpose horizontally
is the inclusion of all people in such a cooperative community
and the height of it upward is the raising of all people to a full
consciousness of sonship with God, in a family-fellowship,
living to do his will. Here, once more, the emphasis of Christ is
on life and action, not on theory and definition. The kingdom
of God is something we *do* – not a place to which we go. . . .

We are forever seeking to find ourselves, but our sporadic
quests lead us off on trails that end in some cul-de-sac, or,
as Emerson would say, "up a tree in a squirrel hole." Our
subordinate ends bring and have always brought frustration,
disillusionment, and defeat. Let us once find the real end
for which our nature is equipped and we can live thrillingly
and triumphantly. That real end, according to Christ of the
Gospels, is the kingdom of God, a spiritual organism, a
fellowship of persons, bound together in cooperative love and
forming in union with God the tissue and web of the spiritual
world – the eternal universe. To this end were we born and for

this cause we came into the world, that we might bear witness to this reality and that we might reveal its laws, its principles, and its serene and demonstrative power. ◆

Style of Life

◆ ◆ ◆ ◆ ◆

Christoph Friedrich Blumhardt

FOR THOSE who keep their eyes on God's kingdom, it is not only in the future – it is already coming into being in the present. And it is present, for this faith is today shaping a community of men and women, a society in which people strengthen each other toward this goal. Without such a society, how is faith possible? The kingdom of God must be foreshadowed in a human society. The apostle Paul calls this society the body of Christ, of which Christ is the head (1 Cor. 12:12–27). Peter calls it a building, where each stone fits the next so that the building becomes complete (1 Pet. 2:4–12). Jesus calls it his little flock, where all love one another, where each answers for the others and all answer for the one. As such, we are fighters for the future, through whom the earth must become bright. We know what we believe; therefore we testify to it, and live it out. In this way God's kingdom comes into the present, just as it shall be in the future.

In order to form such a society in Christ there must be people who are resolute and free from anxiety. Right from the beginning, when the apostles began to preach, Christians sought this freedom from worry. But do not misunderstand this. You can't just say to your neighbor, "Don't worry!" When a person lives utterly alone and nobody is concerned about him, when other people kick him around or want nothing to do with him, when a person is excluded from everything that lends dignity to life, when there is nothing for him to do but earn his bread with much worry, toil, and burden, then it is a sin to say to him, "Don't worry!"

Today it is coldly said of millions, "They shouldn't worry. If they would only work, they would earn their wages." Those who talk like this pass right by such folks without caring a jot for them. The majority of working people still do not have jobs worthy of a human being. They live scattered and isolated lives. What a misery it is to have to beg, or to work two jobs. Yet how many people have to do it! What an unworthy existence it is for people who want to meet their obligations and be respected, but who cannot pay their taxes or their bills or are unable to serve society in any meaningful way. How can I say to such a person, "Don't worry"? What coldness of heart!

At present the whole world, including the wealthiest of nations, lies deep in worries and cares. But within the society and organism that proceeds from Christ, worries can and should cease. There we should care for one another. When the apostle Paul says, "Do not worry," he takes it for granted that these are people who are united by a bond of solidarity so that no one says anymore, "This is mine," but all say, "Our solidarity, our bond, must take away our worries. All that we share together must help each one of us and so rid us of anxiety." In this way the kingdom of heaven comes. First it comes in a small flock free from anxiety. Thus Jesus teaches: "I tell you, do not worry about your life, what you will eat or drink; or about your body, what you will wear. . . . But seek first God's kingdom and his righteousness, and all these things will be given to you as well" (Matt. 6:25–34). From the beginning, ever since Christ was born, people have sought such a society, a fellowship of the kingdom, free from cares and worries. There is an enormous strength when people stand together, when they unite in a communal way. The idea of private property falls away, and they are so bound together in the Spirit that each one says, "What I have belongs to the others, and if I should ever be in need, they will help me" (2 Cor. 8:13–15). This firm and absolute solidarity in a shared life where each is responsible for the other is the kind of life in which you can indeed say, "Don't worry!"

Time and again, people have attempted to live together in this way. Yet it has never come fully into being. And this is the reason why Christianity has become so weak. To be sure, people throughout the ages have known that this building up of a social order in which one need not worry anymore was originally Christ's will. Christ told us not to seek after riches or the honors of this world. He said this precisely because he took it for granted that his united people would always have the necessary means for life. He told his followers that their oneness in love, their lifestyle of sharing, would provide them with sufficient food and clothing.

Again and again people have thought that this is the way society should be. But because it does not fully come about, they give it up eventually and settle for charity, where those who have offer something to those who have not out of a charitable urge. This is the way it has always been. Many people find ways, with their extra means, to help the poor here and there. Yet this is not what Jesus Christ wants. Just the opposite! What worries are caused by the many charitable institutions of our day! Millions of people continue to worry how they can get a little here and a little there. Often they are turned away by charity itself. Does this surprise you? Do not be taken aback when the philanthropists of this world fail to give help. Charity is not the way; it still holds back what is essentially needed. Therefore we must join together. A united company of Jesus must come about.

How will this happen? We have lost the feeling for it. One reason why Christ's followers did not remain organically bound together, as at Pentecost, is that they wanted to draw in too many foreign elements. The members wanted to convert the whole world before they themselves were fully converted. It is simply not possible to gather hundreds of thousands of people into common fellowship before the members themselves are ready for this. This is especially so if you draw in people who are materialistic, envious, unfree, and unwilling to go the whole way. It would be better if they remained outside and had the cares of the world. They are not yet fit to be co-fighters.

Freedom of the heart must be there first, a freedom from all the worldly pleasures that might attract us. Then we can shed all worries. How much people are able to do once they are freed from all cares and do not worry about their daily bread! It does not take much, only that people are so bound together that they know, "When I get into need, the others will be there." But if I say, "I will save enough for myself so that I will never have to depend on others," then this is the ruin of any Christian community. It is a mockery of Christ's body.

For this reason I do not think much of "spiritual communities." They do not last. People are friends for a while, but it eventually ends. Anything that is going to last must have a much deeper foundation than some kind of spiritual experience. Unless we have community in the flesh, in things material, we will never have it in spiritual matters (1 John 3:16–18). We are not mere spirits. We are human beings of flesh and blood. Every day we need to eat. We need clothing for every season. We must share our tools; we must work together; we must work communally and not each for himself. Otherwise we can never become one in the love of Christ, can never become the flock, the community of Jesus that stands up in the world and says, "Now things must become quite different. Now the individual must stop living for himself. Now a society of brothers and sisters must arise."

This is the way Jesus calls us to set aside our worries. Yet we Christians somehow expect people to have faith in the most impossible of situations, in conditions where they nearly perish in need and misery, where they exist in wretched hovels, hardly knowing how to keep the wolf from the door. And we come along and call out to them, "Simply believe!" To shout into this kind of distress, "Believe! Then everything will be added unto you – heaven awaits you!" is a demand that simply cannot be carried out (James 2:14–18). No, the kingdom of God must not be only a kingdom of the future. In Christ's church community we should strive to become united, and begin to become free in such a way that, at least in the circles where we love one another, cares cease. ◆

4

Embodiment

◆ ◆ ◆ ◆ ◆

Gerhard Lohfink

ONE OF THE FUNDAMENTAL PROBLEMS of the church is that faith no longer saturates the whole of life, but only a narrow sector. Out of an entire week we often have no more than sixty minutes on Sunday for "faith." Our employment has long since become a world in itself with its own rule and ways of behaving. It has scarcely anything to do with Christian existence. All the efforts of Christian societies and church efforts toward a "lay apostolate" have not changed this. In the same way leisure time has also become a world unto itself, as have education, the economy, culture, and all the other spheres of life. Faith is drying up. It no longer has any material that it can transform. It has become unworldly and therefore ineffectual.

For many Christians it would not be a turning point in their lives if they decided, one day, to stop praying tomorrow, to leave off going to church next Sunday, and at the next opportunity to stop the church magazine. Their lives would continue according to the very same social rules, norms, styles of behavior, and models as before. Nothing would change because, long before that, their faith already would have become unworldly, inconsequential, and ultimately futile. It was, in fact, not faith at all. Where faith is really faith it cannot be shoved to the margins of life.

Christian faith, just like Jewish faith, subjects *all* of life to the promise and claim of God. Its nature is such that it inter-penetrates all aspects of the lives of believers and gives them a new form. Of itself it demands that social relationships must change and that the material of the world must be molded. Faith desires to incorporate all things so that a "new creation" can come to be.

At the same time faith tends toward a more and more inten-sive communion among believers, for only in the community, the place of this communion, only in the place of salvation given by God can the material of the world really be molded and social relationships really transformed. It would there-fore be essential to Christian faith that individual believers should not live alongside one another in isolation but should be joined into a single body. It would be essential that they weave together all their gifts and opportunities, that in their gatherings they judge their entire lives in light of the coming of the reign of God and allow themselves to be gifted with the unanimity of *agapē*. Then the community would become the place where the messianic signs that are promised to the people of God could shine forth and become effective.

All this is part of the tendency of faith to embodiment. Christian faith of itself produces an impulse to bind believers in communion and by way of that communion to draw all spheres of life into God's new creation. This integrating tendency is a property of faith itself. It is not something added secondarily at some time or place. An individual cannot first begin to believe alone and then, afterward, join the church community. Accepting faith already means desiring the communion of believers. Accordingly, the transformation of world and society is not an obligation that is added to faith as something secondary. Instead, where faith is a living thing, it transforms the world from the very outset.

The communion of believers thus is not something that is merely spiritual and intellectual. It must be embodied. It needs a place, a realm in which it can take shape. Perhaps we must read again, with new eyes, how often Paul's letters and the Acts of the Apostles speak of "houses." It is amazing how many houses are known to us by name simply in connection with the apostolic work and journeys of Paul: the house of Lydia the seller of purple cloth in Philippi (Acts 16:14–15, 40), the house of Jason in Thessalonica (Acts 17:5–7), those of Titius Justus and Gaius in Corinth (Acts 18:7; Rom. 16:23), the house of the evangelist Philip in Caesarea (Acts 21:8–14), and the house of Mnason of Cyprus in Jerusalem (Acts 21:15–17).

In these and many other houses of the early Christian era unfolded a crucial piece of the life of the first Christian communities. The *natural* family, which constituted the central focus of the several houses, was opened and joined into a broader context: the *new* family of the community. In these houses catechumens were instructed, journeying brothers and sisters in the faith were welcomed as guests, the community gathered for its meetings and the celebration of the Lord's Supper, unemployed Christians found work, and for the most part the first contacts were made with Gentiles who wanted to become acquainted with a Christian community. When they did so they did not learn merely a set of abstract principles of faith, but Christian life.

In this context we should also consider the following: the ancient house cannot simply be compared to modern houses; the function of the latter is almost exclusively to furnish a mere dwelling place. In contrast, in antiquity and for a long time thereafter the house was a larger social unit. It contained not only the family in the narrow sense but also other people who lived and worked there. Frequently the house was also a place of production. Larger production facilities separate from the house were rarely found. This meant that in Christian houses like that of Aquila and Priscilla faith and life, or faith and work, constituted a unity. Priscilla's family saw how Paul worked with his hands, and those to whom Paul preached the gospel in connection with his artisanal work at the same time experienced a Christian family.

Something else must be added: the houses in which Paul dwelt were often those belonging to the first converts in a given city. This was true of Lydia's house in Philippi and that of Jason in Thessalonica, and probably also of Gaius's house in Corinth. It was precisely in the houses of the first converts, then, that the community usually gathered. In that way those houses embodied a bit of living community history that was made present in every assembly – not only in the rooms themselves, but in the people as well. . . .

We would love to have much more detailed information about the lives of those early communities, but our sources for the most part offer us little. Nevertheless, we know enough that we are in no danger of glorifying the community life of those times. Above all, Paul's two letters to the Corinthians show us a community in which there was uncertainty, arrogance, slanted theology, and serious social conflicts. It would have been no different in other places.

What distinguishes those communities is not their moral integrity or the power of their faith, still less their unanimity. Nevertheless, Paul calls them "the saints" in the introductions to his letters, "the called," "God's beloved," "sanctified in Christ Jesus," the *"ekklēsia* of God." He thus expresses the conviction that what is crucial is not the mistakes that are made; there will always be those. Theological foolishness is also not decisive; there will never be a lack of that. Not even sin and guilt are the most important things, however dreadful they often are; they can be forgiven.

What is decisive, after all, what everything depends on, is that the community knows that God has called it to make the divine plan visible and to be a place of reconciliation in the world as the body of Christ. It is already that body, anterior to any of its own efforts. The spirit of God promised for the end time, the spirit of Jesus Christ, has already been given to it and has made it one body. Nevertheless it must know that its task is still to become that body. ◆

5

Brothers, Sisters

◆ ◆ ◆ ◆ ◆

Hal Miller

THE CHURCH IS NEVER defined in the New
Testament. Rather, it is pictured by dozens and
dozens of metaphors. One author counts ninety-six
different ones, but there are probably even more than that. . . .

Many renewal movements have focused on the metaphor of
the body. . . . [They] have come to rely on the body metaphor
for a number of reasons. One is that they are, more or less
consciously, returning to the New Testament for nourishment.
And in the New Testament, the body metaphor is obvious.
Paul, for example, has spun out the body metaphor at greater
length than any other. He is more specific than Jesus and
certainly develops this idea more fully than the little snatches
of other imagery we get here and there.

The body metaphor also pictures the church as having a
variety of interdependent roles. As renewal movements have
moved away from a one-dimensional concentration on the

pastor or priest as the sole actor in the church, the body metaphor has been very helpful. . . .

Other images, however, can rise to fill the need. Though
renewal movements have tended to concentrate on the body,
the family is the New Testament's single most common
metaphor for the believers in Jesus. For the New Testament
writers, family imagery falls effortlessly from their minds onto
paper. They call each other "brother" and "sister"; we enter the
kingdom of God by a "new birth" and are "children of God";
Paul claims to be "once again in childbirth" with the Galatian
Christians; he tells the Corinthians "they have many teachers
but not many fathers." Again and again, New Testament
writers assume they are a family with other Christians and act
on the basis of that vision.

Consider some of the ways the family metaphor may help us
where the body metaphor either lets us down or distorts our
vision. Although there may be many more than these – and
other applications are (as engineering books say) left as an
exercise for the reader – four stand out.

First, the way a body is one and many is different from the
way a family is one and many. The uniqueness of individuals,
for instance, is much more strongly portrayed in a body than
in a family. The eye is not an arm and so (obviously) cannot
have the same function. But, though a brother is not a sister, in
the family, the role distinctions blur: anyone can do the dishes
or carry out the garbage. Old family acquaintances say to me,
"Oh yes, you're Ray Miller's boy." They might have said the
same about either of my brothers, for, seen in the family, our
roles were not all that distinct.

In an age of independence and struggle for identity, it is
no wonder we have latched onto the body metaphor with its

strong affirmation of the indispensability of each part. But I wonder whether we have not played that particular melody enough. Perhaps it's time to hear the counterpoint: we are all children of the same God, and we share that relationship in common. Maybe that's all the identity I need: to be the Creator's boy instead of emphatically a particular, unique individual. Renewing the family metaphor can help us come to terms with the things we all share in common, which are just as important as the things which make us each unique.

Second, although differences in a body are cast in terms of role and function, in a family, differences are primarily in terms of maturity. Children listen to mothers and fathers not (in the first place) because parents have a different abstract role but because they are more mature, wiser, and better able to cope with the unpredictability of life; children trust their parents. The body metaphor has as its goal to get people involved in doing what is uniquely theirs to do; the family metaphor teaches them how to do it. In a family, the older members are often better able to do the things that the younger members also do, and the younger members look to the older for guidance and models of living. Understanding the church as family will mean that the younger members will learn to take their cues from those who are older and wiser.

Similarly, the body focuses more on accomplishing tasks, but the family more on day-to-day existence. Thinking about the church as family makes a person's specific gifts less relevant. It doesn't matter what your gifts are; the fact is we need someone to take out the garbage, and here you are. The same thing is true of relationships. In a family, it doesn't matter what another person's gifts are; we are loving them or putting up with them or nourishing them because we are part of the same family, not because they have a particular gift.

This brings out a third significant difference between the body image and the family image: the church as body is oriented toward tasks while the church as family expresses and nurtures our need for community. American culture has almost entirely fragmented the extended family. As a result, we experience a deep longing for the things the extended family used to provide: a network of close relationships outside the immediate, the stimulation of others who are different and yet closely related, a sense of security in having options beyond the immediate ones (just in case things don't quite work out).

The church as family can be a way of incarnating an answer to these longings. Perhaps the reason Paul and others did not spin out the family metaphor is that it seemed so obvious to them. Because they experienced extended households as a fact of life, it was easy to see how church repeated that pattern. As children in a family learn most (for good and ill) by imitating, so new Christians learn not what their gifts are but how to exercise them, discovering what they are in the process. Children imitate the way you eat, the way you deal with others, and the things you deem important. What we mean by Christian growth is largely just this process, a process which in the church as family is a spontaneous, not a programmed, one.

Church as family also points to both the tragedy and the fallacy of one of the important decisions of Christian life for us: finding the right church. Seeing church as family doesn't even acknowledge that there is such a decision. Being in a given family isn't a matter of choice at all; you just end up there. The family to which you belong gives you both your possibilities and limitations. It gives you people with whom you must deal. People in a family are not necessarily friends, they may not go bowling with each other, and they may not even particularly like each other. But they are still family.

In fact, of course, we do have a choice about church, which seeing church as family can obscure. Nonetheless, the family metaphor can help us see that we should not constantly be looking for the "perfect church" any more than we should for the perfect family. . . .

The vision of the church as a body has been very important for Christians to catch hold of. We shouldn't ignore the insights it gives, but enrich them with the insights that envisioning the church as family can give us. It can show us how we touch the world. It can teach us about Christian nurture. It can show us the dynamic way in which new groups of believers form and gain integrity. . . .

But the need is not met merely by saying, "Yes, family is a good metaphor for church," and leaving it at that. Rather, we need to look into that metaphor and bring out its implications just as Paul did with the body metaphor. We might even be surprised at some of the things which come out. ◆

Joseph H. Hellerman

JESUS' EARLY FOLLOWERS were convinced that the group comes first – that I as an individual will become all God wants me to be only when I begin to view my goals, desires, and relational needs as secondary to what God is doing through his people, the local church. The group, not the individual, took priority in a believer's life in the early church. And this perspective (social scientists refer to it as "strong group") was hardly unique to Christianity. Strong-group values defined the broader social landscape of the ancient world and characterized the lives of Jews, Christians, and pagans alike. . . .

Early Christian communities, moreover, represented a specific kind of strong-group entity. Historians have struggled for generations to situate early Christianity in its social world. Were churches like Jewish synagogues or Greco-Roman voluntary associations or what? As it turns out, the social model that best accounts for the relational expectations reflected in our New Testament epistles is the Mediterranean family. Most of us are familiar with the surrogate kinship language (brother, sister, Father, child, inheritance) that permeates the New Testament. Family remained the dominant metaphor for Christian social organization in the writings of the church fathers, as well. . . .

Stories of the ancient church living out its family values appear throughout early Christian literature. For example, sometime around AD 250, a marvelous thing happened in a small church in the rural town of Thena, just outside the Roman metropolis of Carthage in North Africa: An actor converted to Christ. We do not know his name, but let's refer to him as Marcus. Marcus's conversion created a stir in the church in Thena.

Theater performances in antiquity were typically dedicated to a pagan god or goddess, and the plays often ran as part of larger public religious festivals. Scenes portraying blatant immorality were commonplace. All this proved rather troubling to the early church. Christian leaders, such as Tertullian, spoke out in opposition to the idea of believers going to the theater:

> Why is it right to look on what it is disgraceful to do? How is it that the things which defile a man in going out of his mouth, are not regarded as doing so when they go in at his eyes and ears – when eyes and ears are the immediate attendants of the spirit? You have the theater forbidden, then, in the forbidding of immodesty.

Thus, when an actor converted to Christ in third-century Carthage, the church demanded that he quit his profession.

Marcus did just that. Our new convert now faced an economic dilemma, however, since he was no longer gainfully employed. So, instead of acting, Marcus opened an acting school. This apparently created quite a stir among Marcus's fellow Christians, and the surviving letters exchanged by his pastor and the church's bishop paint a portrait of the church truly living out its strong-group family values.

Marcus's pastor, Eucratius, naturally wondered how it could be acceptable for Marcus to teach others what he himself was forbidden to do. Yet Marcus had already made a tremendous sacrifice to follow Jesus. So Eucratius wrote to his spiritual mentor, Cyprian of Carthage, to ask "whether such a man ought to remain in communion with us."

Cyprian's reaction to Marcus was unequivocal: "It is not in keeping with the reverence due to the majesty of God and with the observance of the gospel teachings for the honor and respect of the church to be polluted by contamination at once so degraded and so scandalous."

No compromise. No drama teaching. Marcus must either leave the church or quit his job – again.

Marcus's story has the "strong-group" aspect of the strong-group, surrogate family written all over it. It is Cyprian's conviction that "the honor and respect of the church" must take priority over Marcus and his acting academy. Marcus, on his part, finds himself answering to the church for his whole vocational and financial future.

Cyprian's handling of Marcus's dilemma grates harshly against modern social sensibilities, since we tend to prioritize the needs and goals of the individual over the viability of any group to which he or she belongs. But for all his hard-nosed strong-group convictions, Cyprian is not unaware of the suffering Marcus will face. As Cyprian's comments clearly demonstrate, the intense emphasis on personal holiness that characterized the North African church had a beautiful complement: a genuine concern for those whose livelihoods might be adversely affected by assenting to the church's demanding moral standards. In short, Cyprian tells Pastor Eucratius that the church should provide for Marcus's material needs:

> His needs can be alleviated along with those of others who are supported by the provisions of the church. . . . Accordingly, you should do your utmost to call him away from this depraved and shameful profession to the way of innocence and to the hope of his true life; let him be satisfied with the nourishment provided by the church, more sparing to be sure but salutary.

And if this is not enough, Cyprian concludes by telling Eucratius that Cyprian's church will foot the bill if the rural church in Thena lacks the resources to meet Marcus's basic needs:

But if your church is unable to meet the cost of maintaining those in need, he can transfer himself to us and receive here what is necessary for him in the way of food and clothing.

Cyprian made sure that the church would serve as the economic safety net for any brother or sister whose finances were adversely affected by their willingness to follow Jesus. Why? Because the church was family, and this is what families in the ancient world did.

The conviction that church members should meet one another's material needs is, of course, central to the New Testament understanding of church family life: "How does God's love abide in anyone who has the world's goods and sees a brother or sister in need and yet refuses help?" (1 John 3:17).

Can we recapture in our churches the biblical vision for authentic Christian community as reflected in the strong-group, surrogate family model that characterized the early church? ◆

6

Pentecost

◆ ◆ ◆ ◆ ◆

C. Norman Kraus

PENTECOST AS IT IS REPORTED in Acts is the climax of the three-act drama of incarnation. Act one presents various scenes in the ministry of Jesus. Act two is the Passion of the Christ. Act three is the triumphant advance of the victorious Lord. At Pentecost "the promise of the Father" was fulfilled (Luke 24:49; Acts 1:4). The ministry, death, and resurrection were not the completion of the promise. That is why Jesus told his followers to wait in Jerusalem. Jerusalem was the point of departure for the triumphant mission – "beginning at Jerusalem" – and they were to "sit tight" until the promise had become full reality (Luke 24:47–49). It was not simply a matter of their receiving an individual spiritual capability for service and witness to what Christ had finished. No, they were not to begin their mission because the Father had not yet completed the formation of the new body through which the Christ would continue and expand his presence and ministry.

The drama of incarnation does not conclude with a final act that neatly wraps up the loose ends of the story and draws the curtain. Rather it ends with an open future for those involved. Pentecost is a commencement in the same sense that we use the word to describe a graduation. It is simultaneously climax and beginning. It concludes with the assurance that this is not the end but the beginning. Christ is not dead or absent in some far-off spiritual realm. The kingdom he announced is not set aside to some future millennium but enters a new era of fulfillment. His ministry is not concluded but universalized through his new body. Surely this is part of the good news! . . .

Luke makes clear what he understood to be of central importance in the account. He does this both by the language he uses and by the way he constructs the account. His summaries in 2:42–47 and 4:32–37 highlight preceding developments and act as a bridge to the next sections of the story. These summaries indicate clearly what Luke thought had really happened. Further, just as there are parallelisms between the birth, life, and ministry of Jesus (Luke) and the church (Acts) so there are in both accounts fairly obvious allusions and parallelism with the story of the exodus and formation of Israel into a people of God. Both of these literary devices indicate the same answer to our question. *What really happened at Pentecost was the forming of the new covenant community of the Spirit.* Let us look more closely at the significance of these characteristics of Luke's account.

The teaching that the church was born at Pentecost is, of course, not new. Nor is the idea of continuity as well as discontinuity with Israel new, although this has been a matter of dispute within evangelicalism. What has not been sufficiently recognized is that the new thing that happened on Pentecost is *the new community*. It is this parallelism with the formation of Israel from a "mixed multitude" into a "people" that Luke's many allusions to Exodus seem to underscore.

The immediate manifestations of the Spirit's presence were fire, wind, and speaking in other tongues. All three have a rich and varied symbolic use in the Old Testament and other Jewish literature. No doubt Luke consciously alludes to this tradition. To make exodus symbolism primary is not to rule out all other possible allusions, but rather to highlight the fundamental significance in his account.

As the Israelites left Egypt the special presence of the Lord leading his people was manifested in the "pillar of fire" (Exod. 13:21–22; 14:24). Now the presence appears again and disperses itself, resting on each one in the representative new Israel (Acts 2:3). The mysterious "violent wind" which dried up the waters of the Red Sea (Exod. 14:21) and whipped in the faces of the Israelites as they crossed to Sinai now again filled the house with a roar and is fully identified as God's Spirit. The play on words in the original language of the Bible makes this more obvious. Both *ruach* (Hebrew) and *pneuma* (Greek) have the double meaning of wind and spirit. . . .

The symbolism of speaking and hearing in different dialects is also multifaceted. It most likely alludes to the confusion of languages at Babel (Gen. 11:7–9). The Spirit's presence reverses Babel, and as Saint Paul said, in Christ there are no "barbarians," that is, those of uncouth languages (Col. 3:11). It also indicates the universality of the salvation message and therefore the mission and nature of the new people being formed. The connection with Exodus and Sinai is not so apparent until we learn that there was a Jewish tradition that the Mosaic Law had been given in seventy languages simultaneously, indicating the universal scope of its authority. Luke's account of the new covenant's being announced in many languages may well be a parallel to this Jewish tradition. . . .

In his sermon at Pentecost, Peter explained all this as the fulfillment of Joel's prophecy. Jesus, the true Messiah, has sealed the new covenant in his death. Now, risen and victorious, he is forming his new people. Just as the Israelites were "baptized in the sea" (1 Cor. 10:2), marking decisively their separation from their old family identity in Egypt, so Peter called upon his audience to be baptized and to save themselves from the old "crooked generation." Just as Israel received their new identity as the people of God at Sinai through *the gift of the law,* so the new people is constituted through *the gift of the Spirit.* And just as great signs accompanied Israel's deliverance and formation into a covenant nation, so "signs and wonders done through the apostles" accompanied the birth of the new community of the Spirit. . . .

On the day of Pentecost, to be saved meant to join the messianic community. On that day, baptism in the name of Jesus Christ was a public act of acknowledging that Jesus was truly the Messiah, the rightful leader of God's people, and a declaration of allegiance to him by *throwing in one's lot* with the original apostolic band. To be as explicit as possible let me perhaps overstate the point. It was not a matter of "receiving Jesus into their hearts" and then being urged to find a church (voluntary society) of their choice for fellowship. It was not a matter of an inner experience of justification or even of conversion that made them members of the spiritual or invisible body of Christ to be followed by baptism and "joining the church."

It was not a matter of "saving their souls" and then gathering them into conventicles or visible religious societies.

Within the new group defined by allegiance to Jesus Christ they received the Holy Spirit, for it was the victorious Messiah and Lord of the new community who was giving the Spirit (Acts 2:33). The Spirit of the ascended Christ now became the Spirit of his new body. Peter's promise that following repentance and baptism they would receive the gift of the Holy Spirit (2:38) was not the promise of a "second experience" but the announcement that it is within the community of the Spirit that the new reality is to be found. ✦

7

Christian Communism

• • • • •

Ulrich Stadler

THERE IS ONE communion of all the faithful in Christ and one community of the holy children called by God. They have one Father in heaven, one Lord Christ; all are baptized and sealed in their hearts with one Spirit. They have one mind, opinion, heart, and soul as having all drunk from the same fountain, and alike await one and the same struggle, cross, trial, and, at length, one and the same hope in glory. . . . In this community everything must proceed equally, all things be one and communal, alike in the bodily gifts of their Father in heaven, which he daily gives to be used by his own according to his will. For how does it make sense that all who have here in this pilgrimage to look forward to an inheritance in the kingdom of their Father should not be satisfied with their bodily goods and gifts? . . . Therefore, they also live with one another where the Lord assigns a place to them, peaceably, united, lovingly, amicably, and fraternally,

as children of one Father. In their pilgrimage they should be
satisfied with the bodily goods and gifts of their Father, since
they should also be altogether as one body and members one
toward another.

Now, if then, each member withholds assistance from the
other, the whole thing must go to pieces. The eyes won't see,
the hands won't take hold. Where, however, each member
extends assistance equally to the whole body, it is built up and
grows and there is peace and unity, yea, each member takes
care for the other. . . . In brief, *one, common* builds the Lord's
house and is pure; but *mine, thine, his, own* divides the Lord's
house and is impure. Therefore, where there is ownership and
one has it, and it is his, and one does not wish to be one with
Christ and his own in living and dying, he is outside of Christ
and his communion and has thus no Father in heaven. . . .

But the wickedness of men has spoiled everything. For as
the sun with its shining is common to all, so also the use of
all temporal things. Whoever appropriates them for himself
and encloses them is a thief and steals what is not his. For
everything has been created free in common. Of such thieves
the whole world is full. May God guard his own for them. To
be sure, according to human law, one says: that is mine, but not
according to divine law. ◆

José P. Miranda

"ALL THE BELIEVERS together had everything in common; they sold their possessions and their goods, and distributed among all in accordance with each one's needs" (Acts 2:44–45). "The heart of the multitude of believers was one and their soul was one, and not a single one said anything of what he had was his, but all things were common. . . . There was no poor person among them, since whoever possessed fields or houses sold them, bore the proceeds of the sale and placed them at the feet of the apostles; and a distribution was made to each one in accordance with his needs" (Acts 4:32, 34–35).

Anticommunist commentators allege that this is Luke's personal point of view, and that the other New Testament writers fail to corroborate it. . . . We shall see that the hypothesis is false, for Jesus himself was a communist. But let us place ourselves hypothetically in the worst possible position: that only Luke teaches communism. With what right, indeed with what elemental logic, is it thereupon asserted that communism is incompatible with Christianity? . . . If at least the Lucan part of the New Testament teaches communism, how is it possible to maintain that communism is at odds with Christianity?

Let us suppose (not concede) that there are parts of the New Testament which lend footing to the projection of social systems different from Luke's. Well and good. That some

Christians today may prefer these other parts of the Bible to Luke's is their affair. But with what right do they deny the name Christian to what the Lucan part of the Bible teaches emphatically and repeatedly? The origin of the communist idea in the history of the West is the New Testament, not Jamblicus or Plato. . . .

A second anticommunist allegation against the texts we have cited from Luke is that the communism of the first Christians failed. It is flabbergasting that sermons, documents of the magisterium, books, and bourgeois public opinion should brook the notion that this is an argument. The Sermon on the Mount failed too, but this does not deprive it of its normative character. . . . What should concern us is to find out why it broke down, and bring communism to realization without committing whatever error caused the first Christians to break down. This would be the logical conclusion if our objectors had the flimsiest desire to be guided by the Bible. But what our objectors have done is make an antecedent and irreformable decision to disagree with the Bible, and to this purpose they bring forward every pretext, even if it tramples upon the most elemental logic.

To cite that initial failure is pure pretext. It is as if we told ourselves we were eliminating the Ten Commandments because they failed in history. . . .

The third objection runs as follows: the communism of the first Christians was optional, as can be seen from Peter's words to Ananias, "Was it not still yours if you kept it, and once you sold it was it not yours to dispose of?" (Acts 5:4). . . .

According to Luke, what is optional is not communism, but Christianity. Peter does not tell Ananias that he could have come into the Christian community without renouncing the private ownership of his goods. Nor could he say such a thing after it was explicitly emphasized that of the Christians "*not a single one* said anything was his.*"* Ananias lied to the Holy Spirit by pretending to become a Christian via a simulated renunciation.

The objection belongs to the type of reader who thinks a work can be understood without understanding the thought of the author. Luke would have to have been a very slow-witted writer if he claimed to assert, in the Ananias episode (5:1–11), the optional character of communism, when four verses earlier he has insisted that "*whoever* possessed fields or houses sold them," and so on, and two verses above that, "and *not a single one* said anything was his," and still earlier, "*all the faithful* together had everything in common." This is the Luke who had recorded these words from the lips of Jesus: "Every one of you who does not renounce all he has cannot be my disciple" (Luke 14:33). . . .

Let it be well noted that this last verse cited is concerned with the simple fact of being disciples of Christ, and not of some "special vocation" or other. See the beginning of the passage: "Many crowds accompanied him, and he, turning, said to them . . . " (Luke 14:25). He is not addressing the Twelve, but the crowd. It is a simple matter of the conditions for being a Christian, exactly as in the texts we cited in Acts. What is optional is to be a Christian, to be a disciple of Christ. ◆

40

Helmut Gollwitzer

W E S H O U L D N O T in the very least weaken Luke's text. The commentaries of some New Testament scholars make the meaning quite clear, while others try to smooth it away. They say, for instance: It turned out very badly for the first church in Jerusalem, what they did there. The hasty distribution of the little bit of property they had eventually resulted in their having nothing at all. Then among all the Christians of that time they were called "the poor of Jerusalem," and a collection had to be made for their support.

All right, Luke might have said, perhaps in their enthusiasm they did not do it very cleverly. Then you do it better, more effectively. Think out a communism in which one does not become poor but through which all people are really helped! Enthusiasm must also include some common sense.

Other commentaries say, and probably we too: Yes, that was a voluntary communism, a communism of love, not a horrible communism of force like we saw in the Soviet Bloc!

Quite right, says Luke, so show me your free-willingness. Where is your communism of love? Perhaps it has come to this forced communism because the hungry people have waited in vain for two thousand years for the Christians' communism of love!

Others argue along a different set of lines, claiming that it is not the abolition of private property that concerns Luke but rather an inner freedom from possessions.

True, Luke might say, they may have retained title deeds over the disposal of their property, as the historians claim. But what belonged to them they put at the disposal of the church with the one goal, as it says here, that none among them went short. So keep the titles to your private property, but come along with what belongs to you, with the one goal – that no one among us suffers need! . . .

What, then, is the result of taking seriously Luke's nice, edifying account of this time of first love? The whole thing is beyond us, people say. It may have been possible in their small circles at that time, first in Jerusalem, then in Corinth and Philippi, that no one was in need. That was a shining sign of the resurrection, and others pointed to it and said, "See how they love one another; no one suffers need among them!" But today, when we can't help seeing the millionfold need of humankind, it is no longer possible.

This can only mean one thing: becoming a Christian today is beyond us. Tasks come in from all sides and we see our feeble strength and vanishing means, our egotism and the fetters of private property, and don't know how to go on. We can understand why today many Christians suggest one should understand the gospel altogether differently, that one should not apply it to social relationships, but only to community with God and the consolation of the forgiveness of sins.

Oh, yes! The consolation of the forgiveness of sins is very important, especially when we notice in such an account that our sins consist not only of personal thoughts and deeds in opposition to God, but also our involvement in the public sins of this order of death. This terrible social order, which in reality is a disorder, has had from the very beginning the slogan, "That belongs to me!" The possessors defend their possessions against those who have less or nothing at all.

Here we are ensnared, and none of us can get out because we have to take care of ourselves, our families, and our old age. How can we escape this appalling, sinful social order? When we think about this, how can we still laugh and enjoy our gardens? How can we drink our coffee at breakfast when we know that it is offered to us at a reasonable price through the infamous policies of our governments, at the expense of the hungry in coffee-producing countries? In such blind alleys, the consolation of the forgiveness of sins is certainly necessary. But forgiveness of sins can never mean, "Carry on just as before." The same goes for the individual sins for which we need forgiveness – the promise of forgiveness is always at the same time both comfort and thorn. This thorn says: demand freedom, try freedom, at least begin to seek freedom, simply refuse to cooperate! This thorn, this thorny question, asks: What can we do so that everything does not simply go on as before? This thorny question sinks right into our hearts through Luke's report. . . .

"They had all things in common, and distribution was made to each as any had need, and there was not a needy person among them." The praising of God and the sharing of possessions, the Lord's Supper and the common table, the vertical and the horizontal – a complete life – is present in the true resurrection church. And the horizontal is the manifestation of what happens, concealed, in the vertical. The horizontal – our relationship with others – is the test of the genuineness of the vertical – our relationship with God.

It is all one freedom: the freedom of rejoicing in God, our freedom toward other people, and the freedom never to say, "That belongs to me." We have been promised such freedom, which is the answer to our longing for a fellowship in which "ours" belongs to everyone, no one suffers need, and we are there for the others in a meaningful life.

Therefore we pray, Lord, lead us into this real, practical life of resurrection. Break the fetters and make us free for a new life! ◆

8

A Visible Reality

◆ ◆ ◆ ◆ ◆

Dietrich Bonhoeffer

A TRUTH, A DOCTRINE, or a religion needs no space for itself. They are disembodied entities. They are heard, learned, and apprehended, and that is all. But the incarnate Son of God needs not only ears or hearts, but living people who will follow him. That is why he called his disciples into a literal, bodily following, and thus made his fellowship with them a visible reality. That fellowship was founded and sustained by Jesus Christ, the incarnate Lord himself. It was the Word made flesh which had called them and created their bodily fellowship with him. Having been called, they could no longer remain in obscurity, for they were the light that must shine, the city set on the hill, which must be seen.

Their fellowship with him was visibly overshadowed by the cross and passion of Jesus Christ. In order that they might enjoy that fellowship with him, the disciples must leave everything else behind and submit to suffering and persecution.

Yet even in the midst of their persecutions they receive back
all they had lost in visible form – brothers, sisters, fields, and
houses in his fellowship, the church consisting of Christ's
followers manifest to the whole world as a visible community.
Here were bodies that acted, worked, and suffered in fellowship with Jesus. . . .

The fellowship between Jesus and his disciples covered every
aspect of their daily life. Within the fellowship of Christ's
disciples the life of each individual was part of the life of the
brotherhood. This common life bears living testimony to the
concrete humanity of the Son of God. The bodily presence
of God demands that for him and with him we should stake
our own lives in our daily existence. With all the concreteness
of our bodily existence, we belong to him who for our sake
took upon himself the human body. In the Christian life the
individual disciple and the body of Jesus belong inseparably
together.

All this is confirmed in the earliest record of the life of the
church in the Acts of the Apostles (Acts 2:42–47; 4:32–37).
"They continued steadfastly in the apostles' teaching and
fellowship, in the breaking of bread and the prayers." "They
that believed were of one heart and soul and . . . had all
things in common." It is instructive to note that fellowship is
mentioned between Word and Sacrament. This is no accident,
for fellowship always springs from the Word and finds its goal
and completion in the Lord's Supper. The whole common
life of the Christian fellowship oscillates between Word and
Sacrament, it begins and ends in worship. It looks forward in
expectation to the final banquet in the kingdom of God.

When a community has such a source and goal it is a
perfect communion of fellowship, in which even material

goods fall into their appointed place. In freedom, joy, and the power of the Holy Spirit a pattern of common life is produced where "neither was there among them any that lacked," where "distribution was made unto each according as anyone had need," where "not one of them said that aught of the things which he possessed was his own." In the everyday quality of these events we see a perfect picture of that evangelical liberty where there is no need of compulsion. They were indeed "of one heart and soul." . . .

The first disciples learned the truth of the saying that where their Lord is, there they must also be, and where they are, there also will their Lord be until the world comes to an end. Everything the disciple does is part of the common life of the church of which he is a member. That is why the law, which governs the life of the body of Christ, is that where one member is, there the whole body is also. There is no department of life in which the member may withdraw from the body nor should he desire so to withdraw.

Wherever we are, whatever we do, everything happens "in the body," in the church, "in Christ." The Christian is strong or weak "in Christ" (Phil. 4:13; 2 Cor. 13:4), he works and rejoices "in the Lord" (Rom. 16:9, 12; 1 Cor. 15:58; Phil. 4:4), he speaks and admonishes "in Christ" (2 Cor. 2:17; Phil. 2:1), he shows hospitality "in Christ" (Rom. 16:2), he marries "in the Lord" (1 Cor. 7:39), he is in prison "in the Lord" (Phil. 1:13, 23), he is a slave "in the Lord" (1 Cor. 7:22). Among Christians the whole range of human relationships is embraced by Christ and the church. . . . When people are baptized into the body of Christ not only is their personal status as regards salvation changed, but so are the relationships of daily life.

The slave Onesimus had run away from his Christian master, Philemon, after grievously wronging him. Now Onesimus has been baptized, and Saint Paul writes to ask Philemon to receive him back again forever, "no longer as a servant, but more than a servant, a brother beloved . . . both in the flesh and in the Lord" (Philem. 8–21). "In the flesh" a brother, says Paul with emphasis, thus warning Philemon against those misunderstandings to which all "privileged" Christians are liable. Such Christians are prepared to tolerate the society of Christians of lower social standing in church, but outside they give them the cold shoulder.

Instead, Philemon must welcome Onesimus as a brother, nay, as if he were Paul himself, and since Onesimus is his brother, Philemon must not seek repayment for the damage he suffered at his hands. Paul asks Philemon to do this voluntarily, though if necessary he would not shrink from ordering him to do it outright, and says he knows that Philemon will exceed in kindness beyond what is asked of him. Onesimus is a brother in the flesh because he has been baptized. Whether he stays on as a slave or not, the whole relationship between master and slave has been radically changed.

And how had this come to pass? Master and slave are now both members of the body of Christ. Their common life is now a tiny cell in the body of Christ, the church. "As many of you as were baptized into Christ did put on Christ. There can be neither Jew nor Greek, there can be neither bond nor free, there can be no male nor female: for ye are all one man in Christ Jesus" (Gal. 3:27–28 ASV; cf. Col. 3:11). In the church, people look upon one another no longer as freemen or slaves, as men or women, but as members of Christ's body. To be sure, this does not mean that the slave is no longer a slave nor the man a man. But it does mean that in the church no one has to be considered in his special capacity, whether he be Jew or Greek, freeman or bondservant. Any such respect of persons must be excluded at all costs. . . . Wherever Christians live together, conversing and dealing with one another, there is the church, there they are in Christ. This is what transforms the whole character of their fellowship. The wife obeys her husband "in the Lord"; by serving his master the slave serves God, and the master knows that he too has a Lord in heaven (Col. 3:18–4:1), but they are all brethren "in the flesh and in the Lord."

This is how the church invades the life of the world and conquers territory for Christ. For whatever is "in Christ" has ceased to be subject to the world of sin and the law. No law of the world can interfere with this fellowship. The realm of Christian love is subject to Christ, not to the world. The church can never tolerate any limits set to the love and service of the brethren. For where the brother is, there is the body of Christ, and there is his church. And there we must also be. ◆

9

Counterculture

◆ ◆ ◆ ◆ ◆

Howard A. Snyder

J ESUS COULD HAVE LEFT a book of instructions or
set up an organization. He could have created a ready-
made system so that when the thousands of converts
appeared, the church would have known exactly what to do.

But Jesus worked at a more fundamental level. He gathered
a community of believers, working intensively with them so
that they would understand who he was and why he had come.
God, through Jesus Christ, had such confidence in the Twelve
that he left it to them and their fellow disciples to figure out
organizational questions. They could handle the problems as
they came up, guided by the Holy Spirit and following Jesus'
teaching and example. In the Book of Acts we see believers
using their own intelligence but guided by the Holy Spirit in
nurturing the growth of the church.

Here is a vital lesson about church life and structure, about
wine and wineskins. It is easy to look at Pentecost and see the

spirit but miss the structure. It is easy to be amazed at what was new but blind to what was old. At Pentecost the disciples clearly got a taste of new wine. But Jesus also provided the basis for new wineskins in the community he had formed – wineskins created not out of thin air but from patterns, customs, and understandings derived from centuries of God's acts in history. As he delights to do, the Ancient of Days did a new thing. Jesus drew on centuries, even millennia, of God's work in forming his new community – and then baptized the little group with his spirit at Pentecost.

And so the first disciples did what Jesus did. As Jesus had been with them in small groups, and as they had met together outdoors and in homes, so did the first Christians. The early church took shape primarily in the homes of the believers. Its life was nourished in homes in two ways. First, the church was built through normal family life, drawing on the strength of the family in that day. Second, it was fed through *koinonia* groups, cells of people who met together for prayer, worship, and the Eucharist and who passed on Jesus' teaching by example and word of mouth.

As the church developed and spread through the Roman world, its experience of community was complemented by the sense of being a distinct people. The Epistles reveal a strong countercultural consciousness in the early church, a consciousness that developed and deepened as the church spread across the empire. Initially Jewish Christians saw themselves simply as Jews who accepted the Messiah. But as the church grew and spread, it learned that God's plan was not just for the Jews. It was for the Gentiles, for all peoples, nations, and classes. The Book of Acts shows the gospel spreading beyond Jewish confines and the church beginning to develop a consciousness as a new people.

This consciousness dawned gradually; it didn't come all at once. Through the ministry of Peter, Paul, Barnabas, Philip, and others the church came to see that it was a new community and people. The Holy Spirit was poured out equally on Jew and Gentile (Acts 10:44–47; 11:15–18; 19:5–6). The believing community was not just a sub-community among the Jews but a new work of God in history. Christians began to think of themselves as a third race: neither Jew nor Gentile, but something new transcending both. They were the new Israel, the new people of God fulfilling Old Testament promises and expectations, but as a new social reality transcending the separate identities and allegiances of Jew and Gentile, slave and free, male and female. The church became not just a subculture within the dominant culture, but a new counter-culture, a contrast community in the Greco-Roman world. Christians were "neither Jew nor Greek, slave nor free, male nor female," but "all one in Christ Jesus" (Gal. 3:28; cf. 1 Cor. 12:13; Eph. 2:14; Col. 3:11). This was not merely spiritual renewal. It was social revolution. . . .

In his study of the Sermon on the Mount, *Christian Counter-Culture,* John Stott writes, "If the church realistically accepted [Jesus'] standards and values as here set forth, and lived by them, it would be the alternative society he always intended it to be, and would offer to the world an authentic Christian counterculture." Instead of doing this, the church throughout history has too often developed clever ways of explaining why Jesus didn't really mean what he said or why his teachings are not to be applied to the present time. Fortunately, there have been prophetic exceptions to this pattern of unfaithfulness.

As applied to the church, being a contrast community possesses both a positive and a negative aspect. Perhaps the negative side is more obvious: The church takes its stand *against* surrounding culture. The Christian community must be in some sense "other than" the world around it, maintaining fundamental points of antithesis.

On the positive side, the church offers a genuine alternative to the dominant culture. In fundamental ways, it claims to be not only other than but also better than the world's culture. In offering a clearly delineated, visible alternative, the church pushes society to self-examination, self-criticism, and very often self-defense. Hidden or only dimly perceived questions rise to the surface. In this way it has a significant social impact, good or bad. . . .

In what sense should the church be a contrast community? Is the fidelity of the church to the kingdom a matter of a counter-cultural existence? Or is this an unwholesome, negative way to picture the church's life?

The answer depends on the biblical image of the church. Does the Bible picture the church counterculturally? Five portions of Scripture help answer the question.

John 15:18–19 —*In the world, not of it.* This passage shows that Jesus' disciples must maintain a critical tension: *in* the world but not *of* it. Christians are neither to withdraw from the world nor to become one with it. Jesus said, "My kingdom is not of this world" (John 18:36), but he made it plain that it is *in* the world (Luke 17:21). Jesus plants us in a place of tension. We are to maintain that tension against the strong pull to a more comfortable position either out of the world or totally of the world. This is the tension of incarnation, and it requires the church to be in some sense contrary to the broader culture.

Romans 12:2 —*Conformed to Christ, not the world.* The church is to be a community of people who are conformed to the pattern of Jesus, not to the pattern of the world's culture. Is this merely another way of saying that we are to be in the world but not of it? Certainly Paul's statement here presupposes what Jesus said in John 15 and 17. But we find an added note: Jesus calls us to *be* conformed to himself, to be like him. Jesus' disciples are not of the world *just as* Jesus himself was not of the world (John 17:16). We are to be conformed to the image of God. We are "in all things" to "grow up into him who is the head, that is, Christ" (Eph. 4:15). So here conformity to Christ means nonconformity to the world's culture. The church is not only "other than" but "contrary to" the world.

Luke 12:29–32 —*The flock of the kingdom.* Here Jesus pictures his disciples as the flock of the kingdom, the kingdom community. What an amazing contrast of weakness and strength – a flock and a kingdom! You are a little flock, Jesus says, but in your very weakness and dependence on me you will inherit the kingdom of God, no less! (cf. 2 Cor. 12:9). The church pledges its allegiance to a sovereign different from that of the citizens of this world kingdom, the dominion of darkness. This goes beyond what has been said already, adding two more elements. First, the church's distinctness from the world is not merely a difference; it is warfare, a world struggle. A battle is raging between the kingdom of God and the powers of the enemy. Second, in this warfare the church must be faithful to its King and Lord. It must be faithful to the new covenant. As a covenant community, the church has pledged itself to live by the values of God's kingdom and to renounce the values of the world's culture. This is the basis for its concern with justice, truth, reconciliation, and God's new order.

John 17:18 —*Sent into the world.* Many scriptures teach that Christians are sent into the world as Christ's witnesses and ambassadors. In his prayer recorded in John 17 Jesus says, "As you sent me into the world, I have sent them into the world." We are sent to be witnesses and to make disciples in all nations. In other words, the church is to be engaged aggressively with the world in winning the allegiance of increasing numbers of people away from the world and to Jesus as Lord and King. Its task is to win people not just to the church but to the full kingdom and economy of God. This comes about through the regenerating work of the Holy Spirit in human lives. We are called to make disciples, not just converts, and disciples of the kingdom, not just of the church. The church is not merely to be in the world; it is to pursue the mission of God in the world. It is the agent of God's kingdom in bringing all things under the headship of Jesus Christ (Eph. 1:10).

Revelation 21:23–27 —*The glory of the nations.* We may not understand all this passage means, but one thing is strikingly clear. The holy city – the consummated kingdom of God – will include "the glory and honor of the nations." This suggests a positive evaluation of cultural diversity and of human cultural works. All that is good in human works – whatever is pure, lovely, true, honorable, and harmonious – will be brought into the city of God. Everything false, ugly, and distorted will be rejected. God will somehow gather all our cultural works, purify them, and use them in his kingdom. This means Christians themselves have a positive contribution to make to culture. The church can legitimately be engaged in cultural works that add beauty, harmony, and ecological health to the world. This also is kingdom work. When we speak of the priesthood of all believers and the ministry of all God's people, we must understand that kingdom ministry is not confined to religious things or church work. It includes all good work in the world that holds potential for glorifying God.

The danger of a countercultural model is that it may lead inward, away from worldly engagement. The antidote to this danger is a deep consciousness that the church exists for the kingdom. The notion of a contrast community is essentially negative, despite its positive possibilities. It is therefore an inadequate model by itself. But as part of the total picture of what it means to be the church in a hostile world, it is an important perspective. The church can be free for the kingdom only if it is sufficiently detached and distinct from the world's culture to maintain obedience for the kingdom.

The key fact, then, is the church as a *kingdom community*. In most cultural settings, a faithful church will be a contrast community. The more important point, however, is simply that the church be faithful to the kingdom, whatever this means for its position in society. . . . If the church poses no threat to the enemy, its allegiance to Jesus Christ is deeply suspect. We are, after all, involved not merely with a religious organization but with the *people* of God, the *community* of the Spirit, and the *kingdom* of Jesus Christ, our sovereign Lord. ◆

10

The Way

• • • • •

Alden Bass

THE HISTORY of committed Christian community is a story of roads. The first followers of Jesus called themselves "the Way," a name that echoes Jewish *halakha,* the "way of life" enshrined in the Torah, as well as the disciples' belief that Jesus was "the way" to God the Father.

The earliest community that formed in Jerusalem after Jesus' execution was composed of the original disciples and pilgrims who had traveled to Jerusalem to celebrate the holy days. United by the conviction that Jesus' resurrection was a sign of covenant renewal and the new creation, these Jews marched through the Red Sea of baptism into a radically new way of life, one in which all possessions were held in common, there were no needy persons, and all members were "of one heart and mind." The spirit of ancient Israel engulfed the Holy City, and for a brief period of time the utopian community of the Jubilee was reconstituted.

Eventually, war drove all the Christians and Jews from the land. Still, the traces of that original movement were so impressed in their memory that the disciples who fled Jerusalem continued to establish countercultural communities of economic sharing, scripture study, participatory worship, and service to the poor.

These first Christians wended the path pioneered by Jesus. They were not the only people to live intentionally; in the early centuries of the Common Era there were other fraternal associations of mutual aid, organized by profession, religious devotion, or simply voluntary adherence. Christian communities differed from them, as Tertullian observed in the third century, in their charity to the underserved (*Apology* 39.5–6). Groups of Christians organized themselves into economic communities called parishes, a word derived from the Greek *paroikia,* which meant "neighbor" but also "sojourner" or "pilgrim." So, just as "parish" is similar to "pariah" in English, the name would have reminded Christians they were outcasts and exiles in a foreign land.

Palestinian roads were treacherous, consisting of packed earthen pathways, usually narrow and winding around the many mountains in the region. Persecution forced whole families of Christians to follow these dusty trails to new cities, where they formed tightly-knit communities of a few dozen people. In times of difficulty, Christians relied on one another for basic needs. For instance, if Christians were imprisoned, they counted on the community to bring them food and care for them. Such pressures bound the parish together into a family unit, sometimes called "the household of faith."

The development of Roman highways – between eight and thirty feet wide; built in courses of gravel, sand, and pavement; engineered to efficiently drain water away – not only made life easier but also aided the spread of Christianity throughout the empire. As external pressures relaxed, Christians' dependence on one another likewise waned. By the end of the third century, the parish had morphed from a countercultural community into an administrative jurisdiction of the institutional church. This shift occurred at different rates in different regions, but by the end of the fourth century Christianity was the official religion of the Roman Empire and firmly established in major urban areas. From this point until the modern period, Christians in Europe would live in tension between a supposedly "Christian" society and the communal ideal of the early church.

Ironically, one man credited with the renewal of Christian community spent most of his life living as a hermit in the Egyptian desert. Anthony was born in 250 to an affluent family in Lower Egypt. His parents died while he was young, and Anthony received a significant inheritance. One day, entering a church just as the gospel was being read, he heard the lector say: "If anyone would be perfect, go, sell what you have, and give it to the poor, and you will have treasure in heaven; and come, follow me." Immediately Anthony sold his possessions and distributed the money to the poor. He lived as an outcast on the margins of the village, seeking God alone in the wilderness. For twenty years, he prepared the way of the Lord through prayer, fasting, and vigils. As his reputation grew, others followed him down the deserted highway into the wilderness, settling in individual cells near him. These pilgrims were called "monks," from the Greek *monos,* which means "alone."

Although Christianity was now accepted throughout the empire, some Christians believed the faith to be weakened, diluted by its social respectability and assimilated to prevailing cultural norms. Inspired by Anthony's example to recover the original vision of Jesus' followers, many divested themselves of property and worldly concerns, leaving even the security of marriage to pursue a simple life of prayer and manual labor. For them, commitment to God was not a matter of words (they spoke few) but of action. They eschewed luxury in all forms, preferring simple food, plain dress, and basic shelter. They even surrendered their autonomy by submitting themselves to the oversight of a spiritual elder called an abbot (from *abba,* "father"). These decisions eventually evolved into the three monastic vows of poverty, chastity, and obedience.

The "way of the Lord" was soon jammed with traffic as waves of would-be monks entered the deserts of Egypt, Syria, and Palestine. The men began to join together in large colonies, meeting occasionally for prayer and communion. This common life was given form by Pachomius, who organized the monks into communal houses under the leadership of an elder. The men ate together, held their goods in common, and followed a common order of communal prayer, manual labor, and later, bible study. Their way of life was called cenobitic, from the Greek *koinos biosi,* "common life." Within a few years, Pachomius had three thousand followers, and by the mid-fourth century there were several men's houses and, situated on the other side of the Nile, at least one house for women. After Pachomius died his followers wrote down his communal rules, which were published in Latin by Jerome and became well known, the first of many such communal covenants.

At the time, most of the monks who left the city for the desert were uneducated laymen dissatisfied with the worldliness of the church. Basil of Caesarea, a well-educated nobleman from Cappadocia, was an exception. He attempted to incorporate monastic principles in an urban setting under the guidance of church leaders. He wrote his own *Rule* and established a community at his family's estate near the Black Sea. His goal was to balance the individualism and personal holiness of the desert monks with Jesus' call to engage the world with acts of justice and mercy. To that end, Basil built one of the world's first hospitals in his community, a place to offer hospitality especially to those who could not afford medical care. The hospital was an integral part of the intentional community, which was named the Basiliad after its founder. Physicians and nurses lived on the grounds, as did students studying at the attached medical school. The complex also included space to host travelers and provide education. Basil's *Rules* remain the basis for monastic life in the Orthodox churches of Turkey, Greece, Syria, and Russia.

Until the fourth century, communal activity was concentrated in the east, but all roads lead to Rome. Monastic ideals arrived by way of travelers from Egypt and Syria and through stories being published about the monks. John Cassian lived among the eastern monks for years, then wrote several influential books in Latin about what he had learned. His audience was a new generation of urban Christians forming communities in cities across Europe. Many were inspired to retread the Palestinian roads Jesus had walked, including a number of aristocratic Roman women. Under the guidance of Jerome, this circle of heiresses adopted a life of simplicity, common prayer, fasting, and charitable works. One of the women, Melania the Elder, moved to Jerusalem in 378 and led a community of about fifty women on the Mount of Olives. Many of these women took vows of celibacy and devoted themselves to biblical study. Another community was established at Bethlehem. Back in Italy, the bishop Ambrose formulated policies for the many young women who wanted to live out the gospel around Milan.

Like Basil, the French bishop Caesarius of Arles believed that monastic ideals should be integrated into the life of the parish church. Caesarius preached hundreds of sermons to his congregation on prayer, fasting, chastity, compassion, and social justice throughout the fifth century. He exhorted all the Christians in the twenty-five or so rural parishes of his diocese to practice mutual love and responsibility for one another – to be communities. His sermons continued to circulate for centuries after his death, inspiring generations of Christians to live out radical Christian values in their everyday lives.

Outside of the New Testament, perhaps no text has been as important to the development of Christian community as the *Rule of Benedict*, written in the early sixth century and shaped by the writings of John Cassian and the anonymously written *Rule of the Master*. Benedict, a Roman nobleman, left Rome for the countryside, where he established several monastic communities. Everyone in the community shared the responsibilities of tending the farm and the kitchen. Work was punctuated eight times each day by common prayer called "the hours." Benedict's vision for common life – which integrated work and prayer, solitude and community, personal responsibility and authority – was extraordinarily successful, and remained the paradigm for Christian communities for well over a millennium. His emphasis on stability and fidelity to a particular locality would become hallmarks of intentional Christian community.

As the roads of the crumbling empire fell into disrepair, the monasteries became isolated, scattered outposts. The monks were fantastically successful – erudite and wealthy – but they lost themselves in contemplation. The monastic life of prayer and study became professionalized and the way of simplicity and manual labor was eventually lost. Caricatures of fat monks began to appear in this period. A series of reforms in the Middle Ages struggled to recover Benedict's original vision, first the Cluniac reforms in the tenth century, then the Carthusians in the eleventh. The Cistercians likewise attempted to restore the simplicity of the original Benedictine spirit; they made time for more manual labor, stripped their chapels of rich art and décor, and adopted a simple worship style. Much later, the Trappists would re-reform the Cistercians, adding their own emphasis on silence.

Despite these reforms, the monasteries could not contain the radical impulse of Christianity. Europe was undergoing major social and economic change during the twelfth century, moving from a feudal, village-centered society to an urban economy. The ancient cities, dormant since the time of Benedict, were awakening with new commerce. The Roman roads were cleared and rebuilt. Yet as trade increased, the division between rich and poor also widened. Alongside a rising urban middle-class of merchants, bankers, and lawyers grew an underclass of poor and underemployed. Beginning with monks such as Rupert of Deutz (who wrote a little treatise titled *On the Truly Apostolic Life*) a movement arose to restore the model of the Jerusalem community for the entire church. Others, such as Gerhoh of Reichersberg, argued that if monasticism is the pattern for the church, then all Christians should be monks of a sort; God's call to the Christian life is universal, not limited to the cloister. The apostolic life, they said, was not simply a life of prayer and devotion but of social and economic justice. Ordinary Christians should reconcile economic divisions through solidarity with the poor, banding together with those marginalized by the new economy through fraternal charity, scripture study, voluntary poverty, and active proclamation of the faith.

This awakening led to the formation of small evangelical communities across Europe. In western France, Robert d'Abrissel gathered a diverse group of men and women, including a number of former prostitutes, into a community at Fontevrault known as Christ's Poor. In southern France, groups of Christians known as the *cathari,* or "pure ones," organized radical communities which rejected sexual relations, the eating of meat, and hierarchical authority. The Cathars were regarded as heretics because of their denigration of the material creation, and were relentlessly persecuted. Northern Italy produced a movement called the *humiliati,* or "humble ones," in which both clerics and laypeople attempted to conform their lives to the gospel call to simplicity. The movement included both celibate and married people, many of whom were drawn from the thriving garment industry in the area. Though the communities produced rich cloth in the textile industry, they wore only plain, undyed clothes. They refrained from political engagement, served the disadvantaged, and prayed the Benedictine hours. By the end of the thirteenth century, there were communities of Humiliati in most cities in northern Italy.

In southern France, a wealthy merchant named Peter Waldo led a similar movement. In a story not unlike Anthony's, Waldo gave up his business, made reparation for his dishonest dealings, and began distributing bread in the streets of Lyons. Others followed his example of poverty and commitment to studying the Bible, and they became known as the Poor Men of Lyons. The "Waldensian" movement spread quickly to Germany and Italy, where it eventually merged with the Humiliati. Small communes formed which engaged in common work and gospel preaching; some remain to this day.

Saint Francis became the most famous exemplar of the apostolic life. Like so many earlier community leaders, Francis was a scion of aristocrats, who relinquished all his wealth, even the clothes on his back (he literally went naked for a time). Exchanging rich silk garb for a rough woolen habit, Francis and his friends traipsed across Europe preaching and exhorting people to follow Jesus' way. Before long the roads of medieval Europe were clogged with tens of thousands of friars singing, preaching, and begging for daily bread. The Franciscan movement spread throughout the continent, spilling over into North Africa and the Middle East, where friars initiated some of the first interfaith conversations with Muslims. Besides celibate communities of men and women, confraternities of married people with children who vowed to follow the simple way of the gospel grew up in major cities.

Farther north, in what is now Belgium, groups of single women inspired by Francis joined together to form communities within the great urban centers of Leuven, Ghent, and Bruges. Known as Beguines, they established "towns within towns" that contained houses, workshops, churches, hospitals, and dorms for poorer members of the community. The women practiced celibacy, daily prayer, and simplicity, wearing plain beige dresses. Most worked in the Belgian textile factories, spending their extra time with the poor and sick. Unlike traditional nuns, the Beguines took no formal vows and shared no rule of life, but each woman promised obedience to the local community and the local pastor. Similar communities of men called the Beghards soon followed their lead. A little later, in the fourteenth century, the Brethren of the Common Life flourished in the Netherlands and Germany. Like the Beguines and the Beghards, the Brethren did not take formal vows. They roomed together in large houses and ministered to others by preaching (some were priests) and producing devotional literature. The most well-known example is *The Imitation of Christ*, by Thomas à Kempis, a book on the devotional life that has guided many people to the Way.

Such movements to "monasticize" all of Christian society climaxed in the Great Reformation. The Reformers mounted a devastating critique of the "monkish" life, which was already suffering under the weight of internal problems. Luther, himself an Augustinian monk, renounced his vows, marched out of the monastery, and married a nun. Calvin likewise opposed traditional monasticism as morally and spiritually bankrupt, believing it represented a double standard for Christians – all should strive for moral perfection. Monks and nuns in reformed lands were released from their vows, and many married and joined secular life.

Meanwhile, more radical Reformers such as Michael Sattler (a former Benedictine prior) organized new apostolic communities that rejected military service and political involvement and revived the ancient practice of believer's baptism. Among these "Anabaptists," the Mennonites considered it a mark of the true church that there should be no poor among them. The Hutterites went further, abolishing private property altogether and practicing full economic sharing. The egalitarian spirit was manifest in the practice of calling other members "brother" and "sister"; hence some groups in Moravia and Switzerland were simply called "Brethren." Persecuted across Europe by Catholics and Protestants alike, Anabaptist communities saw themselves as following in the footsteps of the persecuted early church.

The "age of exploration" opened the pathways of the sea and connected the world in previously unimaginable ways. Wherever Christians sojourned, intentional communities developed. Hundreds of Baptists and other dissenters left their homes in England and Scotland in order to build a Christian society in the New World. Both the Pilgrims who settled Plymouth Colony in 1620 and the Puritans who established the "Bible commonwealth" in the Massachusetts Bay Colony in 1630 attempted to create cohesive Christian communities. The Plymouth Pilgrims practiced the discipline of shared property in the first generation of their colony; all shared a high standard of moral discipline. The idealism of these founding communities directly influenced the formation of America's distinct sense of mission and left a legacy of utopian community, both Christian and non-Christian, in the New World.

Many of these New World communities had a millenarian cast – they believed the Second Coming was at hand. The austere community of Bohemia Manor, founded in the 1680s in Pennsylvania by the followers of Jean de Labadie (the "second Calvin"), had no private property and shared common work on the estate; food and dress were plain. A few years later, the Seventh Day Baptists established a community, also in Pennsylvania, called Ephrata Cloister. Perhaps most successful were the Shakers, established right before the Revolutionary War. By the 1830s they had attracted some four thousand members to more than sixty celibate communes called "families" in nearly twenty different settlements from Maine to Indiana. One community remains, at Sabbathday Lake, Maine. Other North American communities likewise attracted thousands: German Pietists flocked to communities such as Harmony and Economy in Pennsylvania, and New Harmony in Indiana. Another German sect, the Inspirationists, built seven communal villages in Amana, Iowa, in the 1850s, which survived until the Great Depression. The largest intentional Christian communities in the New World are the Hutterites, who fled oppression in Europe and established expansive farming colonies on the western plains of the United States and Canada. Today there are around forty thousand Hutterites living in more than four hundred colonies.

The twentieth century witnessed a revival of radical Christian community. Communal life focused on discipleship was seen as a way to heal the wounds left by centuries of religious strife and political turmoil. In response to the church's complicity in war, Eberhard Arnold founded the Bruderhof community in Sannerz, Germany, in 1920. A few years later, in 1933, Dorothy Day and Peter Maurin founded the Catholic Worker, a community committed to serving the homeless poor. In 1934, Dietrich Bonhoeffer started the experimental underground Christian community in Finkenwald, which would become the subject of *Life Together*. In 1938, a Presbyterian pastor named George MacLeod founded the Iona Community in Scotland, in order to close the gap between middle- and working-class Christians. In 1946, Roger Schütz, known as Brother Roger, founded the Taizé Community in France as an ecumenical religious order of Catholics and Protestants. A year later, Basilea Schlink, a Lutheran, founded the Evangelical

Sisterhood of Mary in Darmstadt, Germany, with a mission to repent for the Holocaust and work for reconciliation between Jews and German Christians. Around the same time, the Focolare movement was emerging in Italy, and what is now the Catholic Integrated Community began in Germany. Nineteen sixty-four saw the founding of L'Arche, an international community consisting of households of people with disabilities and their helpers. Many charismatic and activist communities also sprang up in this period, centered on Jesus' Sermon on the Mount and transcending old denominational lines. In the last several decades the New Friars, the New Monastics, and a plethora of similar urban and neo-Anabaptist missional endeavors in North America have blended elements of the active and contemplative traditions in an effort to incorporate God's kingdom into everyday life.

The communities mentioned here are but a sampling of the thousands of groups of Christians who have determined to live lives of intentional discipleship in communities modeled on the Jerusalem church. The stories of many of these communities, especially those outside of Europe and North America, remain to be told. And doubtless many communities quietly serving others will remain forever unknown. Though each community's narrative is of value in itself and worthy of remembrance, each is also a chapter in the overarching and ongoing story of Christians on the Way, a people walking many different roads with the same intention and the same destination, each group seeking to experience the presence and power of God in the shared life of community, a preparation for great communion to come. ◆

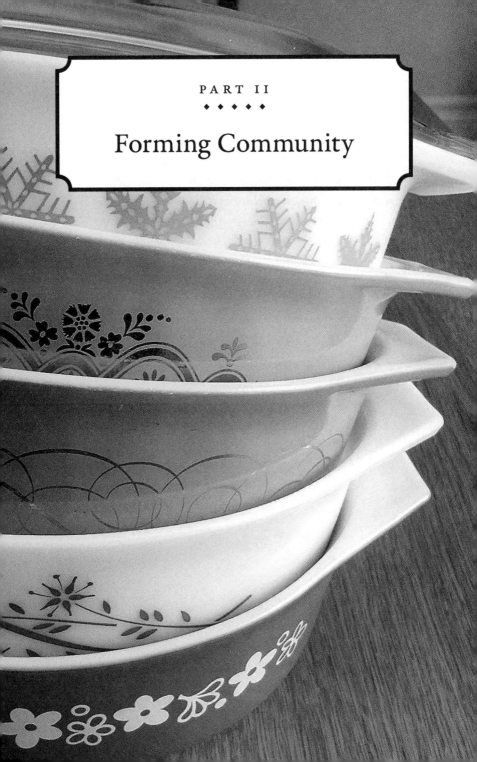

PART II
• • • • •

Forming Community

Efforts to organize community artificially can only result in ugly, lifeless caricatures. Only when we are empty and open to the Living One – to the Spirit – can he bring about the same life among us as he did among the early Christians. The Spirit is joy in the Living One, joy in God as the only real life; it is joy in all people, because they have life from God. The Spirit drives us to all people and brings us joy in living and working for one another, for it is the spirit of creativity and love.

EBERHARD ARNOLD, Why We Live in Community

II

A Vision

• • • • •

George MacDonald

"UNCLE," SAID RACHEL, "may I read your visions of the shops in heaven?"

"Oh no, Rachel. You are not able to read tonight," said her uncle deprecatingly.

"I think I am, uncle. I should like to try. It will let the gentlemen see what you *would* think an ideal state of things.

"Mr. Wingfold, it is something my uncle once dictated to me, and I wrote down just as he said it. He can always do better dictating than writing, but this time he was so ill with asthma that he could not talk much faster than I could write; and yet to be so ill I never saw him show so little suffering; his thinking seemed to make him forget it.

"Mayn't I read it, uncle? I know the gentlemen would like to hear it."

"That we should," said both men at once.

"I will fetch it you then," said Polwarth, "if you will tell me where to find it." Rachel gave him the needful directions, and presently he brought a few sheets of paper and handed them to her.

"This is no dream, Mr. Wingfold," he said. "It is something I thought fairly out before I began to dictate it. But the only fit form I could find for it was that of a vision – like the Vision of Mirza, you know. Now read, Rachel, and I will hold my tongue."

After a little arranging of the sheets, Rachel began. She read not without difficulty, but her pleasure in what she read helped her through.

"And now," said my guide to me, "I will bring thee to a city of the righteous, and show thee how they buy and sell in this the kingdom of heaven." So we journeyed a day and another day and half a day, and I was weary ere we arrived thither. . . .

. . . One great noon-day, my conductor led me into a large place, such as we would call a shop here, although the arrangements were different, and an air of stateliness dwelt in and around the house. It was filled with the loveliest silken and woolen stuffs, of all kinds and colors, a thousand delights to the eye – and to the thought also, for here was endless harmony, and no discord.

I stood in the midst, and my guide stood by me in silence; for all the time I was in the country, he seldom spoke to me save when first I asked of him, and yet he never showed any weariness, and often a half-smile would dwell for a moment upon his countenance.

And first I watched the faces of them that sold; and I could read therein – for be it understood that, according to the degree of his own capacity, a man there could perfectly read the countenance of every neighbor, that is, unless it expressed something that was not in himself – and I could read in them nothing of eagerness, only the calm of a concentrated ministration. There was no seeking there, but a strength of giving, a business-like earnestness to supply lack, enlivened by no haste, and dulled by no weariness, brightened ever by the reflected content of those who found their wants supplied. As soon as one buyer was contented they turned graciously to another, and gave ear until they perfectly understood with what object he had come to seek their aid. Nor did their countenances change utterly as they turned away, for upon them lingered the satisfaction as of one who hath had a success, and by degrees melted into the supervening content.

Then I turned to watch the countenances of them that bought. And there in like manner I saw no cupidity and no meanness. They spake humbly, yet not because they sought a favor, but because they were humble, for with their humility was mingled the confidence of receiving that which they sought. And truly it was a pleasure to see how everyone knew what his desire was, making his choice readily and with decision. I perceived also that everyone spoke not merely respectfully, but gratefully, to him who served him. And at meeting and parting such kindly though brief greetings passed as made me wonder whether every inhabitant of such a mighty city could know every other that dwelt therein. But I soon saw that it came not of individual knowledge, but of universal faith and all-embracing love.

And as I stood and watched, suddenly it came into my mind that I had never yet seen the coin of the country, and thereupon I kept my eyes upon a certain woman who bought silk, that when she paid for the same I might see the money. But that which she had largely bought she took in her arms and carried away, and paid not. Therefore I turned to watch another, who bought for a long journey, but when he carried away what he bought, neither did he pay any money. And I said to myself, "These are well-known persons, to whom it is more convenient to pay all at a certain season." And I turned to a third who bought much fine linen. But behold, he paid not! Then I began to observe again those that sold; whereupon I thought with myself, "How good must be the air of this land for the remembrance of things, for these men write down nothing to keep on record the moneys men owe them on all sides!" And I looked and looked again and yet again, and stood long watching – but so it was throughout the whole place, which thronged and buzzed and swarmed like the busiest of beehives – no man paid, and no man had a book wherein to write that which the other owed!

Then I turned to my guide and said: "How lovely is honesty, and truly from what a labor it absolveth men! For here I see every man keepeth in his mind his own debts, and not the debts of others, so that time is not spent in paying of small sums, neither in the keeping of account of such; but he that buyeth counteth up, and doubtless when the day of reckoning arrives, each cometh and casteth the money he oweth into the merchant's coffer, and both are satisfied."

Then my conductor smiled and said, "Watch yet a while."

And I did as he said unto me, and stood and watched. But the same thing went on everywhere, and I said to myself, "Lo, I see nothing new!" Suddenly, at my side, a man dropped upon his knees and bowed his head to the ground. And those that stood nigh him dropped also upon their knees, and there arose a sound as of soft thunder; and lo, everyone in the place had dropped upon his knees and spread his hands out before him! Every voice and every noise was hushed, every movement had ceased, and I and my guide alone were left standing.

Then I whispered in his ear, "It is the hour of prayer; shall we not kneel also?"

And my guide answered, "No man in this city kneeleth because others do, and no man is judged if he kneeleth not. If thou hast any grief or pain upon thee, then kneel; if not, then love God in thy heart and be thankful, and kneel when thou goest into thy chamber."

Then said I, "I will not kneel, but will watch and see."

"It is well," said my guide; and I stood.

For certain moments all was utter stillness – every man and woman kneeling, with hands outstretched, save him who had first kneeled, and his hands hung by his sides and his head was still bowed to the earth. At length he rose up, and lo, his face was wet with tears; and all the people rose also, and with a noise throughout the place; and the man made a low obeisance to them that were nigh him, which they returned with equal reverence, and then with downcast eyes he walked slowly from the shop. The moment he was gone, the business of the place, without a word of remark on any side concerning what had passed, began again and went on as before. People came and went, some more eager and outward, some more staid and inward, but all contented and cheerful. At length a bell somewhere rang sweet and shrill, and after that no one entered the place, and what was in progress began to be led to a decorous conclusion. In three or four minutes the floor was empty, and the people also of the shop had gone, each about his own affairs, without shutting door or window.

I went out last with my guide, and we seated ourselves under a tree of the willow-kind on the bank of one of the quieter streams, and straightway I began to question him. "Tell me, sir," I said, "the purport of what I have seen, for not yet have I understood how these happy people do their business and pass from hand to hand not a single coin."

And he answered, "Where greed and ambition and self-love rule, money must be; where there is neither greed nor ambition nor self-love, money is needless."

And I asked, "Is it then by the same ancient mode of barter that they go about their affairs? Truly I saw no exchange of any sort."

"Bethink thee," said my guide, "if thou hadst gone into any other shop throughout the whole city, thou wouldst have seen the same thing."

"I see not how that should make the matter plainer to me," I answered.

"Where neither greed nor ambition nor selfishness reigneth," said my guide, "there need and desire have free scope, for they work no evil."

"But even now I understand you not, sir," I said.

"Hear me then," answered my guide, "for I will speak to thee more plainly. Wherefore do men take money in their hands when they go where things are?"

"Because they may not have the things without giving the money."

"And where they may have things without giving money, there they take no money in their hands?"

"Truly no, sir, if there be such a place."

"Then such a place is this, and so is it here."

"But how can men give of their goods and receive nought in return?"

"By receiving everything in return. Tell me," said my guide, "why do men take money for their goods?"

"That they may have wherewithal to go and buy other things which they need for themselves."

"But if they also may go to this place or that place where the things are which they need, and receive of those things without money and without price, is there then good cause why they should take money in their hands?"

"Truly no," I answered, "and I begin, methinks, to see how the affair goeth. Yet are there some things still whereupon I would gladly be resolved. And first of all, how cometh it that men are moved to provide these and those goods for the supply of the wants of their neighbors, when they are drawn thereto by no want in themselves, and no advantage to themselves?"

"Thou reasonest," said my guide, "as one of thine own degree, who to the eyes of the full-born ever look like chrysalids, closed round in a web of their own weaving; and who shall blame thee until thou thyself shinest within thyself? Understand that it is never advantage to himself that moveth a man in this kingdom to undertake this or that. The thing that alone advantageth a man here is the thing which he doth without thought unto that advantage. To your world, this world goeth by contraries. The man here that doeth most service, that aideth others the most to the obtaining of their honest desires, is the man who standeth highest with the Lord of the place, and his reward and honor is to be enabled to the spending of himself yet more for the good of his fellows. There goeth a rumor amongst us even now that one shall ere long be ripe for the carrying of a message from the King to the spirits that are in prison.

"Thinkest thou it is a less potent stirring up of thought and energy to desire and seek and find the things that will please the eye, and cheer the brain, and gladden the heart of the people of this great city, so that when one prayeth, 'Give me, friend, of thy loaves,' a man may answer, 'Take of them, friend, as many as thou needest' – is that, I say, an incentive to diligence less potent than the desire to hoard or to excel? Is it not to share the bliss of God who hoardeth nothing, but ever giveth liberally? The joy of a man here is to enable another to lay hold upon that which is of his own kind and be glad and grow thereby – doctrine strange and unbeliev- able to the man in whom the well of life is yet sealed.

"Never have they been many at a time in the old world who could thus enter into the joy of their Lord. And yet, if thou bethink thee, thou wilt perceive that such bliss is not unknown amongst thy fellows. Knowest thou no musician who would find it joy enough for a night, to scale the tower of a hundred bells and send the great meteors of music-light flying over the care-tortured city? Would everyone even of thy half-created race reason with himself and say: 'Truly it is in the night, and no one can see who it is that ministereth; the sounds alone will go forth nor bear my image; I shall reap no honor; I will not rise and go?' Thou knowest, I say, some in thy world who would not speak thus in their hearts, but would willingly consent to be as nothing, so to give life to their fellows. In this city so is it with all – in shop or workshop, in study or theater, all seek to spend and be spent for the love of all."

And I said, "One thing tell me, sir – how much a man may have for the asking."

"What he will – that is, what he can well use."

"Who then shall be the judge thereof?"

"Who but the man himself?"

"What if he should turn to greed, and begin to hoard and spare?"

"Sawest thou not the man this day because of whom all business ceased for a time? To that man had come a thought of accumulation instead of growth, and he dropped upon his knees in shame and terror. And thou sawest how all business ceased, and straightway that of the shop was made what below they call a church; for everyone hastened to the poor man's help, the air was filled with praying breath, and the atmosphere of God-loving souls was around him; the foul thought fled, and the man went forth glad and humble, and tomorrow he will return for that which he needeth. If thou shouldst be present then, thou wilt see him more tenderly ministered unto than all the rest." . . .

"I think that *could* be!" said the curate, breaking the silence that followed when Rachel ceased.

"Not in this world," said the draper.

"To doubt that it could be," said the gatekeeper, "would be to doubt whether the kingdom of heaven is a chimera or a divine idea." ◆

12

Life's Task

◆ ◆ ◆ ◆ ◆

Eberhard Arnold

F OR THOSE OF US called to community, it is a life's task. We are not simply a society for colonizing, for forming new settlements as if there were not enough without a new one being formed, in which people live as near and yet just as far from one another as in other places. We are also not seeking a general community of humankind, nor do we wish to bring together in community people as they are at present. If by community we mean a life based on mere mutual regard, then all of us could have remained in our own places, for people are to be found everywhere and here we find neither better people nor worse people than elsewhere. If mutual relationships among people are all we seek, then we need not come together in community as we have.

Human relationships can be found everywhere, but community on this basis is never successful. All attempts that rest upon the present conditions of human existence must fail. Right from the beginning they are bankrupt. Left to our natural inclinations, we cannot realize true community. Even the smallest community between husband and wife, which arises out of love, only in the rarest cases shows itself to be a true, lasting spiritual community. Most married couples merely coexist.

It is impossible to build up a true community – a heartfelt unity, a true fellowship of mutual help, and a common task – if it is based on human goodwill. Granted, as long as people's interests do not conflict, things will be all right, but as soon as conflict arises and egos clash, people rise up against one another.

True community will never be achieved if human relationships go on as they are. The community we seek is not based on human nature but on the eternal God. It is fed by divine strength and comes to true unity in God not by reason of our own strength, or even our collective strength, but through a power given from above. Without faith that we will be given this spirit of complete love and fellowship, the spirit of Jesus Christ, we cannot last long in community. In other words, if you do not seek for God with your whole heart, if you do not seek for love and unity, and if this is not the all-important question for you, then in the long run seeking community is pointless.

In every person there is a longing for true righteousness, love, and unity. Our doors, therefore, should be open to everyone. Still, most people are not yet ready for community. There is no point going out on the streets to call everyone to community. It is not cowardice that keeps us from doing this. It would be folly; many people would simply not be in the position to understand such a call. They would not be mature enough in their inner development to follow it. God must call them first. The Spirit must speak the living Word into their hearts. So, since faith is not given to everybody at all times, we must wait for the hour which God gives.

No one should join a community simply to live a friendly life of mutual human relationships. That will never do; it will certainly fail. One can enter into community only if one seeks its religious secret, only if one seeks this with all one's heart, soul, thought, and powers. One need not already fully understand this secret, for in the final analysis no one can understand it. Only one thing is necessary: to seek this religious secret with our whole being.

People have come to join our community who claimed to understand nothing at all of religious words, but they understood the social element. Social justice, brotherhood, unity, and social harmony were their highest concern. In pursuing these things with their whole heart, they were in fact seeking community's spiritual secret without realizing it. And they belong with us in spite of the fact that they have rejected religious language, because what we are seeking together is not any dogma, any stringing together of religious words, but a power. The essence of this elementary power is love and unity, a love and unity that extends into the outermost aspects of life and action and work. Whoever seeks for this wholeheartedly should be welcome to stay with us.

But why is it that some people seek and do not find? That even after pledging themselves to others in community, they fail? That even though they are ready to fight to the death, it is not given to them? . . . That is not our concern. It would be judging our friends if we wished to discover the reason their faith had not held out, and Jesus has told us not to judge. We know that anyone else could have become equally unfaithful. The term used by the early Christians is grace. To one it is given, to the other not. More than that we do not know.

We must not be surprised when people come who do not find an inward relationship to life in community. We cannot hope to come to the deepest exchange with everyone we talk with. What God does not give, we cannot do. We must also not be shocked if people leave us who have made some steps and attempted to live in community. It has simply not been given them. They could not substitute their own tremendous willpower for that which can only be given to them by God.

We do not want our community to grow by having many people join us who wish to surrender themselves and be stead-fast merely through their own capacity for decision. That will come to nothing, and the sooner the better. There are many who would gladly take part in something that seems great to them and contribute to it their own goodwill and personal gifts. All these people will fail; in their own strength they will not be able to remain faithful.

We can only go the way of complete community if a power comes to us which is not our own power, a source of strength from another world and another future. When people leave us, we must test ourselves deeply as to whether we are called by God to such a radical life witness, or whether perchance we have entered on this way out of our own will and in our own strength. Jesus asked his disciples, "Will you also go away?" (John 6:67). This question should come to mind every time someone leaves.

All this will be alive for us only if our first concern is not personal salvation and happiness or the fulfillment of our personal wishes, but rather that which is great, that which lives beyond us. Only then will we be able to stay true to the very end. Those who seek only their personal happiness, their own salvation and blessedness, will not stand firm. Only those will stand firm whose hearts beat for the cause of justice and peace for all nations, for the brotherhood of all social classes, and for the welfare of all people in all parts of the world. Only those who wish to see the victory of the reign of God as the reign of love and unity, and who lose themselves with a glowing heart in this desire, will be able to remain true to the church of Jesus Christ. Such people will seek first the kingdom of God and its righteousness, and in them will be fulfilled Jesus' words, ". . . and all these things will be given to you as well" (Matt. 6:33).

◆ ◆ ◆ ◆ ◆

IT IS NOT SUFFICIENT for us merely to find an intellectual unanimity of opinion, or to find a common goal toward which all our wills can strive, or to experience together the same subjective feeling in the swing of the emotional pendulum. Something quite different must move in us to lift us out of this purely human level, so that our human sphere and human atmosphere are permeated with a power that comes from an entirely different realm. Just as the rays of the sun constantly stream onto the earth, and as the lightning brings down light and fire from the clouds, so must an element break in upon us which does not originate in us. This element has nothing to do with our abilities. It does not arise from our most lofty and idealistic thoughts or feelings, nor from that which is most holy or noble in our nature. No, that which descends upon us is something which cannot come from us.

Only through the Holy Spirit, which comes upon us, are we enabled to achieve a unity of consciousness, which brings about a complete unanimity of thought, willpower, and emotional experience. Just as a man is in himself a unity of consciousness – and this in spite of his conflicting thoughts, goals, and sentiments – so the descent of this Spirit brings into being a unity of consciousness among those who receive it. Thus the individual person is significant only as a cell which belongs to the whole living organism of this one unity of consciousness of the Spirit. ◆

13

It Takes Work

• • • • •

Charles E. Moore

AT ONE LEVEL OR ANOTHER, all of us want to be connected with others. But what does it mean to connect? What does it take to forge relationships that count? How do we move from living autonomous, self-sufficient lives to a life that is genuinely interdependent and shared?

Superficiality and rootlessness are diseases of our time. Shallow friendships and fragile relationships mark not only our society but also the church. By contrast, we read that the early Christians did not just occasionally fellowship (verb); they *were* a fellowship (noun). They didn't go to church; they *were* the church. Few of us today experience life together as the early Christians did – a common, daily, material life of unity and sharing. Instead, we rush here and there, madly trying to connect with this group or that person, but still living lives that are very much our own. We follow and text each other, but actually share very little of ourselves.

To come across a dismembered human body part, like a finger or a toe, would shock and repulse us. If we would only step back and see how fractured and dismembered our lives are, we might see why restoring our lives to wholeness, as difficult as this might be, is so desperately needed. After all, this is what Christ prayed for, and it is what our world needs. Jesus prayed that we might be a community, that his followers would possess the togetherness and love and unity that he and the Father have for each other (John 17:20–26).

No wonder the reciprocal pronoun "one another" *(allelon)* stands out in the New Testament. This one word highlights the importance of belonging to a group that shares life:

Outdo one another in showing honor (Rom. 12:10)

Live in harmony with one another (Rom. 12:16)

Admonish one another (Rom. 15:14)

Greet one another with a holy kiss (Rom. 16:16)

Wait for one another (1 Cor. 11:33)

Have the same care for one another (1 Cor. 12:25)

Be servants of one another (Gal. 5:13)

Bear one another's burdens (Gal. 6:2)

Comfort one another (1 Thess. 5:11)

Build one another up (1 Thess. 5:11)

Be at peace with one another (1 Thess. 5:13)

Do good to one another (1 Thess. 5:15)

Put up with one another in love (Eph. 4:2)

Be kind and compassionate to one another (Eph. 4:32)

Submit to one another (Eph. 5:21)

Forgive one another (Col. 3:13)

Confess your sins to one another (James 5:16)

Pray for one another (James 5:16)

Love one another from the heart (1 Pet. 1:22)

Be hospitable to one another (1 Pet. 4:9)

Meet one another with humility (1 Pet. 5:5)

Virtually none of the above exhortations make sense unless we share life together and are committed to one another. How are we to bear another person's burden unless the burden is known and unless we are willing to actually carry it? How are we to "put up with each other" unless we relate closely enough to get on each other's nerves? How are we to forgive one another unless we are in each other's lives enough to hurt and let one another down? How can we learn to submit to one another unless we struggle with differences? In other words, if we are to connect (or reconnect) our lives with one another, it will demand much more of us than we normally give. It demands that we *become* a church community, not just occasionally *go* to church or *have* community with others.

Community is a nice ideal, but are we ready to do the work it takes to forge a common, committed life with others on a daily basis, especially if it costs us? If we are honest, we'll recognize that we have been groomed to believe that our lives are ours to do with as we please and that our independence is more important than our involvement in whatever groups we happen to participate in, including the church. But forming community will never happen if we keep hanging on to our independence. Neither will it happen if our schedules only allow us to meet together a couple of hours a week. We will have to form new lifestyle habits and dispense with old patterns of living and thinking. We will have to sacrifice convenience and give up private spaces and personal preferences. We will have to make concerted choices to forgo some of our personal freedom so that others can more naturally be in, and not just around, our lives. It will take work.

Such a life demands that we engage in very concrete practices. Perhaps the first fruit of community is *time.* Those who love one another spend time together. Time is important because without being available to each other, fulfilling the biblical "one anothers" is virtually impossible. Take the construction metaphor of "building one another up." Building is a process that requires effort and persistence. Leaving a project undone will do damage to the materials. Or take the command to "do good to one another." It takes time to discern what is good for another person. Time is crucial if we are to serve one another as Jesus served his disciples. It takes time to wash one another's feet. It takes time to outdo one another in love and good works. It takes time to put another's interests above one's own. It takes time to show one another hospitality. It takes time . . .

As important as time is, so is sharing *space.* This may or may not mean living with one another under the same roof. But it will mean becoming more proximate with each other. The notion of a commuter marriage is an oxymoron. So is a commuter community. Unless we are physically present in each other's lives in the same physical, social space, community will only be skin deep. There are many ways to draw together in closer proximity. Whatever its size or form, any authentic community will find practical ways to live out their life of faith together. This, of course, takes sacrifice.

However, Christian community demands more than sharing time and space. Everything we do must be done in Christ and placed under his authority. For this to happen, we must be governed by the Word and seek to obey it *together*. Christian community means allowing God's Word to shape us *as a people*. Almost all the New Testament epistles are written to churches, not to individuals. And when we think about the various "one another" commands, we are only capable of fulfilling them in the spirit of Christ. Being under the Word is not just a matter of listening to a sermon at some designated hour, but of seeking with each other, by way of dialogue and prayer, what it means to live out Christ's commands together.

This leads to yet another mark of community: eagerly sharing our possessions with one another. In the New Testament, *koinonia* means more than "fellowship." Its predominant use denotes the sharing of resources. The Macedonia and Achaia churches, for example, set up a common fund for the impoverished church in Jerusalem. Since the Gentiles shared in the Jews' spiritual blessing, they in turn helped meet the Jews' material needs (Rom. 15:26–27). "In the midst of a very severe trial, their overflowing joy and their extreme poverty welled up in rich generosity," Paul writes, adding that "they urgently pleaded with us for the privilege of sharing in this service to the Lord's people" (2 Cor. 8:1–15). Such generosity led others to praise God (2 Cor. 9:13). In fact, it was this very practical expression of love that so impressed pagan society. The Christians' love for one another was not in words, but in deeds – real, physical expressions of care and service.

On the question of possessions, it is vital to specify mutual expectations. To break away from the grip of private property

we must remember that Christ's cause, not our own fulfillment or happiness, is at stake. This means going beyond
the usual social expectations and proprieties. We keep our
pocketbooks and bank accounts to ourselves (in more ways
than one). Money matters are nobody's business. But in the
body of Christ, our goods are not our own (Acts 4:32). If we
are serious about forming community *in Christ,* then we need
to start laying everything out on the table (check book, credit
card statements, bills, investments, etc.) and discuss ways in
which we can become more radical in our giving and simpler
in our living. Only in this way can the forces of the workplace
and marketplace, which pull us away from God and each other,
be combatted. We need to be open enough to share where we
find it difficult to cut back or where we overspend, and to help
each other discern what our needs are as opposed to our wants.
We need to give each other honest feedback on how much we
work and why. Only in this way will we get free of the chains
of having to earn and spend. Then the "common life" gets
real and we start to really depend on one another; then God's
justice breaks in.

Laying everything out on the table should also include
other "private possessions" – our sins and burdens, both of
which we are commanded to share with one another (James
5:16; Gal. 6:2). Holding each other accountable is the work of
being our brother's and sister's keeper. Only in this way can the
threads of our separate private lives be knitted together into a
fabric in which Christ makes all things new. Confession means
far more than unloading one's problems on someone else or
striving for personal betterment. We bare our souls before
our brothers and sisters for the sake of building up the body
of Christ. Only by sharing life to this degree can we show the

world that Jesus really does have the power to forgive sins, set burdened people free, and restore broken relationships.

This is what forming community in Christ is about: to give witness every day to Jesus' lordship in every facet of life for every person who longs for a new life. Seeking Christ's kingdom together leads to a revolutionary restructuring of life on all levels. Such a life never comes naturally. It takes work. It means intentionally forgoing the things of this world – its pleasures, pursuits, priorities, and patterns (Rom. 12:1–2) and embarking on a journey with others who also want their lives to be shaped by the joy of the gospel. This kind of life is a gift, for sure – a gift from above. But to experience that gift, it is worth giving everything we have and are. ◆

14

Communion

• • • • •

Thomas R. Kelly

THE FINAL GROUNDS of holy fellowship are
in God. Lives immersed and drowned in God are
drowned in love, and know one another in him, and
know one another in love. God is the medium, the matrix, the
focus, the solvent. As Meister Eckhart suggests, those who are
wholly surrounded by God, enveloped by God, clothed with
God, glowing in selfless love toward him – such people no
one can touch without also touching God. Such lives have a
common meeting-point; they live in a common joyous enslave-
ment. They go back into a single center where they are at home
with him and with one another. It is as if every soul had a final
base, and that final base of every soul is one single holy ground,
shared in by all. Persons in the fellowship are related to one
another through him, as all mountains go down into the same
earth. They get at one another through him. . . .

Two people, three people, ten people may be in living touch with one another through him who underlies their separate lives. This is an astounding experience, which I can only describe but cannot explain in the language of science. But in vivid experience of divine fellowship it is there. We know that these souls are with us, lifting their lives and ours continuously to God and opening themselves, with us, in steady and humble obedience to him. It is as if the boundaries of our self were enlarged, as if we were with them and as if they were within us. Their strength, given to them by God, becomes our strength, and our joy, given to us by God, becomes their joy. In confidence and love we live together in him. On the borders of the experience lie amazing events, at which reputable psychologists scoff, and for which I would not try any accounting. But the solid kernel of community of life in God is in the center of the experience, renewing our life and courage and commitment and love. ◆

Arthur G. Gish

I T IS IRONIC that often it is in the church where we are least open and honest with each other, unable to share and deal with the concerns that touch people most deeply. Part of the meaning of fellowship is to know and be known by others. Within this fellowship we should be able to share from the depths of our souls. There should be no pretending. Before God all our attempts at self-protection are worthless anyway.

We cannot fool God and it is questionable whether we will fool others either. . . .

In community we can take off the masks and give up defense mechanisms, as they are no longer needed. In community we can overcome the gap between our public face and private face, the difference between the way we act at home and the way we act with others. We can feel free to share both who we are and what we have, our strengths and weaknesses, assets and needs. We can completely give ourselves to each other.

Being open with each other is not easy, of course, and we need to seek God's help in this. It is easier to share our possessions than ourselves. We have been conditioned against being honest with others. Sharing means being open to change, being willing to die to the old. We have many fears of being hurt. We need to be especially sensitive to this fear in others and through lots of love and acceptance help them to trust. Sometimes people will use their intellectual ability to hide this fear. Gently we will inform them that we are interested in them, and not only their intellectual theories.

Sharing does involve risk, for as we lower our defenses we become vulnerable to being hurt through being exploited or betrayed. Sharing can be destructive if not based on love. It is nothing to be played with. In community there are many opportunities and possibilities for oppressing others. The human spirit can be crushed to a pulp and the person made unable to respond in any free way. The more sharing we do and the closer we become, the more potential there is for interpersonal conflict, and so the more we need to rely on the guidance of the Holy Spirit and to be forgiving toward each other.

The Bible does not call us primarily to trust each other, but to trust God. People are not always trustworthy. But we can trust God, who will enable us to love people even when we cannot trust them or they cannot trust themselves. Because of this faith we can make ourselves vulnerable. If our faith in God is secure, we can act in a trusting way to those who are untrustworthy just as God loves us even though we are often untrustworthy.

Although it may be difficult, we do have a deep desire to share and be honest. We want community, not polite compliments and formalities. We want to be able to say something ridiculous without be ridiculed. Through faith in God and a loving community we can take the risk of being open and honest.

This openness with each other will include sharing our deepest longings, hopes, and dreams. Not only do we need to share them, but also the community needs to hear them. One of the ways a community moves forward is by responding to these longings. . . .

Sharing involves not only giving but also receiving. Sharing is a two-way experience. Unless sharing is mutual, it leads to paternalism and dependence. Real fellowship is impossible without both giving and receiving, ministering and being ministered to, for that is how the body is built up. Too often because of our pride we want to be self-sufficient and even put a stigma on receiving aid from others. We would never stoop so low as to ask for or admit that we need help from others. This is pride. Only being willing to give and serve may be a way of keeping others at a distance. In pretending that we are the source of all good gifts, we attempt to make ourselves God. God has given us needs and what a joyous blessing it is to have them met.

Another aspect of sharing is to build each other up, encourage each other, and give praise where praise is due. It is easy to criticize and say what is wrong, but it takes a special effort to tell people what is right and how much we appreciate them. Conscious effort needs to be put into sharing our positive feelings toward each other. We should pray for each other and the community every day. ◆

Charles E. Moore

T O LIVE IN COMMUNITY is a gift. God created us to share life and resources and common work with those we call sisters and brothers in Christ. So much can be accomplished and experienced when our lives are shared. And yet living together is not a guarantee that we are actually being woven together by the Spirit.

God created us to know and be known, to love and be loved. We can live and work side by side and even share all things in common but still be miles apart from each other. Not because walls exist between us but because a mutual bond has yet to be forged. Jesus prayed that we might be one as he and the Father are one. "I in them and you in me. May they be brought to complete unity" (John 17:23). Such unity extends well beyond a harmony of purpose and getting along. This kind of unity is deep, an understanding, acceptance, and appreciation of one another that transcends words and deeds.

Too often we forget that life is more than doing deeds for and with each other. Love is more than cooperating and collaborating. Love rests on a trust that confounds costs and benefits. Love gives rise to a joy and a freedom that meld us

together no matter what, whether we accomplish anything or
not. Communion is more than living under the same roof. It is
more than having a relationship with others. It is not a feeling;
it is a connection that truly makes us one.

Within community, each of us is incomplete and in need of
others. Each of us carries needs and wounds we are not meant
to deal with alone. But community can only flourish, in the
deepest sense, when we cease to view others as a means to our
own healing. Genuine community is possible to the extent to
which we give ourselves to others. We move from "community
for me" to "me for the community." This is not a matter of
ignoring or denying our own needs but of making the shift
from self to a common life.

This shift away from ourselves demands moving past our
fears so that we can care for and enter into the need of our
brother and sister. This takes time and acceptance and trust,
but at a certain point we overcome ourselves and discover the
gift of the one we are with – despite differences, despite weaknesses, despite faults and failures. Communion exists when
we find joy in one another not because of what we have done
or can do but because we belong to one another in a common
destiny in Christ.

That destiny is the reconciliation of all things. Though
we have often been torn between our "public selves" and our
"private selves," these two selves no longer have to be divided
when we commit ourselves to one another in Christ. The new
creation that Christ brings makes it possible to be ourselves
and transcend ourselves for the sake of each other. Heart-to-
heart sharing plays a part in all this, but there is something
more that happens. In our mutual vulnerability we are brought
together in mutual trust in God's grace. We find ourselves at

the foot of the cross and experience Christ's uniting power. It is difficult to explain, but such communion is both the source and fruition of sharing life in Christ. Without this deep sharing, community is but a mode and form of life. We can get things done but never really meet. ◆

Idealism

◆ ◆ ◆ ◆ ◆

Dietrich Bonhoeffer

INNUMERABLE TIMES a whole Christian community
has broken down because it had sprung from a wish
dream. The serious Christian, set down for the first time in
a Christian community, is likely to bring with him a very defi-
nite idea of what Christian life together should be and to try to
realize it. But God's grace speedily shatters such dreams. Just
as surely as God desires to lead us to a knowledge of genuine
Christian fellowship, so surely must we be overwhelmed by a
great disillusionment with others, with Christians in general,
and, if we are fortunate, with ourselves.

By sheer grace, God will not permit us to live even for a brief
period in a dream world. He does not abandon us to those
rapturous experiences and lofty moods that come over us like a
dream. God is not a God of the emotions but the God of truth.
Only that fellowship which faces such disillusionment, with all
its unhappy and ugly aspects, begins to be what it should be in

God's sight, begins to grasp in faith the promise that is given to it. The sooner this shock of disillusionment comes to an individual and to a community the better for both. A community which cannot bear and cannot survive such a crisis, which insists upon keeping its illusion when it should be shattered, permanently loses in that moment the promise of Christian community. Sooner or later it will collapse. Every human wish dream that is injected into the Christian community is a hindrance to genuine community and must be banished if genuine community is to survive. He who loves his dream of community more than the Christian community itself becomes a destroyer of the latter, even though his personal intentions may be ever so honest and earnest and sacrificial.

God hates visionary dreaming; it makes the dreamer proud and pretentious. The man who fashions a visionary ideal of community demands that it be realized by God, by others, and by himself. He enters the community of Christians with demands, sets up his own law, and judges the brethren and God himself accordingly. He stands adamant, a living reproach to all others in the circle of brethren. He acts as if he is the creator of the Christian community, as if his dream binds people together. When things do not go his way, he calls the effort a failure. When his ideal picture is destroyed, he sees the community going to pot. So he becomes, first an accuser of his brethren, then an accuser of God, and finally the despairing accuser of himself.

Because God has already laid the only foundation of our fellowship, because God has bound us together in one body with other Christians in Jesus Christ, long before we entered into common life with them, we enter into that common life not as demanders but as thankful recipients. We thank God for what he has done for us. We thank God for giving us brethren who live by his call, by his forgiveness and his promise. We do not complain of what God does not give us; we rather thank God for what he does give us daily. And is not what has been given us enough: brothers, who will go on living with us through sin and need under the blessing of his grace? Is the divine gift of Christian fellowship anything less than this, any day, even the most difficult and distressing day? Even when sin and misunderstanding burden the communal life, is not the sinning brother still a brother, with whom I, too, stand under the Word of Christ? Will not his sin be a constant occasion for me to give thanks that both of us may live in the forgiving love of God in Jesus Christ? Thus the very hour of disillusionment with my brother becomes incomparably salutary, because it so thoroughly teaches me that neither of us can ever live by our own words and deeds, but only by the one Word and Deed which really binds us together – the forgiveness of sins in Jesus Christ. When the morning mists of dreams vanish, then dawns the bright day of Christian fellowship.

In the Christian community thankfulness is just what it is anywhere else in the Christian life. Only those who give thanks for little things receive the big things. We prevent God from giving us the great spiritual gifts he has in store for us, because we do not give thanks for daily gifts. . . . If we do not give thanks daily for the Christian fellowship in which we have been placed, even where there is no great experience, no discoverable riches, but much weakness, small faith, and difficulty; if on the contrary, we only keep complaining to God that everything is so paltry and petty, so far from what we expected, then we hinder God from letting our fellowship grow according to the measure and riches which are there for us all in Jesus Christ. . . .

Christian community is like the Christian's sanctification. It is a gift of God which we cannot claim. Only God knows the real state of our fellowship, of our sanctification. What may appear weak and trifling to us may be great and glorious to God. Just as the Christian should not be constantly feeling his spiritual pulse, so, too, the Christian community has not been given to us by God for us to be constantly taking its temperature. The more thankfully we daily receive what is given to us, the more surely and steadily will fellowship increase and grow from day to day as God pleases.

Christian brotherhood is not an ideal which we must realize; it is rather a reality created by God in Christ in which we may participate. The more clearly we learn to recognize that the ground and strength and promise of all our fellowship is in Jesus Christ alone, the more serenely shall we think of our fellowship and pray and hope for it. ◆

16

Illusions

◆ ◆ ◆ ◆ ◆

Arthur Katz

THERE IS NOTHING MORE IMPORTANT than destroying romantic illusions and fantasies about what we think church as community is. The idea of joining a community of believers lends itself to either total rejection, for fear of becoming a heretical sect, or it is seen as some kind of illusion of tripping off into the rustic wilds. These are terrible distortions, and if there is any romantic idealization of what community is going to confer, or mean for us, we are already in the place of unreality and deception. The enjoyment and appreciation of Christian fellowship with all of its failures and inconveniences, while we are in the process of growing up together, is a much more realistic view of church as community.

Conducting our lives on a daily basis in close proximity to others guarantees that there will be tensions, misunderstandings, individual subjectivities, struggles, and differences of opinion. Our disrespect for one another, our rebellion toward authority, our innate selfishness and insidious self-justifications are revealed. It is a painful but necessary revelation of our hearts. We have to pass through a valley of disillusionment with what we think true fellowship is, what we as God's people are, and not the least, what we ourselves are capable of. In fact, the most painful revelation we need to face is the truth of our own condition. True fellowship is the courage and the willingness to be with one another and bear with one another in all of the above conditions. . . .

In community, our vain illusions will be quickly shattered. But disillusionment is a grace from God, and the only way to be disillusioned is unhappily a painful way, yet far more painful and far more disastrous is to continue in an illusion that is unreal, and which, at the judgment seat of Christ, must be revealed as false. The disillusionment is not just with others; it is recognizing things about yourself that you would not have otherwise been compelled to experience or to see. When it does reveal itself, can we then bear the pain of watching the unraveling of the illusions of another, knowing that we are not to falsely comfort them, or intervene, thus interrupting the redemptive process of God? Can we let the mortification have its full work, and bear the stink of it, while we are alongside that suffering person?

The church is the "pillar and support of truth" (1 Tim. 3:15), and if it is not that, then it is not the church in any true way. Truth has got to be unsparing and total. We cannot allow latitude for illusions and idealism, or any other kind of human-istic tendency. Church as community serves the purpose of putting those things to death. More than one community has been dissolved because the people could not survive the disil-lusionment. They were unprepared for it, and when it came, it took them by surprise and became the end for them because they had wanted to hold on to their illusions.

If we cannot endure a look of indifference, or a seeming rejection, or if we find ourselves reacting in a touchy and hypersensitive manner, how then are we going to be over-comers in the crisis time of the last days when the wrath of the powers of darkness will be vented against God's people in a concentrated way? If we have protective little self-centered egos underlying an outward appearance of spirituality, we will find ourselves constantly hurt, but better to recognize that now, and to submit to the sanctifying work of God in an environment of true fellowship. ◆

Elizabeth O'Connor

WHEREAS CHRISTIAN COMMUNITY is the most difficult to be involved in, it is the most rewarding and the most essential to those on an inward journey. As we grow in depth of relationship with those whose values and experiences are different from ours, the horizons of our little worlds are pushed back. Life comes to have a variety and a richness that was not there before.

In this strange community where commitment is not tentative we become free to act and to speak. We can take risks that we could not take in other situations, which include the risk of getting in touch with our own unfelt feelings. We can afford to express negative reactions and move toward meeting, if we know our words do not cut us off. We can choose to express anger and therefore keep the sun from setting on it. We can take the risk of telling a brother or sister what stands between us, if we know there will be another time when we are together, and that it does not depend on what does or does not happen in this moment.

As for those who irritate us and make us always want to get out of their way, they may be precisely the ones who have the most to tell us about ourselves. Modern psychology teaches that what we object to in others is often what can be found in ourselves. We project onto the other what is in us. . . .

To the extent that a community has a continuing life together we are going to be challenged at the point of our illusions about the kind of people we are. This does not mean that we intentionally seek to break the images of others. The task is always to change ourselves – to deal with that in us which prevents our going forth to meet the other. It is when we are locked in a permanent kind of relationship, however, that the conflicts arise which confront us with ourselves. Peace is not the object of Christian fellowship, though we have thought it was and have maintained "good" relationships at the terrible expense of not being real with each other. When this happens, we forego being a people on a pilgrimage together. . . .

As we will be severely tempted away from an engagement with God and an engagement with self, so will we be tempted away from an engagement with others. The temptation to withdraw will be at the crisis points in our relationships – at times of real confrontation, and at times when we see nothing happening. . . . We will rationalize that it is unprofitable to stick with this particular grouping, when there are more congenial people and more congenial circumstances in other places – "people who think the way I think and feel like I feel" – all of which, when you reflect on it, is rather dull, and in the second place probably fiction, since a sure fact about the next group one joins is that one person there is certain to be the same – saying the same things, doing the same things, and evoking the same kind of response. But of course, we can always move on again when we have settled in enough for the rough edges of another person to rub against our own rough edges. We might even be able to withdraw and maintain the illusion that we still belong to Christ and to his mystical body, but it will remain an unconfirmed opinion.

The New Testament does not know very much about this mystical body. It is concerned with twelve who have a life together. It talks always about the church at Corinth or the church at Rome. The answer that is often made to this is that the church is wherever two or three gather in his name. But this does not only mean the choosing of a few kindred friends with whom to pray. We gather in that name when with other faltering, estranged persons we agree to live a life in depth, which means learning something about forgiveness and what it means to be forgiven. It means staying locked in a concrete, given web of relationship until we come to know ourselves as belonging to one another and belonging to the body of Jesus Christ.

You cannot live in community and hide your problems. In fact, community will bring into light problems which, though they are yours, are often hidden even from you. Relationships in depth will always do that. Christian community probably comes the closest of any community to the family of our child-hood, and all the unassimilated hurts and unresolved problems of that family come to light again in the context of the new "family of faith." Sometimes apparently well-adjusted persons come into the life of the church, people of action, ready to get on with the mission of the church, and then a few months or a year later things do not appear to be as well with them. They are actually much better off, because a lot of their activity had been motivated by anxiety of one kind or another, or simply the need to belong. Others are afraid of relationships in depth and discover that, while they yearn for community, they back away when people get too close. Still others find stirring in them yearnings that had been quieted and are now raised to life by the life around. The reasons are different for each person, but the experience is always pain. No real growth takes place without pain. Nothing is born into the consciousness without suffering. ◆

17

Obstacles

• • • • •

Eberhard Arnold

I F EVERYBODY wants to be in the right, or even if only one person wants to be in the right, it is impossible to live in community. That is egotism or self-love. Touchiness, like opinionatedness, is another form of self-love.

We must seek what brings us together, what is the same for us all. We must think of others with hearts filled with love. If only we could come to the point where we recognize that we are all in the same situation, all in the same state! That we are all equal, and very similar in our situations, is quite amazing. When that becomes clear to us, much of our opinionatedness, our wanting to be in the right, and our touchiness falls away. But that is not yet all. That does not remove the obstacles.

Worst of all is what afflicts people who think about themselves the whole day long: they suffer from a widespread and deadly disease. It destroys body, soul, and spirit. People who have themselves at the center, who relate everything to themselves and see everything from their own point of view, are seriously ill. They are mentally disturbed. They are far from becoming truly human, from becoming true brothers and sisters. They are lost even in the midst of a community household.

All of these things are obstacles to community: touchiness, opinionatedness, self-love, self-centeredness. To have a higher opinion of oneself than of others is a deadly poison. Whoever still does this is completely incapable of community. He or she will not be able to experience the unity of the great cause. This is what is crucial. Of course, it is a help to think of others and of their situation and to look for the best in them. That will help us not to think of ourselves as better than others, but it is not the main thing.

We are still inclined to see the shortcomings of others far out of proportion and thus forget that we ourselves are weak human beings. We should not always try to improve on what another does wrong. We must become reconciled to people's imperfection.

This self-centeredness is a lying spirit; it is out-and-out false. People who have such a high opinion of themselves that they cannot admit a mistake are living in the deepest untruthfulness and insincerity. Egotism must be condemned, not just because it does not fit well in community or because it is morally wrong, but because it is lying and death. It is poisoned through and through and brings destruction. It is the mortal disease. The quarrelsome spirit that destroys community comes from this mortal disease of the soul. Self-centered people are mortally sick. They must be redeemed. ◆

Those who turn around themselves do not know that Christianity has an objective content, that it is actually a cause for which we can completely forget ourselves with our own little egos. Self-importance . . . leads to a hypocritical attitude. We must be freed from all posing, from all affected holiness, otherwise we are utterly lost. The people who are most endangered are the artificial saints who take such pains, yet just these efforts are the root of their hypocrisy. They see God from their own point of view and make God relate to themselves. That is their undoing, because it is utterly untrue. For I am not the truth, and because I am not the truth I cannot and may not place my own person – not even as a Christian – in the center of my thoughts. I would simply make myself an idol. The great cause must be in the center. We must come to true faith in God and the church.

Redemption from the life of self – from wanting to be in the right, from imposing our own ways, from our unfitness for community, from this deadly disease that will be our ruin – can come only through a cause that exists completely outside of our own selves. God's cause is a cause for which we are not needed. We are not indispensable. It is not just that I am unimportant; I am an obstacle. I am an adversary of the cause. Redemption cannot begin until we each recognize this and see ourselves thus in the light of the cause – as adversaries, especially in our own piety. Until that happens we are merely deluding ourselves with our own cramped efforts.

We human beings can recognize light only in contrast to shadow and darkness. We can grasp the cause only through an awareness of its opposite and of its adversaries, for we are not gods but mere mortals. Why do torches give us so much joy? Because they are lit in the night and we become an illuminated circle in the dark. It is the dark background that makes the shining circle of our common life visible at all and allows it to speak to our hearts. Those who are still in love with themselves cannot recognize the cause, nor can those who are still in love with their own religious experience, with their own conversion and rebirth. Not until we see the great cause against the wretchedness of our own little being will we grasp its greatness.

In the early church the Holy Spirit came to those who finally recognized themselves as the murderers of the longed-for Messiah-King, as adversaries of the holy cause for which they had always striven. We are afraid of this awful awakening, especially if we have sought for years or decades to live in a certain holiness and suddenly must recognize ourselves as murderers and adversaries. That is hard but necessary. Paul was blinded when the Spirit came upon him, and it was no subjective exaggeration on his part but his deepest conviction when he said, "I am the worst of all sinners," because he had been personally responsible for the persecution of the church of Jesus Christ and for the murder of the Christian martyrs. That was Paul's experience, this tremendous contrast. He was a persecutor of the church of the Messiah, a persecutor of the kingdom of God. Not until he recognized this could he become an apostle of God's cause. That same contrast helped the early Christians to realize that God's cause is very different from what they had imagined; they would have never grasped it in any other way. Karl Barth says rightly, "The kingdom of God must strike us as being totally other, or it remains closed to us."

This cause, which is totally other from what we ourselves are, alone can free us from our self-centeredness and touchiness. It can free us from our opinionatedness and our quarrelsomeness, from all that we complain makes us unfit to live in community.

Unless we recognize ourselves as adversaries – even in our own piety – we will never grasp the greatness of this cause.

◆ ◆ ◆ ◆ ◆

ONE THING CONCERNS me very much: our powerlessness. Only God is mighty; we are completely powerless. Even for the work that has been given us, we are wholly without power. We cannot fit even a single stone into the church community. We can provide no protection whatsoever for the community when it has been built up. We cannot even devote anything to God's cause by our own power. We are completely without power. But I believe that just this is the only reason God has called us into community: we know we are powerless.

It is very hard to give an account of how it has come about that all of us, especially we older members of the community, know we are so completely powerless. It is hard to describe how all our own power is stripped off us, how our own power has been dropped, dismantled, torn down, and put away. What I wish for our younger members is this same realization, that the dismantling of your own power might be carried out to its full extent. That is not attained so easily and does not happen through a single heroic decision. God must do it in us.

This is the root of grace: the dismantling of our own power. Only to the degree that all our own power is dismantled will God be able to give the fruits of the Spirit and build up his kingdom through us, in us, and among us. There is no other way. If a little power of our own were to rise up among us, the Spirit and authority of God would retreat in the same moment and to the corresponding degree. In my estimation that is the single most important insight with regard to the kingdom of

God. How it actually happens is hard to say. It is as hard to speak of this as it is to speak of the mystic source of all things. The only thing that can be said is that the Holy Spirit produces effects that are deadly for the old life and that at the same time have a wakening and rousing power for the new life which comes from Christ and his Holy Spirit alone.

Let us then give glory to God. Let us pledge to him that all our own power will remain dismantled, and will keep on being dismantled among us. Let us pledge that the only thing that will count among us will be the power and authority of God in Jesus Christ through the Holy Spirit; that it will never again be we that count, but that God alone will rule and govern in Christ and the Holy Spirit. That means we declare our dependence upon grace. This is the testimony we are required to give. Everything we have is the unmerited gift of God. God can give this unmerited gift only to people in whom their own claims and special rights have been dismantled. And for this reason we acknowledge and ask for the grace that appeared in Jesus Christ and that comes to us in the Holy Spirit. ◆

18

Poisons

• • • • •

C. S. Lewis

Possessiveness

Of all the things that can come between people and poison life in community, possessiveness is perhaps the most common. In C. S. Lewis's The Screwtape Letters, *a senior demon, Screwtape, advises his nephew, Wormwood, an inexperienced tempter, on how best to corrupt a human.*

MY DEAR WORMWOOD,
 . . . Men are not angered by mere misfortune but by misfortune conceived as injury. And the sense of injury depends on the feeling that a legitimate claim has been denied. The more claims on life, therefore, that your patient can be induced to make, the more often he will feel injured and, as a result, ill-tempered. Now you will have

noticed that nothing throws him into a passion so easily as to find a tract of time which he reckoned on having at his own disposal unexpectedly taken from him. It is the unexpected visitor (when he looked forward to a quiet evening), or the friend's talkative wife (turning up when he looked forward to a tête-à-tête with the friend), that throws him out of gear. Now he is not yet so uncharitable or slothful that these small demands on his courtesy are in *themselves* too much for it. They anger him because he regards his time as his own and feels that it is being stolen. You must therefore zealously guard in his mind the curious assumption "My time is my own." Let him have the feeling that he starts each day as the lawful possessor of twenty-four hours. Let him feel as a grievous tax that portion of this property which he has to make over to his employers, and as a generous donation that further portion which he allows to religious duties. But what he must never be permitted to doubt is that the total from which these deductions have been made was, in some mysterious sense, his own personal birthright.

You have here a delicate task. The assumption which you want him to go on making is so absurd that, if once it is questioned, even we cannot find a shred of argument in its defense. The man can neither make, nor retain, one moment of time; it all comes to him by pure gift; he might as well regard the sun and moon as his chattels. He is also, in theory, committed to a total service of the Enemy [God]; and if the Enemy appeared to him in bodily form and demanded that total service for even one day, he would not refuse. He would be greatly relieved if that one day involved nothing harder than listening to the conversation of a foolish woman; and he would be relieved almost to the pitch of disappointment if for one half-hour in that day the Enemy said, "Now you may go and amuse yourself." Now, if he thinks about his assumption for a moment, even he is bound to realize that he is actually in this situation every day. When I speak of preserving this assumption in his mind, therefore, the last thing I mean you to do is to furnish him with arguments in its defense. There aren't any. Your task is purely negative. Wrap a darkness about it, and in the center of that darkness let his sense of ownership-in-Time lie silent, uninspected, and operative.

The sense of ownership in general is always to be encouraged. The humans are always putting up claims to ownership which sound equally funny in heaven and in hell, and we must keep them doing so. Much of the modern resistance to chastity comes from people's belief that they "own" their bodies – those vast and perilous estates, pulsating with the energy that made the worlds, in which they find themselves without their consent and from which they are ejected at the pleasure of Another! It is as if a royal child whom his father has placed, for love's sake, in titular command of some great province, under the real rule of wise counselors, should come to fancy he really owns the cities, the forests, and the corn, in the same way as he owns the bricks on the nursery floor.

We produce this sense of ownership not only by pride but by confusion. We teach them not to notice the different senses of the possessive pronoun – the finely graded differences that run from "my boots" through "my dog," "my servant," "my wife," "my father," "my master," and "my country," to "my God." They can be taught to reduce all these senses to that of "my boots," the "my" of ownership. Even in the nursery a child can be taught to mean by "my teddy bear," *not* the old imagined recipient of affections to whom it stands in a special relation (for that is what the Enemy will teach them to mean if we are not careful), but "the bear I can pull to pieces if I like."

And at the other end of the scale, we have taught people to say "my God" in a sense not really very different from "my boots," meaning "the God on whom I have a claim for my distinguished services and whom I exploit from the pulpit – the God I have done a corner in."

And all the time the joke is that the word "mine" in its fully possessive sense cannot be uttered by a human being about anything. In the long run either Our Father [the devil] or the Enemy will say "mine" of each thing that exists, and especially of each man. They will find out in the end, never fear, to whom their time, their souls, and their bodies really belong – certainly not to *them,* whatever happens. At present the Enemy says "mine" of everything on the pedantic, legalistic ground that he made it. Our Father hopes in the end to say "mine" of all things on the more realistic and dynamic ground of conquest.

Your affectionate uncle
Screwtape ◆

Basilea Schlink

Annoyance

WHY DO WE GET ANNOYED AT OTHERS? Because we are not at one with the will of God. That is why everything that does not suit us upsets us. We object to everything. Or demands are made on us which we think are too much. Or someone's request upsets our intentions and we react with annoyance. But we do not realize that all things, large and small, that come from people around us, are actually placed in our daily lives by God. When we get upset, we rebel against God and grieve him. And why do we get annoyed at people, at situations and conditions? Because our ego or our self-will is so big. Everything has to go the way we intended, the way we think is right, the way that is easiest for us. Every wish, opinion, or mistake that others make meets with our opposition. . . .

When we are annoyed, our faces are sullen and we reproach others. Annoyance hinders joy and ruins life together. But the kingdom of Jesus Christ is a kingdom of joy and peace. Annoyance does not fit in. Therefore, it has to be overcome; it cannot have any more room in our lives.

We often try to make excuses for being annoyed. We say it is due to weak nerves [i.e., stress] or because we are "down." But irritation and annoyance come from our evil hearts and ultimately do not have anything to do with fatigue or weak nerves. Having weak nerves or being overworked just brings out what is really deep down in our hearts. When we get into such situations, we have no reason to excuse ourselves or even to pity ourselves. But we have every reason to repent and to call upon the name of Jesus. In this way we will be set free from these evil things that come from our hearts, are expressed by our tongues, and disrupt the peace.

Envy

Envy is a poisonous root in our soul that can kill others. . . . When God has given someone else something that he has denied us, we seldom stop at just having hurt feelings. This poison oozes out of our hearts in word and deed. In the more harmless cases we are unfriendly to others; we repel them; we

quarrel with them and make life difficult for them. . . . We try
to humiliate them somehow, to take them down a peg or two
in the sight of others, or to put them out of the limelight as
best we can. Sometimes we are unconscious of this, because we
pretend that we have impartial reasons for resisting them. And
if we become conscious of our envy, perhaps we try to make it
seem harmless or we even feel sorry for ourselves, because God
has not given us something that he has given to others. If we do
so, we are justifying our envy. . . .

The main roots [of envy] are usually in our selfishness or in
our cravings, whether they be for physical or spiritual goods.
Therefore, we must ask ourselves, "Are we willing to surrender
our selfishness and our claims on possessions and talents to
Jesus and to be poor with him in the way of material goods,
abilities, love, and respect? Are we willing to believe that God
will always endow the poor and that they are the ones who are
really rich?"

[Another] root of envy is mistrust against God. It is
comparing ourselves with others, as though the Father in
heaven had been unjust when he distributed his gifts and
burdens. Therefore, it is a matter of renouncing our rebellious,
mistrustful thoughts. Instead we must trust that God, because
he is love, always gives us what is best for us. He always leads
us the best way. If he had a better way for us, he would have
chosen it.

No matter how he leads us, whether he gives us something
or not, it is always best for us, because it comes from the
hands of the Father who loves us. We must believe that firmly.
Besides, we can never judge the pleasures and burdens of
others, because we cannot see the background. Perhaps we
envy someone for something that is merely a difficult task for
him or her. . . .

Therefore we must begin to give thanks for everything that we have received and then there will be no more room for envy. If we give thanks to God for the gifts that others receive, the poison of envy must yield.

Mistrust

Behind every mistrustful thought, even toward other people, there is something serious, namely an unspoken accusation. We think the other person does not have our best interests in mind; he or she does not want us to have anything good. This poison of mistrust spoils the relationship of trust to our heavenly Father and also to our neighbor. For if we mistrust the love and wisdom of God, we will unintentionally come into the same mistrustful, prejudiced attitude toward one another and will become guilty. This guilt, however, will accuse us before the judgment seat of God if it is not brought into the light, repented of, and forgiven through the blood of Jesus.

But if we are mistrustful toward one another, we will be judged now in our everyday life together. Because the relationship of trust is destroyed, we will no longer receive the love and the good things that we would otherwise have to bring to each other. We become unhappy. This is the consequence of sin. Mistrust separates us from God and one another and poisons our whole life. For this reason we have to get rid of it. . . .

In the fight against mistrust we first have to be shown what the root of our mistrust is. It is ever-present concern for our ego. Will we get what we deserve? Will we be loved and respected enough? That is why we mistrust the leadings of God. That is why we suspect one another. We think we are constantly in danger of getting a bad deal, or having others say negative things about us, or not receiving the love and respect we think we deserve. We imagine that while others appear friendly to us, they are in reality against us. We always suppose that others have ulterior motives. We even attribute evil to someone who only wants to do us good. And whenever there are misunderstandings, we immediately suppose that there is something bad. So we cannot be happy. Mistrust prevents bonds of love from being tied, for love believes all and does not think evil of others, even taking the risk of being disappointed.

Because egoism nourishes mistrust, it is very important, if we want to be freed from this, to make a serious, sober commitment such as, "I do not want to be respected by certain people; I do not want to be admired. Lord, accept my commitment today. I do not want to worry about whether I get a bad deal; I do not want to be involved in myself. I want to trust that you will not let anything happen to me that would not be for my good. I always want to think the best of my brother and sister and not give way to any mistrustful thoughts again. . . ." Then we should go and seek ways to bring love and trust to those whom we have mistrusted. That will help us; for if we give others love, we will no longer center around ourselves. ◆

19

Listening

◆ ◆ ◆ ◆ ◆

Henri J. M. Nouwen

BY REVEALING THE UNIQUE GIFTS of the other, we learn to empty ourselves. Self-emptying does not ask of us to engage ourselves in some form of self-castigation or self-scrutiny, but to pay attention to others in such a way that they begin to recognize their own value.

Paying attention to our brothers and sisters in the human family is far from easy. We tend to be so insecure about our self-worth and so much in need of affirmation that it is very hard not to ask for attention ourselves. Before we are fully aware of it, we are speaking about ourselves, referring to our experiences, telling our stories, or turning the subject of conversation toward our own territory. The familiar sentence, "That reminds me of . . ." is a standard method of shifting attention from the other to ourselves. To pay attention to others with the desire to make them the center and to make their interest our own is a real form of self-emptying, since to be able to receive others into our intimate inner space we must be empty. That is why listening is so difficult. It means our moving away from the center of attention and inviting others into that space.

From experience we know how healing such an invitation can be. When someone listens to us with real concentration and expresses sincere care for our struggles and our pains, we feel that something very deep is happening to us. Slowly, fears melt away, tensions dissolve, anxieties retreat, and we discover that we carry within us something we can trust and offer as a gift to others. The simple experience of being valuable and important to someone else has a tremendous recreative power.

If we have been given such an experience, we have received a precious kind of knowledge. We have learned the true significance of Paul's words, "Always consider the other person to be better than yourself" (Phil. 2:3). This is not an invitation to false humility or to the denial of our own value, but it is a call to enter Christ's healing ministry. Every time we pay attention we become emptier, and the more empty we are the more healing space we can offer. And the more we see others being healed, the more we will be able to understand that it is not through us but through Christ in us that this healing takes place.

◆ ◆ ◆ ◆ ◆

IN OUR WORDY WORLD we usually spend our time together talking. We feel most comfortable in sharing experiences, discussing interesting subjects, or arguing about current issues. It is through a very active verbal exchange that we try to discover each other. But often we find that words function more as walls than as gates, more as ways to keep distance than to come close. Often – even against our own desires – we find ourselves competing with each other. We try to prove to each other that we have something to show that makes us special. The discipline of community helps us to be silent together. This disciplined silence is not an embarrassing silence, but a silence in which together we pay attention to the Lord who calls us together. In this way we come to know each other not as people who cling anxiously to our self-constructed identity, but as people who are loved by the same God in a very intimate and unique way.

Here – as with the discipline of solitude – it is often the words of scripture that can lead us into this communal silence. Faith, as Paul says, comes from hearing. We have to hear the word from each other. When we come together from different geographical, historical, psychological, and religious directions, listening to the same word spoken by different people can create in us a common openness and vulnerability that allow us to recognize that we are safe together in that word. Thus we can come to discover our true identity as a community, we can come to experience what it means to be called together, and we can recognize that the same Lord whom we discovered in our solitude also speaks in the solitude of our neighbors, whatever their language, denomination, or character. In this listening together to the word of God, a true creative silence can grow. This silence is a silence filled with the caring presence of God. Thus listening together to the word can free us from our competition and rivalry and allow us to recognize our true identity as sons and daughters of the same loving God and brothers and sister of our Lord Jesus Christ, and thus of each other. . . .

Community makes us persons; that is, people who are sounding through to each other (the Latin word personare means "sounding through") a truth, a beauty, and a love which is greater, fuller, and richer than we ourselves can grasp. In true community we are windows constantly offering each other new views on the mystery of God's presence in our lives. . . . Community is obedience practiced together. The question is not simply, "Where does God lead me as an individual person who tries to do his will?" More basic and more significant is the question, "Where does God lead us as a people?" This question requires that we pay careful attention to God's guidance in our life together and that together we search for a creative response. Here we come to see how prayer and action are indeed one, because whatever we do as a community can only be an act of true obedience when it is a response to the way we have heard God's voice in our midst. ◆

Dietrich Bonhoeffer

J UST AS LOVE TO GOD begins with listening to his Word, so the beginning of love for brothers and sisters is learning to listen to them. It is God's love for us that he not only gives us his Word but also lends us his ear. So it is his work that we do for our brother and sister when we learn to listen to them. Christians, especially ministers, so often think they must always contribute something when they are in the company of others, that this is the one service they have to render. They forget that listening can be a greater service than speaking.

Many people are looking for an ear that will listen. They do not find it among Christians, because these Christians are talking where they should be listening. But the one who can no longer listen to his brother and sister will soon be no longer listening to God either; they will be doing nothing but prattle in the presence of God too. This is the beginning of the death of the spiritual life, and in the end there is nothing left but spiritual chatter and clerical condescension arrayed in pious words. One who cannot listen long and patiently will presently be talking beside the point and be never really speaking to others, albeit they will be not conscious of it. Those who think that their time is too valuable to spend keeping quiet will eventually have no time for God and their brother and sister, but only for themselves and for their own follies. . . .

There is a kind of listening with half an ear that presumes already to know what the other person has to say. It is an impatient, inattentive listening, that despises the other and is only waiting for a chance to speak and thus get rid of the other person. This is no fulfillment of our obligation to listen, and it is certain that here too our attitude toward our brother or sister only reflects our relationship to God. . . . Christians have forgotten that the service of listening has been committed to them by him who is himself the great listener and whose work we should share. We should listen with the ears of God that we may speak the Word of God. ◆

20

Surrender

◆ ◆ ◆ ◆ ◆

Arthur G. Gish

CHRISTIAN COMMUNITY is a result of surrendering our lives to God's kingdom. Our commitment to our brothers and sisters is an expression of our commitment to God and his will for our lives. Membership in Christian community involves a serious claim of God upon our lives. In Christian community this claim is recognized and accepted. Christian community is not like a service club which competes with other groups for the loyalty of its members. Commitment must be total. To participate in the kingdom of God we must give up all loyalties and commitments that in any way conflict with or hinder our commitment to God.

Christian community is more than an association of independent individuals, for membership involves the very heart of a person's being in all its dimensions. One is not truly in community unless all is committed and shared. Community always includes a price. It means giving up something else, being here rather than there, giving up other options. But the sacrifices are nothing in light of what is received. In fact, the more we give up and the higher the cost for us, the more valuable and significant community will be for us. Those who give little also receive little. The degree of success of intentional communities is directly related to the strength of commitment in those communities.

Commitment in Christian community is the degree to which a person has given up self-interest for the good of the larger community, the amount of personal investment and sense of belonging in the community, and the degree to which one's whole future is seen as linked with that of the community. This sociological definition is not enough for Christian community, however.

Christian commitment in community is not based on the extent to which we see the community fulfilling our own needs or the extent to which the interest of the total community matches our self-interest, but rather the extent to which we have given up self in order to live the new life to which God has called us. Unless we are prepared to die for each other we are not ready to love and live for each other.

Community has many benefits, but they come at the cost of death of the old person in each of us. Just as we must give up self to know Christ (Phil. 3:7–11), so we must die to ourselves to enter God's kingdom. The old self must die for the new to be born, for us to become the new people we are called to be. . . .

One of the main hindrances to doing God's will is our unwillingness to give up self, our constant desire to have our own way. Even most people who do good want to keep control of their own lives and instruct God on how he can help them in doing more good. All too often we pray to God primarily to give us strength to do what we want to do.

God will do little in our lives unless we surrender our wills to him and allow God's will to become our will. Then we can say with Paul, "It is no longer I who live, but Christ who lives in me" (Gal. 2:20). As we offer ourselves wholly to the Lord our will becomes identified with that of Christ. Then we can pray, "Lord, do what you want with my life." As long as we hold back something for ourselves we cannot receive the power, victory, and freedom that God would give us. It is those who have nothing to lose who are most free to be faithful.

God keeps asking more of us than we are able to give. After it seems like we have given every last bit of ourselves and our energy, God still asks more of us. But every time it happens, God gives us new strength we never expected.

Our lives are demanded of us not only when we face persecution, but just as much in good times. When things are going well we are also called to surrender all to God and our brothers and sisters. The Christian calling is a cross on which all our desires, ambitions, and possessions are put to death. Holding on to the smallest thing and being unwilling to surrender it is as bad as the pride of the richest of the rich. This is not just a surrender of our outer nature so that the "pure inner nature" may shine through, but a surrender of everything, including our innermost selves.

The German word for this is *Gelassenheit*. *Gelassenheit* is what is left after you have turned over everything to God and are not holding back anything for yourself. It means surrender, yieldedness, let-go-ness, defenselessness, resignation, vulnerability, serenity, and peace. It is the meekness of those who have been broken by the Spirit. . . .

To surrender everything to God is a deep act of self-affirmation, for it is a recognition that God does love and care for us. How different this is from egoism, with all its deceit and fear! What freedom it is to no longer need to be at the center, to be right, or to prove our worth! What freedom not to need to pretend to be all-powerful, all-wise, and above most human limitations. All of us have tried to create our own little world with ourselves in the center. The history of our lives is the story of our attempts to manipulate everything according to our own wills and dreams. Sometimes we are willing to fit God somewhere into our plans, but often there is little room for God.

The reality we create, however, seldom corresponds with the real world, or with God's desire for us and the world. The result is frustration, alienation, fear, distrust, anxiety, and bitterness. We have set out on a path that cannot lead to life. We are defeated from the start. And no wonder, for we were never meant to be in the center of the world. Only God is big enough for that. Our place is to be gathered together in a circle around God, at peace with others, self, and God's creation.

Here is the basis for living in Christian community. Only as our rebellious, conceited self-wills are broken by the Spirit can we participate authentically in community. Only then are we ready for what God wants to give to us. When King Uzziah died, Isaiah's hopes were shattered, but it was then that God spoke to him (Isa. 6:1). The more we are broken by the Spirit, the more open and sensitive we can be to God's will and to our brothers and sisters.

We cannot of ourselves give up our self-will, for that also requires self-will. But we can allow God to take it away. The point is not to try to be humble, but to be humbled by our relationship with God. To the extent we are broken, we are no longer obsessed with ourselves and are available for God to use us.

One of the reasons faith and community are so difficult for us is that we hold back and refuse to surrender so much. It may be secret sins, an unwillingness to do what we know needs to be done, our pride, our ambition, or maybe our intellectualism. The greatest obstacle to community is refusal to surrender our wills. How hard it is to give up our own opinions, our stubbornness, our conceit, our cleverness! How difficult it is to pray, "Not my will, but thine be done." It is possible to give away all our possessions and still hold on to our will. The struggle with self-will is a daily struggle, confronting us again and again with decisions regarding whether we will live in love. . . .

It is important that we come to terms with our own selfishness. Unless we do that, our communities will be little more than reflections of the old society we hoped to overcome. It is not enough to reject the selfishness and materialism of the larger capitalist society. The cause of the human condition is not only the corrupt environment in which we live, but also the condition of our inner selves which needs to be transformed.

The life of the community must be a manifestation of the new life in Christ which has become real in the experience of each member of the community. We cannot simply come together in community and carry the cancer of the old society with us. Community is possible only to the extent that we leave our old selves behind and are cleansed. To become a member of the new community we need to be converted and reborn. ✦

21

The Center

◆ ◆ ◆ ◆ ◆

Dietrich Bonhoeffer

CHRISTIANITY means community through Jesus Christ and in Jesus Christ. No Christian community is more or less than this. Whether it be a brief, single encounter or the daily fellowship of years, Christian community is only this. We belong to one another only through and in Jesus Christ.

What does this mean? It means, first, that a Christian needs others because of Jesus Christ. It means, second, that a Christian comes to others only through Jesus Christ. It means, third, that in Jesus Christ we have been chosen from eternity, accepted in time, and united for eternity. . . .

One is a brother to another only through Jesus Christ. I am a brother to another person through what Jesus Christ did for me and to me; the other person has become a brother to me through what Jesus Christ did for him. This fact that we are brethren only through Jesus Christ is of immeasurable significance. Not only the other person who is earnest and devout, who comes to me seeking brotherhood, must I deal with in fellowship. My brother is rather that other person who has been redeemed by Christ, delivered from his sin, and called to faith and eternal life. Not what a man is in himself as a Christian, his spirituality and piety, constitutes the basis of our community. What determines our brotherhood is what that man is by reason of Christ.

Our community with one another consists solely in what Christ has done to both of us. This is true not merely at the beginning, as though in the course of time something else were to be added to our community; it remains so for all the future and to all eternity. I have community with others and I shall continue to have it only through Jesus Christ. The more genuine and the deeper our community becomes, the more will everything else between us recede, the more clearly and purely will Jesus Christ and his work become the one and only thing that is vital between us. We have one another only through Christ, but through Christ we do have one another, wholly, and for all eternity.

That dismisses once and for all every clamorous desire for something more. Those who want more than what Christ has established do not want Christian brotherhood. They are looking for some extraordinary social experience which they have not found elsewhere; they are bringing muddled and impure desires into Christian brotherhood. Just at this point Christian brotherhood is threatened most often at the very start by the greatest danger of all, the danger of being poisoned at its root, the danger of confusing Christian brotherhood with some wishful idea of religious fellowship, of confounding the natural desire of the devout heart for community with the spiritual reality of Christian brotherhood....

Perhaps the contrast between spiritual and human reality can be made most clear in the following observation: Within the spiritual community there is never, nor in any way, any "immediate" relationship of one to another, whereas human community expresses a profound, elemental, human desire for community, for immediate contact with other human souls, just as in the flesh there is the urge for physical merger with other flesh. Such desire of the human soul seeks a complete fusion of I and thou, whether this occur in the union of love or, what is after all the same thing, in the forcing of another person into one's sphere of power and influence. . . .

Human love is directed to the other person for his own sake, spiritual love loves him for Christ's sake. Therefore, human love seeks direct contact with the other person; it loves him not as a free person but as one whom it binds to itself. It wants to gain, to capture by every means; it uses force. It desires to be irresistible, to rule.

Human love has little regard for truth. It makes the truth relative, since nothing, not even the truth, must come between it and the beloved person. Human love desires the other person, his company, his answering love, but it does not serve him. On the contrary, it continues to desire even when it seems to be serving. There are two marks, both of which are one and the same thing, that manifest the difference between spiritual and human love: Human love cannot tolerate the dissolution of a fellowship that has become false for the sake of genuine fellowship, and human love cannot love an enemy, that is, one who seriously and stubbornly resists it. Both spring from the same source: human love is by its very nature desire – desire for human community. So long as it can satisfy this desire in some way, it will not give it up, even for the sake of truth, even for the sake of genuine love for others. But where it can no longer expect its desire to be fulfilled, there it stops short – namely, in the face of an enemy. There it turns into hatred, contempt, and calumny.

Right here is the point where spiritual love begins. This is why human love becomes personal hatred when it encounters genuine spiritual love, which does not desire but serves. Human love makes itself an end in itself. It creates of itself an end, an idol which it worships, to which it must subject everything. It nurses and cultivates an ideal, it loves itself, and nothing else in the world. Spiritual love, however, comes from Jesus Christ, it serves him alone; it knows that it has no immediate access to other persons.

Jesus Christ stands between the lover and the others he loves. I do not know in advance what love of others means on the basis of the general idea of love that grows out of my human desires – all this may rather be hatred and an insidious kind of selfishness in the eyes of Christ. What love is, only Christ tells in his Word. Contrary to all my own opinions and convictions, Jesus Christ will tell me what love toward the brethren really is. Therefore, spiritual love is bound solely to the Word of Jesus Christ. Where Christ bids me to maintain fellowship for the sake of love, I will maintain it. Where his truth enjoins me to dissolve a fellowship for love's sake, there I will dissolve it, despite all the protests of my human love. Because spiritual love does not desire but rather serves, it loves an enemy as a brother. It originates neither in the brother nor in the enemy but in Christ and his Word. Human love can never understand spiritual love, for spiritual love is from above; it is something completely strange, new, and incomprehensible to all earthly love.

Because Christ stands between me and others, I dare not desire direct fellowship with them. As only Christ can speak to me in such a way that I may be saved, so others, too, can be saved only by Christ himself. This means that I must release the other person from every attempt of mine to regulate, coerce, and dominate him with my love. The other person needs to retain his independence of me, to be loved for what he is, as one for whom Christ became man, died, and rose again, for whom Christ bought forgiveness of sins and eternal life. Because Christ has long since acted decisively for my brother, before I could begin to act, I must leave him his freedom to be Christ's; I must meet him only as the person that he already is in Christ's eyes. This is the meaning of the proposition that we can meet others only through the mediation of Christ. Human love constructs its own image of the other person, of what he is and what he should become. It takes the life of the other person into its own hands. Spiritual love recognizes the true image of the other person which he has received from Jesus Christ, the image that Jesus Christ himself embodied and would stamp upon all people.

Therefore, spiritual love proves itself in that everything it says and does commends Christ. It will not seek to move others by all-too-personal, direct influence, by impure interference in the life of another. It will not take pleasure in pious, human fervor and excitement. It will rather meet the other person with the clear Word of God and be ready to leave him alone with this Word for a long time, willing to release him again in order that Christ may deal with him. It will respect the line that has been drawn between him and us by Christ, and it will find full fellowship with him in the Christ who alone binds us together. Thus this spiritual love will speak to Christ about a brother more than to a brother about Christ. It knows that the most direct way to others is always through prayer to Christ

and that love of others is wholly dependent upon the truth
in Christ. It is out of this love that John the disciple speaks:
"I have no greater joy than to hear that my children walk in
truth" (3 John 4). ◆

Friedrich Foerster

MANY SAY: "can we not be brothers and sisters
without the Crucified?"
Of course. Such slight claims can be made
of depth and purity of fraternal love that the cross is not
necessary to make possible such community. But if you are in
earnest about becoming a real brother or sister you will also
earn the self-knowledge in this conflict which will open for
you the indispensability of the cross for the perfection of the
bond of brotherhood. You will obtain a sharpness of vision
for the mark of Cain that every person bears upon his or her
brow; you will think of the vast power of envy, ambition, and
jealousy that every community threatens to explode; you will
have before you in their full range the merciless, divisive power
of the little habits and qualities, the bellicosity of the nerves,
the unprincipled hunger for the sweetmeats of life, and all the
hostility of rivals thereby engendered. And finally, you will be
conscious of what it means to keep permanently in honorable
peace opposing natures of strong will, passionate temperament, and firm conviction – without deep-lying falsehood or
falsified cordiality.

Our own self-knowledge does not suffice to reveal to us all the inner limitations of brotherly love. Only in the light of Christ can we know to the roots what there is in our souls that rebels against brotherhood; only in the presence of the Redeemer do we know that a spasm of little emotions keeps us chained as soon as we become involved with others in the division of labor, in suffering, and in joy. And for this reason it remains true that only in Gethsemane and upon Calvary was human society perfected. Without the crucifixion of the natural man all socialization must finally burst asunder in wild hatred. For the natural man cannot really be a brother. Whoever fails to see that doesn't know either what a man or a brother is.

"Of course Christianity is life," says Kierkegaard, "but first it passes through death." Only if we realize through how many deaths everyone must pass who really desires to be a brother can we grasp the ultimate condition of human community and therewith also the eternal reference of the cross to the social question. ◆

22

God's Call

• • • • •

Henri J. M. Nouwen

THE BASIS of the Christian community is not the family tie, or social or economic equality, or shared oppression or complaint, or mutual attraction, but the divine call. The Christian community is not the result of human efforts. God has made us into his people by calling us out of "Egypt" to the "New Land," out of the desert to fertile ground, out of slavery to freedom, out of our sin to salvation, out of captivity to liberation. All these words and images give expression to the fact that the initiative belongs to God and that he is the source of our new life together. By our common call to the New Jerusalem, we recognize each other on the road as brothers and sisters. Therefore, as the people of God, we are called *ekklēsia* (from the Greek *kaleo,* "call," and *ek,* "out"), the community called out of the world into the new.

Since our desire to break the chains of our alienation is very strong today, it is of special importance to remind each other that, as members of the Christian community, we are not primarily for each other but for God. Our eyes should not remain fixed on each other but be directed forward to what is dawning on the horizon of our existence. We discover each other by following the same vocation and by supporting each other in the same search. Therefore, the Christian community is not a closed circle of people embracing each other, but a forward-moving group of companions bound together by the same voice asking for their attention.

It is quite understandable that in our large, anonymous cities we look for people on our "wavelength" to form small communities. Prayer groups, Bible study clubs, and house churches are ways of restoring or deepening our awareness of belonging to the people of God. But sometimes a false type of like-mindedness can narrow our sense of community. We all should have the mind of Jesus Christ, but we do not all have to have the mind of a school teacher, a carpenter, a bank director, a congressman, or whatever socioeconomic or political group. There is a great wisdom hidden in the old bell tower calling people with very different backgrounds away from their homes to form one body in Jesus Christ. It is precisely by transcending the many individual differences that we can become witnesses of God who allows his light to shine upon poor and rich, healthy and sick alike. But it is also in this encounter on the way to God that we become aware of our neighbor's needs and begin to heal each other's wounds.

During the last few years I was part of a small group of students who regularly celebrated the Eucharist together. We felt very comfortable with each other and had found "our own way." The songs we sang, the words we used, the greetings we exchanged all seemed quite natural and spontaneous. But when a few new students joined us, we discovered that we expected them to follow our way and go along with "the way we do things here." We had to face the fact that we had become clannish, substituting our minds for the mind of Jesus Christ. Then we found out how hard it is to give up familiar ways and create space for the strangers, to make a new common prayer possible.

Not without reason is the church called a "pilgrim church," always moving forward. The temptation to settle in a comfortable oasis, however, has often been too great to resist and frequently the divine call is forgotten and unity broken. At those times not just individuals but whole groups are caught in the illusion of safety, and prayer is shriveled into a partisan affair.

◆ ◆ ◆ ◆ ◆

IN AND THROUGH CHRIST, people of different ages and lifestyles, from different races and classes, with different languages and educations, can join together and witness to God's compassionate presence in our world. There are many common-interest groups, and most of them seem to exist in order to defend or protect something. Although these groups often fulfill important tasks in our society, the Christian community is of a different nature. When we form a Christian community, we come together not because of similar experiences, knowledge, problems, color, or sex, but because we have been called together by the same God. Only God enables us to cross the many bridges that separate us; only the Lord allows us to recognize each other as members of the same human family, and frees us to pay careful attention to each other. This is why those who are gathered together in community are witnesses to the compassionate God. By the way they are able to carry each other's burdens and share each other's joys, they testify to God's presence in our world.

Life in community is a response to a vocation. The word vocation comes from the Latin vocare, which means "to call." God calls us together into one people fashioned in the image of Christ. It is by Christ's vocation that we are gathered. Here we need to distinguish carefully between vocation and career. In a world that puts such emphasis on success, our concern for a career constantly tends to make us deaf to our vocation. When we are seduced into believing that our career is what counts, we can no longer hear the voice that calls us together. . . .

A vocation is not the exclusive privilege of monks, priests, religious sisters, or a few heroic laypersons. God calls everyone who is listening; there is no individual or group for whom God's call is reserved. But to be effective, a call must be heard, and to hear it we must continually discern our vocation amidst the escalating demands of our career. ◆

Eberhard Arnold

IT IS CLEAR that the war of liberation for unity and for the fullness of love is being fought on many fronts with many different weapons. So too, the work of community finds expression in many different ways.

Some might be tempted to believe that a life without personal property in community of goods is the only way to be a follower of Jesus and a member of his church on earth.

But this would be an error. We must recognize the astounding diversity of tasks and vocations that belong to the church militant. Still, for each one of us there is a certainty of purpose for every stretch of the way we are called to go. Only where there is direct certainty about one's vocation can there be loyalty and an unerring clarity (even in little things) to the very end. Only those who hold firm can bear the standard; but to those unable to endure, nothing can be entrusted.

Accordingly, humans do not receive some high commission from God without also receiving a specific, defined task. Obviously, a greater, more comprehensive vocation can absorb a former, more limited one (this is the only way one vocation can supplant another). . . . What is decisive is that any specific vocation leads only to Christ: that it serves the whole of the church and advances the coming kingdom.

Wherever people see their particular task as something special in itself, they will go astray. But anyone who serves the whole in his own specific place and in his own characteristic way can rightfully say: "I belong to God and to life in community," or to God and any other calling. Before our human service can become divine service, however, we must recognize how small and limited it is in the face of the whole. Then a special calling – living in community, for instance – must never be confused with the church of Christ itself. . . .

That is why, in the life of a community, people will be confronted by several decisive questions again and again: How am I called? To what am I called? Will I follow the call? Only a few are called to the special way that is ours. Yet those who are called – a small, battle-tried band, who must sacrifice themselves again and again – will hold firmly for the rest of their lives to the common task shown them by God. They will be ready to sacrifice life itself for the sake of the common life.

People tear themselves away from home, parents, and career for the sake of marriage; for the sake of wife and child they risk their lives. In the same way it is necessary to break away and sacrifice everything for the sake of our calling to this way. Our public witness to voluntary community of goods and work, to a life of peace and love, will have meaning only when we throw our entire life and livelihood into it. ◆

Andreas Ehrenpreis

WE CAN SEE many clear signs that show the way to true love and community. But it is quite wrong to accuse us of making life in community a matter of compulsion. By no means. It is Another who demands it and compels us to it; but neither he nor we want to force anyone. Never! Whoever is not driven by love and an inner calling should leave it alone. It is an urgent longing for enduring life and joy, it is fear of God's wrath, that drives us and urges us to obey God. That is the source of community life. It is not we ourselves. It is not our invention. It cannot be our undertaking. Many of us have had a livelihood and property and a strong self-will. We liked it all too. We felt comfortable in it. But love for Christ and for the poor drove us to do what we do and confess to now. It was the recognition of God. So we found out the truth of the saying, "If you want the one you must let the other go." We recognized the truth that no one can obey two masters. We cannot belong to God and mammon at the same time. . . .

Jesus wants more than our good will. He wants us to have joy in it, the joy of one who has lost something of little value and found a priceless treasure, like the man in the parable of the kingdom who, in pure joy and without any compulsion, sells all he has for the sake of his new treasure. It means more to him than all the money, all the riches, and all the property in the world. Therefore we should not set store by what is petty and worthless, but give it up for the sake of the one and only treasure. That is the best exchange we can make in life. ♦

23

Promises

♦ ♦ ♦ ♦ ♦

Jonathan Wilson-Hartgrove

IN A SPARSE LIVING ROOM, just off a busy street, a young man kneels on a hardwood floor, his head bowed, oil dripping from his hair. Standing around him with their hands on his head, his back, his shoulders, a small group is praying. They are asking God to bless the promise this young man has made – "to persevere with these people in this place." Minutes ago, one of them read from Psalm 133:

> How good and pleasant it is
> > when God's people live together in unity!
> It is like precious oil poured on the head,
> > running down on the beard,
> running down on Aaron's beard,
> > down on the collar of his robe.

This oil is anointing oil, like the oil that marked Aaron as a priest – like the perfume that Mary of Bethany poured on

Jesus' feet, signifying him as one who was set apart for God's service. This is precious oil, dripping down on holy ground. It is precious not so much for its market value as for the commitment it marks.

"Do you promise to submit to the Holy Spirit as discerned in this community?" a leader asked the young man as he presented himself for membership. His "I do" was echoed by the community, who pledged their commitment to him. Now they are touching, united in prayer, the oil of these promises on each of their hands. This is a solemn vow before their God.

If a passerby in this low-income, inner-city neighborhood were to peek in the window and witness this scene, she would probably be suspicious. Who besides gangs and cults performs ritual acts of initiation, asking members to commit their whole life to something? If she knew this young man, she would likely be concerned. Has he been brainwashed by this group? We are leery of organizations that ask too much of people. We worry about friends who submit to extreme demands. Vows can be dangerous.

Yet, for most of the history of the church, small groups of monks and nuns have welcomed members in ceremonies like this, making lifelong promises in the service of God and the church. In his *Rule,* Saint Benedict of Nursia instructs communities to test those who come seeking membership, leaving them to knock at the door for four or five days. Only if these seekers are persistent should they be invited into the community for a short time, after which the *Rule* is to be thoroughly explained to them. Then, if they want, they can practice living this way of life. Through various stages, this testing continues. But when someone is finally ready to join, the commitment is total: she declares her intent to the group, bows at their feet in prayer, and leaves everything, even the clothes on her back, for the new life she has chosen in community.

Extreme as this may seem to the modern observer, monastic vows sound somewhat familiar to anyone who has been to a wedding ceremony or themselves said "I do" before God and community. In both its commitments of marriage and of celibacy, the church calls its members to make promises about who we will be faithful to in our daily living. Our lives are not our own. We have been made living members of the body of Christ. Nothing could be more extreme, yet our new life gets fleshed out in terms of particular relationships and the promises that make them possible. To learn to live "in Christ" is to learn to make promises and keep them.

But we live in a world marked by infidelity, each of us debilitated in our incapacity to do what we say we will do. While we may suspect others of simply lying when they do not keep their promises, we each know from our own experience that we often fail to do things that we fully intended to do when we said we would do them. Indeed, we may have never consciously chosen *not* to do them. We just forgot. Or got distracted by other things. Yet, in our relationships with other people these broken promises add up, creating walls of mistrust on the already fragmented landscape of our shared existence. We learn to confess both the evil we've done and "the things we have left undone" because we know our will is weak from the start.

Infidelity is a tendency deep within us. But it also comes to us through the constant barrage of powers at work in this world's broken systems. Because sex sells, we are inundated daily by the suggestive poses of women and men to whom we're not only not committed but whom we do not even know. Their images come to our senses not as icons in which we might glimpse the divine but as products to be consumed.

This pornographic imagination is extended to real estate, destinations, entertainment events, and even educational opportunities. Our broken economy does not invite us to ask how we might be faithful to our people and place but rather how we might use them to satisfy our base desires. Infidelity is sold to us as a good.

In his classic text *On Christian Doctrine,* Saint Augustine of Hippo made an important distinction in Christian thinking between something that is to be enjoyed for its own sake and something that is to be used for the sake of enjoying something else. Unlike the modern philosopher Immanuel Kant, who argued that human beings are ends in themselves, Augustine claimed that all creatures – even fellow humans – are to be "used" for the sake of enjoying God. Everything God has made is good, and people are *very* good, according to the creation story. But every good thing is meant to point us toward the greatest Good, the Giver of all good things. The earth, then, is charged with the glory of God, heaven shouting out to us at every turn.

But we defile the holy when we love good things for our own sake, deadening our sense of intimacy and connection with God. When we use people and place to serve ourselves, we are not only untrue to our fellow creatures. We also distance ourselves from the Creator and from the part of ourselves that cries out for connection with the divine. Infidelity unravels the intricate fabric of the universe.

To make promises is to proclaim that a culture of mistrust has been interrupted by One whom we can trust. It is to live as a sign of God's faithfulness, even as we struggle to grow into fidelity ourselves. We make promises because we've glimpsed a picture of hope and know that it points us toward the life we were made for. . . .

A post-college group from a local church is gathered in the living room, just off that busy street, sitting on the hardwood floor where a young man knelt to promise his life to this community. This group is trying to make sense of his commitment, and those of others like him. Why would anyone promise their life to God in community? They are from a dozen states and two other countries – young professionals and graduate students, all of them shaped by a low-commitment culture that nevertheless has lofty ideals. They graduated from schools that told them either they were to go out, work hard, and run the world or they were to go out and work even harder to change it. They are ambitious young people who have, somehow, been fascinated by Jesus. One of them, an accountant, tries to name the tension.

"So, you've committed to stay here. How long are we talking?"

"We're here for life," one community member says.

She tries to clarify: "Is this like a five-year commitment? Ten years?"

"We don't know how long we'll live, but we plan to die here."

For the young accountant, this doesn't compute. She has worked hard to calculate possibilities, to manage futures, to keep her options open in pursuit of the best possible outcome. Ours is a broken world of sharp edges and hard breaks, she knows. She has read of the millions who are dying from poverty, of the wars that are raging in a dozen countries, of the exploitation in human trafficking, of our global environmental crisis. "For God so loved the world," she remembers reading also, and she knows she cannot sit idly in the comfort of her middle-class existence. Surely God wants her to do something. But in a world of so many possibilities, how could anyone commit to one place – and for their whole life long?

Saturated as our story is in covenant, the truth is that all of us – even committed, church-going Christians – are steeped in a culture of contracts that is deeply suspicious of promises. As we've already noted, we are bad at doing what we say we will do, and we know this, each of us. The collective legal codes of cultures all around the world attest to the fact that this tendency to infidelity is not a recent shortcoming in human history. Yet, with the increasing individualism that has emerged from a modern notion of rights and freedom, community safeguards against selfishness and abuse have deteriorated, leaving us with the sole defense of our current legal system – the contract.

To its credit, the contract is excellent at clarifying the terms of commitments. Each party to a contract knows what they are expected to do and what they can expect from others. It is written out in black and white. And because we know that people do not always do what we say we will do, our contracts also spell out terms for what will happen if any party fails to keep their promise. Ultimately, every contract has a dissolution policy that outlines from the very start what the relationship will look like if it ultimately falls apart. Every contract, then, is conditional.

God's story of covenant is an interruption to this logic. God's promise to Noah and to Abraham – to all creation and to all the children of faith – is not conditional. It is a promise that reveals something about who our God is – "gracious and compassionate, slow to anger and abounding in love, and he relents from sending calamity" (Joel 2:13). Though the Mosaic covenant, which fleshes out life with God under a law, does depend on God's people following the good Way that is given to us, the hope of the story is not that we will buckle down and achieve faithfulness, but that a Messiah will come who can establish God's reign and that, as the Lord says through the prophet Jeremiah, "I will put my law in their minds and write it on their hearts" (31:33). We will make promises and keep them because our God is great enough to make faithfulness possible, even among broken people like us.

Do those of us who have been baptized into Christ's body always keep the promises we make? No, we have not been made perfect. In their struggle to "be perfect . . . as your heavenly Father is perfect" (Matt. 5:48), the mothers and fathers of the desert tradition came face-to-face with their weakness and infidelity. In that place of humility, they learned the grace that is given to us in Christ. "It is the property of angels not to fall," Abba Macedonius said. "It is the property of men to fall, and to rise again as often as this may happen." We make promises not because we will always be able to keep them, but because we trust a God who is faithful enough to always help us get up again.

This falling down and getting up, as undramatic as it may seem, is what the story of covenant teaches us to see as the most important thing any of us can ever do. If the God who created the world has indeed redeemed it in Christ, no task is more important than each of us growing up together in Christ. We do this by making promises to particular people, learning to forgive as we are forgiven, and trusting that there is enough grace to sustain us, even when we're not sure how it's all going to work out. Whether it's in a monastery, a community, a church, or a marriage, we make promises in hope that the God who made covenant with Abraham has made faithfulness possible for the whole world in Jesus. Our vows point to Jesus as a sign for the whole world: by grace we are being saved. ◆

Nicholas Ludwig von Zinzendorf

THINGS ARE MUCH freer in the community than in the world. In the world, whoever binds himself in writing to this or that person will not be asked whether he wants to comply with this or not. He must do it, even if he says he acted too rashly. Then people say that if he had considered well at the beginning, he would have had more than one other way of doing things, but now this will not do. . . .

This is the way it works. Such relationships and associations must not take place until people have the heart and mind for it, and not before they have been turned back once, twice, and more times and thus have been put to the test. Then they can be told later, "You did not act because you were humanly persuaded to. At that time you acted in the way a creation who belongs to its Creator God is able to act." People like this who have undergone enough tests, so that their hearts and minds are focused, are received into the community not only for enjoyment but also to work and to suffer for Jesus' sake. . . .

We tell people to stay by themselves for a while first, to consider the matter alone, and to allow the matter to become more difficult for them than it really is. This is so that they are not so taken in by the friendliness and warmth of the community that they enter into a matter out of good will, without sufficient consideration, and only when they are surrounded by difficulties would think, "What have I done?" Then, if they still know that the matter is from the Savior, then the tower will be built with consideration of the costs, and it endures. . . .

When someone said to Jesus, "I want to follow you wherever you go" (Matt. 8:19), he made it difficult for him. He did this simply because he did not want people to be talked into anything more than they had the heart for. He did not want his people to be scorned for having begun to build towers they could not complete. ◆

PART III

Life in Community

Community life is like martyrdom by fire: it means the daily sacrifice of all our strength and all our rights, all the claims we commonly make on life and assume to be justified. In the symbol of fire the individual logs burn away so that, united, its glowing flames send out warmth and light again and again into the land.

EBERHARD ARNOLD, Why We Live in Community

24

Love

• • • • •

Thomas Merton

I T I S N O T E N O U G H for love to be shared: it must be
shared freely. That is to say it must be given, not merely
taken. Unselfish love that is poured out upon a selfish
object does not bring perfect happiness: not because love
requires a return or a reward for loving, but because it rests
in the happiness of the beloved. And if the one loved receives
selfishly, the lover is not satisfied. The lover sees that his or her
love has failed to make the beloved happy. It has not awakened
the capacity for unselfish love.

Hence the paradox that unselfish love cannot rest perfectly
except in a love that is perfectly reciprocated: because it knows
that the only true peace is found in selfless love. Selfless love
consents to be loved selflessly for the sake of the beloved. In so
doing, it perfects itself.

The gift of love is the gift of the power and the capacity
to love, and, therefore, to give love with full effect is also to

receive it. So, love can only be kept by being given away, and it can only be given perfectly when it is also received.

To love another is to will what is really good for him. Such love must be based on truth. A love that sees no distinction between good and evil, but loves blindly merely for the sake of loving, is hatred, rather than love. To love blindly is to love selfishly, because the goal of such love is not the real advantage of the beloved but only the exercise of love in our own souls. . . . It does not seek the true advantage of the beloved or even our own. It is not interested in the truth, but only in itself. It proclaims itself content with an apparent good, which is the exercise of love for its own sake, without any consideration of the good or bad effects of loving.

It is clear, then, that to love others well we must first love the truth. And since love is a matter of practical and concrete human relations, the truth we must love when we love our brothers is not mere abstract speculation: it is the moral truth that is to be embodied and given life in our own destiny and theirs. This truth is more than the cold perception of an obligation, flowing from moral precepts. The truth we must love in loving our brothers is the concrete destiny and sanctity that are willed for them by the love of God. One who really loves another is not merely moved by the desire to see him contented and healthy and prosperous in this world. Love cannot be satisfied with anything so incomplete. If I am to love my brother, I must somehow enter deep into the mystery of God's love for him. . . .

The truth I must love in my brother is God himself, living in him. I must seek the life of the Spirit of God breathing in him.

And I can only discern and follow that mysterious life by the action of the same Holy Spirit living and acting in the depths of my own heart.

A selfish love seldom respects the rights of the beloved to be an autonomous person. Far from respecting the true being of another and granting his personality room to grow and expand in its own original way, this love seeks to keep him in subjection to ourselves. It insists that he conform himself to us, and it works in every possible way to make him do so. A selfish love withers and dies unless it is sustained by the attention of the beloved. When we love thus, our friends exist only in order that we may love them. In loving them we seek to make pets of them, to keep them tame. Such love fears nothing more than the escape of the beloved. It requires his subjection because that is necessary for the nourishment of our own affections.

Selfish love often appears to be unselfish, because it is willing to make any concession to the beloved in order to keep him prisoner. But it is supreme selfishness to buy what is best in a person, his liberty, his integrity, his own autonomous dignity as a person, at the price of far lesser goods. Such selfishness is all the more abominable when it takes a complacent pleasure in its concessions, deluded that they are all acts of selfless charity.

A love, therefore, that is selfless, that honestly seeks the truth, does not make unlimited concessions to the beloved.

May God preserve me from the love of a friend who will never dare to rebuke me. May he preserve me from the friend who seeks to do nothing but change and correct me. But may he preserve me still more from the one whose love is only satisfied by being rebuked.

If I love my brothers according to the truth, my love for them will be true not only to them but to myself.

I cannot be true to them if I am not true to myself.

There is no true intimacy between souls who do not know how to respect one another's solitude. I cannot be united in love with a person whose very personality my love tends to obscure, to absorb, and to destroy. Nor can I awaken true love in a person who is invited, by my love, to be drowned in the act of drowning me with love.

If we know God, our identification of ourselves with those we love will be patterned on our union with God, and subordinate to it. Thus our love will begin with the knowledge of its own limitations and rise to the awareness of its greatness. For in ourselves we will always remain separate and remote from one another, but in God we can be one with those we love.

We cannot find them in God without first perfectly finding ourselves in him. Therefore we will take care not to lose ourselves in looking for them outside him. For love is not found in the void that exists between our being and the being of the one we love. There is an illusion of unity between us when our thoughts, our words, or our emotions draw us out of ourselves and suspend us together for a moment over the void. But when this moment has ended, we must return into ourselves or fall into the void. There is no true love except in God, who is the source both of our own being and of the being we love.

We are obliged to love one another. We are not strictly bound to "like" one another. Love governs the will; "liking" is a matter of sense and sensibility. Nevertheless, if we really love others it will not be too hard to like them also.

If we wait for some people to become agreeable or attractive before we begin to love them, we will never begin. If we are content to give them a cold, impersonal "charity" that is merely a matter of obligation, we will not trouble to try to understand them or to sympathize with them at all. And in that case we will not really love them, because love implies an efficacious will not only to do good to others exteriorly but also to find some good in them to which we can respond. ◆

Søren Kierkegaard

W HEN WE SPEAK about the works of love, it must mean either that we implant love in the heart of another or that we presuppose that love is in the other person's heart and with this presupposition build up love in him or her. One of the two must exist for building up love. But can we implant love in the heart of another? No. It is God alone, the creator who himself is love, who can implant love in a person. All energetic and self-assertive zeal in this regard, all thought of creating love in another person, does nothing to build up. It is unthinkable. No, true love presupposes that love is in the other person's heart, no matter how hidden, and by this very presupposition builds love up – from the ground up.

Love is not what you try to do to transform the other person or what you do to compel love to come forth in him; it is rather how you compel yourself. Only the person who lacks love imagines himself able to build up love by compelling the other. The one who truly loves always believes that love is present; precisely in this way he builds up. In this way he only entices forth the good; he "loves up" love; he builds up what is already there. For love can and will be treated in only one way – by being loved forth.

To love forth love means to believe that love is present at the base. The builder can point to his work and say, "This is my work." But love has nothing it can point to, for its very work consists only in presupposing. If you ever did succeed (by presupposing) in building up love in another person, when the building stands, you must step aside and humbly say, "Indeed, I knew it was there all the time."

Alas, love has no merit at all, for love's building does not stand as a monument to the skill of the builder or, like the pupil, as a reminder of the teacher's instruction. Those who love accomplish nothing; they only bring forth the love that is already there. Those who love work quietly and earnestly, and yet it is the powers of the eternal, not the strength of their love, which are set in motion. The humility in love is the secret of its power.

Love makes itself inconspicuous, especially when it works hardest. In love's work, our labor is reduced to nothing. The building up of love can thus be compared to the work of nature. While we sleep, creation's vital forces keep on. No one gives a thought to how they carry on, although everyone delights in the beauty of the meadow and the fruitfulness of the field. This is the way love conducts itself. It presupposes that love is present, like the germ in a kernel of grain, and if it succeeds in bringing it to fruition, love is modest, as inconspicuous as when it worked day and night.

Therefore, "love is patient." Patience means perseverance in believing that love is fundamentally present. Those who judge that another lacks love take the groundwork away, and thus cannot build up. Love builds up with patience. Neither "is it irritable or resentful," for irritability and resentment ultimately deny love in another. In fact, love bears others' misunderstanding, their thanklessness, and their anger.

"Love does not insist on its own way," neither does it "rejoice at wrong." Those who seek their own way push everything else aside. They demolish in order to make room for their own way, which they want to build up. Yes, the one who seeks to tear down must be said to rejoice at wrong. But love rejoices in knowing that love is already present; therefore it builds up. "Love bears all things." When we say of a very healthy person that he can eat or drink anything, we mean that in his strength he draws nourishment out of even the poorest food. In the same way love bears all things, continually presupposing that love is fundamentally present, despite resistance – and thereby it builds up.

"Love believes all things." Yes, to believe all things means to believe that love is there – even though love is not apparent, even though the opposite is seen. Mistrust takes the very foundation away. Unlike love, mistrust cannot build up. "Love hopes all things." Despite all appearances to the contrary, love firmly trusts that love will eventually show itself, even in the deluded, in the misguided, and in the lost. The father's love won the prodigal son again just because he hoped all things, believing that love was fundamentally present. What more can we say? "Love endures all things. It is not jealous or boastful; it is not arrogant or rude; it is not irritable or resentful . . ."

Love builds up simply because it knows beyond any doubt that love is present. Have you not experienced this yourself? If anyone has ever spoken to you in such a way or acted toward you in such a way that you felt yourself built up, was it not because you quite vividly perceived that he or she presupposed love to be present in you? We know that no one can bestow the ground of love in another person's heart. Love is the ground, and we build only from the ground up, only by presupposing love. Take love away, cease from presupposing it – then there is no one who builds up nor is there anyone who is built up. ◆

Deeds

· · · · ·

Mother Teresa

WHAT WE NEED is to love without getting tired. How does a lamp burn? Through the continuous input of small drops of oil. What are these drops of oil in our lamps? They are the small things of daily life: faithfulness, small words of kindness, a thought for others, our way of being silent, of looking, of speaking, and of acting. Do not look for Jesus away from yourselves. He is not out there; he is among you. Keep your lamp burning and you will recognize him.

These words of Jesus, "Even as I have loved you, also love one another," should be not only a light to us, but they should also be a flame consuming the selfishness that prevents the growth of holiness. Jesus "loved us to the end," to the very limit of love: the cross. This love must come from within, from our union with Christ. Loving must be as normal to us as living and breathing, day after day until our death.

We do not need to carry out grand things in order to show a great love for God and for our neighbors. It is the intensity of love we put into our gestures that makes them into something beautiful for God.

Peace and war start within one's own home. If we really want peace for the world, let us start by loving one another within our families. Sometimes it is hard for us to smile at one another. It is often difficult for the husband to smile at his wife or for the wife to smile at her husband.

In order for love to be genuine, it has to be above all a love for our neighbor. We must love those who are nearest to us, in our own family. From there, love spreads toward whoever may need us.

It is easy to love those who live far away. It is not always easy to love those who live right next to us. It is easier to offer a dish of rice to meet the hunger of a needy person than to comfort the loneliness and the anguish of someone in our own home who does not feel loved.

I want you to go and find the poor in your homes. Above all, your love has to start there. I want you to be the good news to those right around you. I want you to be concerned about your next-door neighbor. Do you know who your neighbor is?

Always be faithful in little things, for in them our strength lies. To God nothing is little. . . . Practice fidelity in the least things, not for their own sake, but for the sake of the great thing that is the will of God. . . .

Do not pursue spectacular deeds. We must deliberately renounce all desires to see the fruit of our labor, doing all we can as best we can, leaving the rest in the hands of God. What matters is the gift of your self, the degree of love that you put into each one of your actions.

Do not allow yourselves to be disheartened by any failure as long as you have done your best. Neither glory in your success, but refer all to God in deepest thankfulness.

If you are discouraged, it is a sign of pride, because it shows you trust in your own powers. Never bother about people's opinions. Be humble and you will never be disturbed. The Lord has willed me here where I am. He will offer a solution.

If you are working in the kitchen do not think it does not require brains. Do not think that sitting, standing, coming, and going, that everything you do, is not important to God.

God will not ask how many books you have read, how many miracles you have worked; he will ask you if you have done your best, for the love of him. Can you in all sincerity say, "I have done my best"? Even if the best is failure, it must be our best, our utmost.

If you are really in love with Christ, no matter how small your work, it will be done better; it will be wholehearted. Your work will prove your love.

You may be exhausted with work, you may even kill yourself with work, but unless your work is interwoven with love, it is useless. To work without love is slavery. ✦

Thomas E. Powers

A PRIME RULE OF ANY and all community is that there is work to do, and all members except the very young, the very old, and the disabled do their share of the work. In secular communities it is the thing to avoid this rule as much as possible; some work gets done, but wherever possible work is avoided; the rich are considered lucky because they can avoid it; ten thousand devices are used to get out of work, partly or entirely; indeed all secular communities have a considerable, and sometimes a huge, population of able citizens who will not work and must be supported by their fellows.

In sacred community, the requirement of faithful work is among first things. The healing and cleansing begin here and are carried forward through many months and years, while the tendencies to evade, to stuff, to sabotage, and to complain are being exposed and reduced in the fires of blessed simple labor.

A man or woman who won't work, or won't work responsibly, falls into mental and physical sickness. You can't be well if you do not find rest; it is necessary before all else to find refreshment in rest. But if you won't work, you can't rest. No work or poor work means no sleep or poor sleep. The most fundamental of all rhythms is involved here. And the person who doesn't work doesn't respect himself. He runs a bad conscience. He has bad feelings about himself as a human being. God has made us so, and has given us among the first of his instructions the command to work.

There is joy in work, there is sweet and deep satisfaction in work, but above all there is *sanity* in work. It is a great milepost on the road of return to our real home.

For those who find it difficult or impossible to work right, sacred community offers an opportunity to learn how. How to value work so that you can endure it; then how to find the spiritual and physical gold in it: the strength and stability and profound enjoyment in reconnecting with the humming loom of the creation. What seemed to be among the greatest of all hardships and troubles turns out to be among the greatest of the gifts of him who the ancients called Philanthropos – lover of humankind. ✦

Eberhard Arnold

WORKING TOGETHER WITH others is the best way to test our faith, to find out whether or not we are ready to live a life of Christian fellowship. Work is the crucial test of faith because such a life can come into being only where people *work* for love. Love demands action, and the only really valid action is work. Christian fellowship means fellowship in work.

✦ ✦ ✦ ✦ ✦

THE COMMON LIFE can only exist where people work together, work hard together, enthusiastically and joyfully. A job done

wholeheartedly and with love involves all our feelings and
thoughts; such work is possible only when it encompasses the
whole horizon of life. . . . We have only one weapon against
the depravity that exists today. This weapon of the Spirit is
constructive work carried out in the fellowship of love. We do
not acknowledge sentimental love, love without work. Neither
do we acknowledge dedication in the practical work if it does
not daily give proof of the heart-to-heart relationship among
those who work together, a relationship that comes from the
Spirit. The love of work, like the work of love, is a matter of
the Spirit. ◆

John F. Alexander

I N C O M M U N I T Y our task is simple and clear. We're to
serve. We're to be good brothers or sisters. We're to clean
the toilets. . . . Like the janitor when you were in third
grade.

That's about all we have to do. Is that really so hard? This
is not a requirement that we leap over buildings in a single
bound. But take care of this minimum, contentedly, and the
rest will take care of itself. (As long as it's not a compulsive
way to keep busy, and as long as you're aware of resentments
you have about it. Those are huge provisos that deserve a lot of
attention, but I'm not going to deal with them here.)

Which is why Jesus washed his disciples' feet. Contentedly.
Or do you think he was annoyed to have to do that just before

he was murdered? It was almost the last thing he did with
them. He wanted them to learn that much.

The great danger of talk about gifts is that we all use
our gifts as weapons, to enhance our power or importance.
(Selfishness can ruin almost anything.) In churches people
moan endlessly, especially new people, about their gifts not
being used enough. Often they're right. Churches have to keep
reminding themselves to identify the full range of gifts the
Holy Spirit has given us.

Nonetheless, the main gift the Spirit has given each person
is the ability to clean the toilet (a contemporary equivalent
of washing feet). We are clear on that for others but often
not for ourselves. So in the body of Christ, it has to be an
incantation: for each of us, our task is to clean the toilet, wash
the dishes – in short, be a good brother or sister. That's our
mission. Clean up after the party, and when the baby down the
hall starts crying at night, go get her. Or take the person with
disabilities to the movies, hang out with your sisters in the
evening, study the Bible to the extent of your abilities, and pray
for your housemates.

Wash their feet. And don't worry much about using your
other gifts. Is that so hard? ◆

26

Vocation

• • • • •

John F. Alexander

THE SINGLE MOST important thing distracting
faithful people from being the church is our culture's
views on jobs and vocation. We get so busy with our
jobs that we have little time left over for being the people of
God. And much of the problem grows out of the Reformation.

The standard Roman Catholic position in the Middle Ages
was that God calls people only to jobs in the church. . . . The
Reformers reacted to the Catholic position by saying that since
God created the whole universe, all legitimate work is God's
work. Being a farmer or soldier is just as good as being clergy,
just as much a calling of God. The only question is whether
you're trying to do God's will, whether you're caring for God's
creation. Within this perspective, the work you do can be a
primary avenue for serving God and transforming the world.

By contrast, Anabaptists taught that our only calling is to
be disciples of Christ in a local church. We're not called to

be shoemakers, farmers, doctors, or even professional clergy; we're called to be fully functioning members of the body of Christ. Of course, Christians have to earn a living, but we are not called to particular trades, careers, or jobs. So Christians should choose those jobs that will best let them serve the body of Christ (where the body of Christ is understood as local churches). Our actual employment is of limited importance.

Which view of vocation are we to take? The Anabaptist argument is that in the New Testament, "calling" or "vocation" doesn't refer to employment but to what we are to be spiritually. We are called, for example, to "eternal life" (1 Tim. 6:12), "into the fellowship of his Son" (1 Cor. 1:9), "out of darkness into his marvelous light" (1 Pet. 2:9), not "to impurity but in holiness" (1 Thess. 4:7). God "called us with a holy calling" (2 Tim. 1:9), and "Those whom he predestined, he also called, and those whom he called, he also justified" (Rom. 8:30).

Nowhere in the Bible is anyone called to a trade or job outside the church: Paul was called to be an apostle (Rom. 1:1; 1 Cor. 1:1), and he and Barnabas were called to be missionaries (Acts 13:2–3). Meanwhile, the Bible records that Paul was a tentmaker (Acts 18:3), but nowhere does it say or imply that Paul was called to be a tentmaker. . . .

Of course, though the Bible doesn't use the word we translate "call" in relation to standard jobs, it might use some other word for the same meaning. It might use a word like sent, ordained, placed, set apart, anointed, or chosen. Such words would convey God's special choice of a job for a person. However, a study of such words gives the same conclusion. In the Bible people aren't set apart for jobs except in the church. . . . No one is ever said to have anything remotely resembling a vocation to be a farm laborer, craftsman, tax collector, doctor, or shepherd. Occasionally people are told to give up such work (Matt. 4:18–22; 9:9; Luke 5:27–28) but never to take it up. . . .

If the primary way people are meant to do God's work today is through local churches, then taking secular jobs seriously will distract us from our main task. Everything except church is secondary, or maybe even tertiary – career, family, politics, financial aid to the poor, learning, creating great music, inventing a cure for AIDS, personal holiness, whatever. Then church is 95 percent of what God plans for us to do; everything else combined is only 5 percent, so to speak. So in the view I'm spelling out, people are doing God's work in direct proportion to their faithfulness in using their gifts in a local church. And insofar as they are not doing that, they are not doing God's work. So those who are not part of a local church can scarcely be doing anything substantial for God.

In this view the primary way to influence society is to call people into some church and nurture them and ourselves into increasing maturity. So the primary way to fight oppression is to call the oppressed and the oppressor to repent and become part of the church. Demonstrations against oppression have a place, but primarily as a way of calling oppressed and oppressor into the church. The way to transform political structures is not primarily by lobbying, but by inviting people into some church (that is, evangelism). Lobbying has a place, but primarily as a way of calling people into the church. That's why Paul didn't attack slavery as an institution. He didn't consider it acceptable, but he believed that the way to do away with slavery was by getting as many people as possible into church and understanding that their master is in heaven.

The Reformation view, by contrast, is that the church universal and invisible is one of many ways God intends us to do his work. It is the most important way, but business, family, politics, financial aid to poor non-Christians, learning – all are significant in their own right. The church is 55 percent of God's plan for people, so to speak, but the rest combined is nearly as important. If people are Christian, then they're automatically part of the church universal, and if they are pursuing their employment with integrity and to the best of their ability, then they are to that extent making a substantial contribution to the kingdom. . . .

For the Reformation, your employment is meant to be a major way of serving God. Whether it intersects with a church or not, it's something sacred. People who believe that would be unlikely to give up a successful career to become full-time overseers in their local church, and they would think careers in politics or medicine are considerably more significant than driving a taxi.

But from an Anabaptist perspective, employment is of no great significance; it's not a calling of God, but a way to put food on the table, like Paul's tent making. A physicist might well be *called* to give up her career if her gifts were seen to be at overseeing the local church. She might end up driving a taxi at night if that facilitated her oversight. If this seems bizarre, it may merely show our skewed priorities. This makes more sense if you believe that all important problems are at bottom spiritual, and that church is the center of spirituality. Then your role in church is more important than any job outside church, no matter how "important" the outside job may seem. . . .

But how could anyone think that being church is such a big deal? How much time does it take to be an usher? Church is only a few hours a week. What are you supposed to do when no meeting is in process?

Such questions suggest that we don't know what church is. Church is more than a building or the meetings in the building, and working in church is more than ushering or teaching Sunday school or attending weekly meetings of the session. Church is lying awake at night trying to figure out how to help your brothers and sisters in your church grow into "the measure of the stature of the fullness of Christ" (Eph. 4:13). It means eating and drinking and breathing ways to encourage others in your church in their walks as Christians. . . .

So what is our work? First, our most important work is living in reconciliation with our sisters and brothers in a church, and lying awake at night trying to figure out how to help others do the same. Second, we should take whatever paid or unpaid employment will do most to help our brothers and sisters live in unity.

From this it follows that many of us will be freed to work less than full time. Ideally, we're so devoted to our brothers and sisters and those who may become our brothers and sisters that our material concerns will be rather minimal, and we will therefore be free to spend little time earning money. That, I suggest, is the primary reason why Jesus and the New Testament are so concerned about money. They want us to be free from serving money so it won't take our time and energy away from serving the people of God.

To look at it differently, we'll choose work that pays as much as possible so that we can spend minimum time and energy at work and maximum time and energy with our brothers and sisters. If I can get $100 an hour as a lawyer or $5 an hour as a delivery boy, I will (other things being equal) choose the job as a lawyer. Then I can work fewer hours or give more money to God's people. Or perhaps I'll work full time, and my large income will allow me to share money with my brothers and sisters so they won't have to work as much.

But many professional careers present real problems. Some careers tend to demand heart and soul and therefore get in the way of a person's role in the church. So Christians with professional careers need to hold them loosely. And that in itself rules out some careers. After all, those serious about the church won't be available at work for repeated fifty-hour weeks; we won't be available to move at the behest of our career; we won't be available for travel that has us away from our church so much that being reconciled scarcely means anything. The point is simply that our minds and hearts won't be on our career (they'll be on our church), and so our attention will wander from work. And some careers and professional jobs just won't tolerate that.

Whereas being a delivery boy doesn't require as much concentration. . . .

But the main point is that our vocation is to live as a reconciled people. ◆

Acceptance

• • • • •

Jürgen Moltmann

THERE IS AN OLD PRINCIPLE for human community which was already stated by Aristotle: "Birds of a feather flock together." To be sure, this kind of sociality combines human beings with one another, but only human beings who are alike: whites with whites, Christians with Christians, healthy with healthy, students with students, professors with their colleagues. To those who are "in," this seems to be the most natural thing in the world. But those on the "outside" feel excluded, degraded, and wounded. We get in a stew about showing special care for those people who are included in our own circle – and then we "stew in our own juices."

"Birds of a feather flock together." But why? People who are like us, who think the same thoughts, who have the same things, and who want the same things confirm us. However, people who are different from us, that is, people whose thoughts, feelings, and desires are different from ours, make us feel insecure. We therefore love those who are like us and we shun those who are different from us. And when these others live in our midst expressing their need for recognition, interest, and humanity, we react with defensiveness, increased self-confirmation, anxiety, and disparagement. This anxiety is indeed the root of racism, anti-Semitism, discrimination against people with disabilities, and not least of all, the lack of relationships in the congregation. "Birds of a feather flock together": that is nothing other than the social form of self-justification and the expression of anxiety. This form of self-justification, therefore, never appears without aggressions against that which threatens its security. It has no self-confidence. It has no ego-strength.

"Accept one another." As we have seen, this imperative unfortunately has its limitations. The roots of these limitations lie deep within ourselves. They appear in our anxiety about ourselves, and then in the self-justification which is so deeply ingrained in us.

"Accept one another, then, just as Christ accepted you" (Rom. 15:7). Only this attitude can give us a new orientation and break through our limitations so that we can spring over our narrow shadows. It opens us up for others as they really are so that we gain a longing for and an interest in them. As a result of this we become able actually to forget ourselves and to focus on the way Christ has accepted us. How have we been accepted in Christ?

To say it quite simply: God suffers because of us, for he wants to suffer us. This is more than a word play. Indeed, everything may be at stake in this saying: he wants to suffer us, and we are indeed suffered by him. Can we suffer those who are different from us? May the others suffer us? Can we suffer ourselves? Whom can we "not endure"? We are always causing suffering for each other: siblings, husbands and wives, parents and children, neighbors and colleagues. These spheres of suffering are deeply implicated in the church and politics. If we ourselves are not able to suffer, then nothing can possibly please us. But if we are able to suffer, then we take nothing amiss. The love of God which is infinitely capable of suffering reaches us in Christ. His love is passion: passion for human beings and their worth, passion for the creation and its peace. Through his suffering because of us and through his death for us Christ has accepted us and brought us to the glory of God. We must again and again become deeply absorbed in the passion of Christ if we are to know that he suffers because of us, for he wants to suffer us. In the depths of his suffering we perceive the greatness of his passion for us. We are disarmed whenever we recognize the suffering of God which has borne and still bears his passion to us.

We are freed from the cramped life of self-confirmation. We lose anxiety about ourselves and become open for others. Prejudices fall from us as scales from our eyes. We become alert and interested, we share in life and give a share of life. Then we no longer feel that we are made insecure by others because we no longer need self-confirmation. The person who is different becomes for us, precisely because of that difference, a surprise which we gladly accept. We can mutually accept each other because Christ has accepted us to the glory of God. And because he has already accepted the others and us, the whole vista of life is opened wide before us. We stand on firm ground wherever we accept, recognize, and confirm each other. We cannot go far enough. In view of the life that has been passionately confirmed and accepted by God, there is no longer any worthless life, no "second-class" citizen. The suffering of God's love has changed everything, and the more we go outside of ourselves, the more we will discover and experience this change ourselves. ◆

Adele J. Gonzalez

A FEW YEARS AGO I went to the White Mountains of New Hampshire with my family. Anyone who has been there knows the beautiful trails that fill a hiker's heart with joy. The children were young and full of energy and so we took on the challenge. What I had not shared with anyone was that for several weeks I had been suffering from an ingrown toenail in my big toe. I had tried the usual home remedies but nothing seemed to improve the condition.

After a couple of hours in my hiking boots my toe was throbbing. I could hardly walk and was slowing down the group. The ordeal continued as my pain was becoming unbearable, and the children were getting more frustrated with my pace. Finally, my brother stopped and said, "Sit on that rock and give me your boot." In shock, I watch him cut off the entire top front part of my boot with his hunting knife. After a few minutes of handiwork, he gave it back to me and said, "Here, the toe won't bother you anymore; it has all the space it needs to move freely without hurting." The rest of the trip was uneventful.

The experience has stayed with me all these years. How many "ingrown toenails" are there in the church? How many members of the body seem to bring only pain, infection, and frustration to the rest of us? The image of my brother working on my shoe to accommodate my toe taught me a lesson.

What do we do with the members of the body of Christ who cause us pain? Do we try to heal them and make them comfortable? Do we give them some space so that they do not hurt so much? Or do we ignore, reject, and get rid of them? Do we punish them with our indifference or neglect?

The Letter to the Romans tells us, "None of us lives for oneself, and no one dies for oneself" (14:7). And 1 Corinthians adds, "If one part suffers, all the parts suffer with it; if one part is honored, all the parts share its joy. Now you are Christ's body, and individually parts of it" (12:26–27).

My ingrown toenail showed me how poorly I deal with the members of my other body, the church. I get impatient and do not even offer them an ointment or a Band-Aid for their pain. The Christian God revealed by Jesus is full of compassion and demands that same compassion from us.

The measure of the quality of a Christian community is the way in which its weakest members are treated and its willingness to welcome everyone as an important part of the body of Christ. ◆

28

Irritations

• • • • •

Anthony de Mello

HOW COULD YOU go about creating a happy, loving, peaceful world? By learning a simple, beautiful, but painful art called the art of looking. This is how you do it: Every time you find yourself irritated or angry with someone, the one to look at is not that person but yourself. The question to ask is not, "What's wrong with this person?" but "What does this irritation tell me about myself?" Do this right now. Think of some irritating person you know and say this painful but liberating sentence to yourself: "The cause of my irritation is not in this person but in me." Having said that, begin the task of finding out how you are causing the irritation. First look into the very real possibility that the reason why this person's defects or so-called defects annoy you is that you have them yourself. But you have repressed them and so are projecting them unconsciously into the other. This is almost always true but hardly anyone recognizes it. So search for this person's defects in your own heart and in your unconscious mind, and your annoyance will turn to gratitude that his or her behavior has led you to self-discovery.

Here is something else worth looking at: Can it be that you are annoyed at what this person says or does because those words and behavior are pointing out something in your life and in yourself that you are refusing to see? Think how irritated people become with the mystic and the prophet, who look far from mystical or prophetical when we are challenged by their words or their life.

Another thing is also clear: You become irritated with this person because he or she is not living up to the expectations that have been programmed into you. Maybe you have a right to demand that he or she live up to your programming, as for instance, when he or she is cruel or unjust, but then stop to consider this. If you seek to change this person or to stop this person's behavior, will you not be more effective if you are not irritated? Irritations will only cloud your perception and make your action less effective. Everyone knows that when a sportsman or a boxer loses his temper, the quality of his play goes down because it becomes uncoordinated through passion and anger. In most cases, however, you have no right to demand that this person live up to your expectations; someone else in your place would be exposed to this behavior and would experience no annoyance at all. Just contemplate this truth and your irritation will vanish. How foolish of you to demand that someone else live up to standards and norms that your parents programmed into you!

And here is a final truth for you to consider: Given the background, the life experience, and the unawareness of this person, he cannot help behaving the way he does. It has been so well said that to understand all is to forgive all. If you really understood this person you would see him as crippled and not blameworthy, and your irritation would instantly cease. And the next thing you know you would be treating him with love, and he would be responding with love, and you would find yourself living in a loving world. ◆

Roy Hession

THAT FRIEND OF OURS has got something in his eye! Though it is only something tiny – what Jesus called a mote – how painful it is and how helpless he is until it is removed! It is surely our part as a friend to do all we can to remove it, and how grateful he is to us when we have succeeded in doing so. We should be equally grateful to him, if he did the same service for us.

In the light of that, it seems clear that the real point of the well-known passage about the beam and the mote (Matt. 7:3–5) is not the forbidding of our trying to remove the fault in the other person, but rather the reverse. It is the injunction that at all costs we should do this service for one another. True, its first emphasis seems to be a condemnation of censoriousness, but when the censoriousness in us is removed, the passage ends by saying, "Then shalt thou see clearly to cast the mote out of thy brother's eye." ...

First, however, the Lord Jesus tells us that it is only too possible to try to take the tiny mote, a tiny speck of sawdust, out of the other's eye when there is a beam, a great length of timber, in ours. When that is the case, we haven't a chance of casting out the mote in the other, because we cannot see straight ourselves, and in any case it is sheer hypocrisy to attempt to do so.

Now we all know what Jesus meant by the mote in the other person's eye. It is some fault which we fancy we can discern in him; it may be an act he has done against us, or some attitude he adopts towards us. But what did the Lord Jesus mean by the beam in our eye? I suggest that the beam in our eye is simply our unloving reaction to the other man's mote. Without doubt there is a wrong in the other person. But our reaction to that wrong is wrong too! The mote in him has provoked in us resentment, or coldness, or criticism, or bitterness, or evil speaking, or ill will – all of them variants of the basic ill, unlove. And that, says the Lord Jesus, is far, far worse than the tiny wrong (sometimes quite unconscious) that provoked it. A mote means in the Greek a little splinter, whereas a beam means a rafter. And the Lord Jesus means by this comparison to tell us that our unloving reaction to the other's wrong is what a great rafter is to a little splinter! Every time we point one of our fingers at another and say, "It's your fault," three of our fingers are pointing back at us. God have mercy on us for the many times when it has been so with us and when in our hypocrisy we have tried to deal with the person's fault, while God saw there was this thing far worse in our own hearts.

But let us not think that a beam is of necessity some violent reaction on our part. The first beginning of a resentment is a beam, as is also the first flicker of an unkind thought, or the first suggestion of unloving criticism. Where that is so, it only distorts our vision and we shall never see our brother as he really is, beloved of God. If we speak to our brother with that in our hearts, it will only provoke him to adopt the same hard attitude to us, for it is a law of human relationships that "with what measure ye mete, it shall be measured to you again."

No! "First cast out the beam out of thine own eye." That is the first thing we must do. We must recognize our unloving reaction to him as sin. On our knees we must go with it to Calvary and see Jesus there and get a glimpse of what that sin cost him. At his feet we must repent of it and be broken afresh and trust the Lord Jesus to cleanse it away in his precious blood and fill us with his love for that person – and he will, and does, if we will claim his promise. Then we shall probably need to go to the other in the attitude of the repentant one, tell him of the sin that has been in our heart and what the blood [of Jesus] has effected there, and ask him to forgive us too.

Very often bystanders will tell us, and sometimes our own hearts, that the sin we are confessing is not nearly so bad as the other's wrong, which he is not yet confessing. But we have been to Calvary, indeed we are learning to live under the shadow of Calvary, and we have seen our sin there and we can no longer compare our sin with another's. But as we take these simple steps of repentance, then we see clearly to cast out the mote out of the other's eye, for the beam in our eye has gone. In that moment God will pour light in on us as to the other's need, that neither he nor we ever had before. We may see then that the mote we were so conscious of before, is virtually non-existent – it was but the projection of something that was in us. On the other hand, we may have revealed hidden underlying things, of which he himself was hardly conscious. Then as God leads us, we must lovingly and humbly challenge him, so that he may see them too, and bring them to the fountain for sin and find deliverance (Zech. 13:1). He will be more likely than ever to let us do it – indeed, if he is a humble man, he will be grateful to us, for he will know now that there is no selfish motive in our heart, but only love and concern for him.

When God is leading us to challenge another, let not fear hold us back. Let us not argue or press our point. Let us just say what God has told us to and leave it there. It is God's work, not ours, to cause the other to see it. It takes time to be willing to bend "the proud, stiff-necked I." When we in turn are challenged, let us not defend ourselves and explain ourselves. Let us take it in silence, thanking the other, and then go to God about it and ask him. If the other person was right, let us be humble enough to go and tell him, and praise God together. There is no doubt that we need each other desperately. There are blind spots in all our lives that we shall never see, unless we are prepared for another to be God's channel to us. ◆

Thomas à Kempis

WHAT WE CANNOT change in ourselves or in others we ought to endure patiently until God wishes it to be otherwise. Perhaps it is this way to try our patience, for without trials our merits count for little. Nevertheless, when you run into such problems you ought to pray that God may find it fitting to help you and that you may bear your troubles well. If anyone who is spoken to once or twice will not listen and change his ways, do not argue with him, but leave it all to God, for he knows well how to turn bad things into good. He knows how to accomplish his will and how to express himself fully in all his servants.

Take pains to be patient in bearing all the faults and weaknesses of others, for you too have many flaws that others must put up with. If you cannot make yourself as you would like to be, how can you expect to have another person entirely to your liking? We would willingly have others be perfect, and yet we fail to correct our own faults. We want others to be strictly corrected, and yet we are unwilling to be corrected ourselves. Other people's far-ranging freedom annoys us, and yet we insist on having our own way. We wish others to be tied down by rules, and yet we will not allow ourselves to be held in check in any way at all. It is evident how rarely we think of our neighbor as ourselves!

If everything were perfect, what would we have to endure from others for God's sake? But now God has so arranged things that we may learn to bear each other's burdens, for no one is without faults, no one is without burdens, no one is wholly self-sufficient, no one has enough wisdom all by himself. That being the case, we must support and comfort each other; together we must help, teach, and advise one another, for the strength that each person has will best be seen in times of trouble. Such times do not make us weak; they show what we are. ◆

Eberhard Arnold

House Rule

THERE IS NO LAW but that of love. Love means having joy in others. Then what does being annoyed with them mean?

Words of love convey the joy we have in the presence of others. By the same token it is out of the question to speak about another person in a spirit of irritation or vexation. There must never be talk, either in open remarks or by insinuation, against others, against their individual characteristics – under no circumstances behind a person's back. Talking in one's own family is no exception.

Without this rule of silence there can be no loyalty, no community. Direct address is the only way possible; it is the spontaneous service of love we owe anyone whose weaknesses cause a negative reaction in us. An open word spoken directly to the other person deepens friendship and is not resented.

Only when two people do not come to agreement quickly in this direct manner is it necessary to talk it over with a third person who can be trusted to help solve the difficulty and bring about a uniting on the highest and deepest levels (Matt. 18:15–20).

Each member of the community should hang this reminder up where he or she works and can see it all the time. ◆

29

Differences

• • • • •

Joan Chittister

O F ALL THINGS unacceptable to the human
psyche, the notion of difference may well be among
the most threatening. We learn sameness very early
in life and find it hard to stray too far from its boundaries,
however old we get, however much we think we've moved away
from such thinking as time goes on.

Sameness becomes a kind of security blanket that wraps
us up in the warm feeling of being acceptable to the groups
with which we identify and whose approval we seek. If we
don't stand out, we can't be criticized. We are safe because we
are just like everybody else. To be socially acceptable we have
allowed ourselves to become socially invisible.

It is an effective technique, a kind of chameleon approach
to life, but it is neither psychologically mature nor spiritually
healthy.

Somewhere along the line we must become who we are meant to be as individuals. We are persons put on earth to contribute to it as well as take from it. Otherwise we doom ourselves to live a life that is only partially alive. Most of all, we must allow others to do the same, as much for our sake as for theirs. It is in the development of our differences that we thrive, that we are gifted by the presence of the other. It is in our respect for the differences of others that we grow. "Sameness," Petrarch wrote, "is the mother of disgust; variety the cure." . . .

Differences not only teach us new ways of doing things; they also make us ask new questions of ourselves about what is really important in life, what really must have priority, and what is true happiness, success, and unity.

Differences are a challenge to our small assumptions about the way the world really goes together. An American world, a white world, a male world, a Western world are all simply small slices of reality attempting to be the whole. Only respect for the Muslim veil, the Chinese smile, the African tribe, the South American campesino can stretch us beyond ourselves, beyond a political imperialism that sets out to corrupt whole peoples in the name of globalization and, in the end, deprives us of the richness of the world community.

But that is the glorious burden of real Christianity: to follow the one who talked to Samaritan women and Roman soldiers, all the time allowing them to be who they were. Clearly, differences were not made to be homogenized; differences were made to be respected, to be honored, to be cherished. . . .

Going along, nodding yes to everything, keeping the norms, thinking by the rules never tests a concept; it only perpetuates it. . . . The truth is that it is only when we think against the mind of another that we find out what we ourselves really think, what we ourselves are willing to support. Anything else leaves us with colorless souls indeed. It is the sparks set off in us by the minds of those around us that fire our own. It is then that we become a real self. We become separate and connected at the same time. In the end, it is our relation to the ideas of the other that determines who we ourselves really are. To speak another truth, our own truth, our uniquely defined truth, however finished, however settled, is to confirm the value of our own existence.

Division of opinion, too often the fault line of human relationships, is, when we embrace it openly, what invigorates thinking and stirs new thought. It is the ground of new beginnings, the beginning of new insight, the foundation of new respect for the other. If anything sharpens the dull edge of a relationship it is often when it ceases to be boringly predictable. It is when everybody on two continents knows what we are going to say next that we know we have stopped thinking. Then we need to have a few old ideas honed. We need to think through life all over again. "Of two possibilities," my mother loved to tell me, "choose always the third."

Creativity, it is too often forgotten, comes out of differences. It is the ability to function outside the lines, beyond the dots, despite the boxes and the mental chains by which we have forever been constrained, that fits us to be the architects of the future. Instead, we want everyone to think alike when what we really need are people who are thinking newly – about theology, about God, about faith, about morality, about science, about life. "You won't find this year's birds in last year's nests," the proverb teaches, but we so easily miss the meaning of it entirely. Life is meant for moving on, the observation implies. . . .

Being able to think differently from those around us and being able to function lovingly with people who think otherwise is the ultimate in human endeavor. It requires three things: a heart large enough to deal with conflict positively, enduringly, and kindly; a keen sense of personal purpose, the notion that there is something on the horizon that is worth debating; and a soul sensitive enough to transcend the tensions of the immediate for the sake of the quality of the future. ◆

Henri J. M. Nouwen

WHEN WE GIVE UP OUR DESIRES to be outstanding or different, when we let go of our need to have our own special niches in life, when our main concern is to be the same, and to live out this sameness in solidarity, we are then able to see each other's unique gifts. Gathered together in common vulnerability, we discover how much we have to give each other. The Christian community is the opposite of a highly uniform group of people whose behavior has been toned down to a common denominator and whose originality has been dulled. On the contrary, the Christian community, gathered in common discipleship, is the place where individual gifts can be called forth and put into service for all. It belongs to the essence of this new togetherness that our unique talents are no longer objects of competition but elements of community, no longer qualities that divide but gifts that unite.

When we have discovered that our sense of self does not depend on our differences and that our self-esteem is based on a love much deeper than the praise that can be acquired by unusual performances, we can see our unique talents as gifts for others. Then, too, we will notice that the sharing of our gifts does not diminish our own value as persons but enhances it. In community, the particular talents of the individual members become like the little stones that form a great mosaic. The fact that a little gold, blue, or red piece is part of a splendid mosaic makes it not less but more valuable because it contributes to an image much greater than itself. Thus, our dominant feeling toward each other can shift from jealousy to gratitude. With increasing clarity, we can see the beauty in each other and call it forth so that it may become a part of our total life together.

Both sameness and uniqueness can be affirmed in community. When we unmask the illusion that a person is the difference she or he makes, we can come together on the basis of our common human brokenness and our common need for healing. Then we also can come to the marvelous realization that hidden in the ground on which we walk together are the talents that we can offer to each other. Community, as a new way of being together, leads to the discovery or rediscovery of each other's hidden talents and makes us realize our own unique contribution to the common life. ◆

30

Conflict

• • • • •

David Janzen

IN TIMES OF CONFLICT – and it is important to
note that conflict is not always bad – our initial reaction,
depending on our personality type, is usually fight or
flight. For some of us the first temptation is to get even, to
gossip and build up a power base of support with our friends
so that we can win when the conflict comes to a head. The
opposite temptation is to protect ourselves by increasing our
distance in the hurtful relationship, or to take the spiritually
superior attitudes of "forgiving in our heart" and perhaps even
"suffering for righteousness' sake." But Jesus has given us a
third way.

In Matthew 18 Jesus outlines a three-step redemptive
process for his disciples to follow whenever conflict arises
in the church community. By putting this "Rule of Christ"
into practice, communities soon accumulate a storehouse of

practical wisdom and memory of reconciled relationships that inform further practice.

The first step is simple and straightforward: "If your brother or sister sins, go and point out their fault, just between the two of you. If they listen to you, you have won them over" (Matt. 18:15). We have all experienced people coming to us with a beef, letting us know that we have hurt or angered them in some way. We have probably encountered people who do this in aggressive outrage, blind to their own part in the dynamic. And we know people who come to us from a more humble concern for the relationship, something like this: "David, I am troubled and hurt by something you said yesterday and want to talk with you about it some more. Here is what I observed. . . . I wonder, how do you see what happened? Help me understand how we can make things right. I want a better relationship with you." With such a conversation opening – one that avoids judgment and shame – mutual confession, forgiveness, and reconciliation usually follow. The Holy Spirit is active in such moments, moving us both to see our faults and to desire unity. This process is easier in community if we have already studied Jesus' teaching in Matthew 18 and agreed that this is how we want to handle the inevitable conflicts that come up between us.

I've lived in community long enough to see others model for me how to listen well when someone is outraged and abusive in sharing his hurt. Here at Reba, Julius Belser is remembered for walking into the home of a hysterical neighbor who was shouting threats and brandishing a gun at the police outside. After half an hour, the two walked out together with the gun in Julius's hand – a standoff diffused. Here is someone I can learn from. He is my mentor.

"The first challenge," Julius explained, "is to just listen, and to keep listening without rebuke until all the emotion has been heard out, until the speaker has gotten to the bottom of his concern and feelings. Ask humble questions until you can repeat the main concern and feeling of offense to his own satisfaction." Some conciliation experts have described this stage as "arriving at accurate empathy."

"Having validated the speaker's concern," Julius continues, "then I can take my turn to speak about the way I experienced events and to suggest how we might repair what has gone wrong. It is amazing how God is present in moments like that to draw us together in forgiveness and a new vision for living at peace. However, if after doing our best, one of us still feels like we have not been heard, it may be time to bring in one or two other persons that we trust, to help us mediate the conflict."

This brings us to the second stage of Jesus' process for reconciling relationships: "But if they will not listen, take one or two others along, so that 'every matter may be established by the testimony of two or three witnesses'" (Matt. 18:16). Sometimes, we have learned, it is acceptable for the process to start at this second stage. Perhaps one of the parties to the conflict is too afraid to talk without a support person at her side. Or the conflict seems so complex (like the story that follows) that everyone agrees to start with a mediator.

Tensions had been growing for the Mustard Seed, making community-planning meetings an increasingly frustrating experience for everyone. As they talked with each other in my presence, I learned that Eric and Betty (a couple) often met with Ruth because they lived next door to each other. From these spontaneous conversations they would go out for coffee or to share a midnight snack, building an intimate

friendship and coming to agreement on directions they hoped
their fledgling community could take. Martin (the designated
community leader) and Eloise (his wife) were never included
in these spontaneous relationship-building and conviction-
forming conversations.

As we talked about this polarizing dynamic and the feelings
of estrangement that had grown up around them, the conversation went a bit deeper. Eric, Betty, and Ruth all assumed that
Martin and Eloise wanted to be left alone because they were
newlyweds. Martin and Eloise acknowledged that this had
been their wish at first, but now they felt ready to widen their
circle of active friendships. Furthermore, Ruth and these two
couples are the only ones who had made a long-term commitment to this young community, while others who came to the
meetings had not. The five came to see their unique leadership
responsibility to the larger group. Their lack of unity was
affecting everyone.

After apologizing and forgiving each other for contributing to the estrangement, they were amazed to suddenly feel a
tender closeness of spirit with one another. They were eager to
build on this moment of reconciliation by getting together on
Friday nights and dreaming together about the future of the
community at times when undecided participants and guests
were not present. They also agreed to fill in the rest of the
group about this meeting and their need for it.

Notice how many things are going on at the same time
in this story. It is not apparent that anyone was deliberately
doing wrong, and yet estrangement was growing. No matter
who feels it first, any source of tension or conflict is reason to
enter into dialogue with reconciling intent. Furthermore, we
cannot know, before we talk, who might be in the wrong or
what needs to be repaired – good reason not to gossip or make

judgments. By talking together, new information comes to light, and ethical discernment becomes possible about the right action for these persons in this specific moment. By talking directly with each other, the community grows in practical wisdom about how to reconcile future hurts. God is really at work in the scene, revealing truth, forgiving sin, healing hurts, restoring love, and giving human beings authority to act in God's name to build up the kingdom. We see how the inevitable conflicts of community can be socially useful when we put Jesus' instructions into practice.

Some of us cringe when we read the third step of the reconciliation process in the Rule of Christ: "If they still refuse to listen, tell it to the church [or the community meeting] and if they refuse to listen even to the church, treat them as you would a pagan or a tax collector" (Matt. 18:17). This is not a "three strikes and you are out" policy – a quick way to kick out troublemakers. Rather, as long as a community member is willing to talk and listen, the process goes on in whatever creative ways the community can devise.

In my experience of forty years in community, I have not seen anyone asked to leave by a united community vote. Rather, when someone no longer listens, that person has usually decided he does not want to belong, and it is helpful for everyone involved to acknowledge this. Sometimes, in a more established community with a long history of relationships, people who want to leave feel trapped because they do not have the financial means or the emotional support to do so. It is best, in such circumstances, to graciously offer the support they need to go, leaving the door open for further dialogue whenever they wish to return. It is essential for a Christian intentional community to be a place of freedom where everyone is present voluntarily. ◆

Sister Penelope Lawson

U NIVERSAL INTERCESSION IS a good antidote
to thoughtlessness and negative indifference to
other people needs. But by no means all our failures
in charity are of that kind. Many of them come from positive
antipathies, and take an active rather than a passive form. They
usually start with something very small. You take offence at
something someone does or says. Much oftener than not, there
is an element of misunderstanding in it, but you are not generous enough to think of or allow for that; you assume the worst
and treat it as a fact. In fact, you have a grudge. Thereafter
you regard that person with a jaundiced eye, which means you
subconsciously at least expect them to offend in the same sort
of way again. Meanwhile the other person is probably feeling
in much the same way about you. So it goes on. And where in
all this is the love of God and of one's neighbor?

In the Anglican liturgy, intending communicants are
expressly required to be in love and charity with all their neighbors. That this is a *sine qua non* of worthy reception is obvious.
Nevertheless, the lives of many otherwise religious people are
spoilt by misrelationships like these. We are far too easy-going
with ourselves about such things. We think they do not matter
very much, and can't be helped, and anyhow the other person
is the most to blame, and we have done our best. But they do
matter. They matter utterly, in any case; and when they are
between Christians, whose duty it is to love each other *as their*

Lord loves them, they are quite damnable and devastating in the harm they do, both to the individuals concerned and to the church, as well as to outsiders who are scandalized. If we want to worship all the time, as we are called to do, and if we do not want to suffer from thrombosis of the soul, we must deal with them and correct them, at whatever cost. Here are a few practical suggestions as to how this may be done.

First and foremost and all the time, let us frankly recognize that, if those blessed twins, the senses of humor and proportion, were always in full working order as they should be in a Christian life, such deplorable situations as we are envisaging simply would not arise. Those senses are intrinsic elements in love, and integral to a full human life. Let us thank God for them, and make full use of them. Where such situations do exist, the following points may be observed.

First, as a necessary safeguard, one should bind oneself by a solemn promise made to God in prayer never to speak of anyone's shortcomings to a third person without real necessity – never, that is, to do so merely to relieve one's feelings and get sympathy. Failure to keep this promise must be confessed as sin.

Second, one must be very brave and honest in searching one's own heart. You can be pretty sure that pride comes into your unfortunate reactions to that person, and there may be jealousy as well. Out with it, then. Admit it and condemn it. If there has been open friction between you and the other, and words have passed between you that are matter for regret, then apologize without delay for your share in the fault. *Someone* has got to begin; it had better be you.

Thirdly, one must take every chance that offers of showing friendliness to the person whom one has annoyed. This approach, however, must be humble, not *de haut in bas.*

Nothing is more alienating to an already exacerbated B than self-conscious magnanimity on the part of A. One should be at least as genuinely ready to put oneself in the other's debt for help and kindness, as to put him in one's own. In some cases this may involve turning a blind eye and a deaf ear to quite a lot for quite a time; but few people's defenses can stand up indefinitely to the assault of genuine, effective love, which is what these tactics are, and many ultimately staunch and lifelong friends have been made and won in this way. Moreover, truly Christian meekness is not weakness; it is strength, for it requires tremendous self-control. You put up with a lot, perhaps, and some may say that you are letting the other person wipe his boots on you and showing lack of spirit. Of course some characters do let themselves be dominated and browbeaten by others of a more aggressive temperament; but that is quite a different thing, and good for neither party.

The generous forbearance that we are advocating here is good for both of you. It is good for A to practice active love to B, and to try "to see the Lord" in him, regardless of his feelings; and it is good for B to have the best believed of him. Further, only the truly humble person in the part of A, the one who is normally forbearing almost to a fault, will have the grace and power on occasion to stand up to B and – as the modern idiom has it – show him where he gets off. Such rare but unequivocal rebuke, given in gentleness and selflessly and prompted by the Spirit, will take effect where a score of heated tellings-off only make matters worse. But no one can hope to act A's part like that, unless he is prepared to take occasional rebuke himself.

Lastly, this line of action is a fulfilment of the "new commandment." To put it mildly, our Lord puts up with a great deal from us. He helps us; yet in his great humility he seeks our help. He fully knows the worst of us, yet he believes the best. He loves us whole. He loves us redemptively, constructively, creatively. ◆

Hans Denck

WHEN YOU HEAR your brother or sister say something that is strange to you, do not immediately argue with them, but listen to see whether they be right and you can also accept it. If you cannot understand them you must not judge them, and if you think that they may be in error, consider that you may be in greater error. ◆

Amy Carmichael

WE ARE TRUSTED *to spread the spirit of love.* Tenderness in judgment, the habit of thinking the best of one another, unwillingness to believe evil, grief if we are forced to do so, eagerness to believe good, joy over one recovered from any slip or fall, unselfish gladness in another's joys, sorrow in another's sorrow, readiness to do anything to help another entirely irrespective of self – all this and much more is included in that wonderful word *love*. If love weakens among us, if it ever becomes possible to tolerate the least shadow of an unloving thought, our fellowship will begin to perish.

Unlove is deadly. It is a cancer. It may kill slowly but it always kills in the end. Let us fear it, fear to give room to it as we should fear to nurse a cobra. It is deadlier than any cobra. And just as one minute drop of the almost invisible cobra venom spreads swiftly all over the body of one into whom it has been injected, so one drop of the gall of unlove in my heart or yours, however unseen, has a terrible power of spreading all through our family, for we are one body – we are parts of one another. If one member suffers loss, all suffer loss. Not one of us lives to herself.

We owe it to the younger ones to teach them the truth that united prayer is impossible, unless there be loyal love. If unlove be discovered anywhere, stop everything and put it right, if possible at once.

Often these misunderstandings are about the merest trifles. You let them grow and grow till your whole day is shadowed. This delights the devil, but it terribly injures your own soul, and it sorely grieves the Spirit of Love. Also, and this is serious, while you are yielding to such feelings you are unconsciously sowing seeds of unlove and distrust in other hearts – in the children's hearts. These seeds will spring to life and grow up to your sorrow one day.

Why don't you keep the Law of the Family and go straight to the one who has (you think) done something wrong? You can't, do you say? You can. Love will find a way....

Some of you remember how in old days if a Prayer Day meeting was lifeless and we could not get anywhere, I used to stop, and we scattered, and any who were not in love met somewhere, perhaps just for a minute under a tree, and then we met again, and *then* the Spirit led us into real prayer. We are too big a Family for that to be possible now, but it is as important now as ever that all should be clear, no one out of love with any other one, no one doubting anyone.

O my children, if only you would make up your minds never to doubt the love of another sister or brother in Christ, but *always* to think the best, to take the best for granted, and never admit an unkind thought in your heart, how happy, how heavenly life would be.

I could not endure it if for one minute I doubted any one of you. It would be like the sting of a wasp in my soul. Why do you endure it? Why do some of you even encourage that wasp to sting? I beseech you to have done with this. Refuse it. Hate it. It may seem like a trifle, but it is of hell.

We are all human. We may forget things we should remember. A message may be undelivered. There may be some mistake or delay about food or some such trifle. Take it as a mistake, not as something intended. I remember once weeks of unhappiness because a certain curry was badly cooked – the cause could have been discovered in five minutes if only there had been loving frankness, and speaking *to* instead of speaking *of* the one who made that curry. Such things are absurd, but they are too sad for laughter, for they do harm. They wound love. ◆

31

Unity

• • • • •

Peter Riedemann

CHRIST'S LOVE and our love one for another are shown to us in the bread and wine. Just as there are many grains of wheat, which are ground by the millstones and become flour, then baked and become bread – and in the bread we no longer distinguish one particle of flour from another – the same thing is true of us human beings, many as we are. When we are ground by the millstone of divine power, believe God's Word, and submit to the cross of Christ, we are brought together, bound with the band of love to one body of which Christ is the head. As Paul puts it, "We who partake of one bread, though many, are one bread and one body" (1 Cor. 10:17).

Those who truly surrender to the Lord become of one mind, heart, and soul. As the grains of wheat unite in the bread, and as Christ, the head, is one with the Father, so the members are of one mind with the head. As it is written, "We have the mind of Christ" (1 Cor. 2:16). But whoever does not have the mind of Christ is not his. And just as each grain of wheat gives the others all it has in order that there may be one loaf of bread, Christ our captain has given himself to us as an example that each should love the other as he has loved us, no longer living for ourselves, but giving ourselves to live for the whole body and serving the others with the gift we have received so that the body may grow and build itself up. . . .

What I have just said about the bread is also true of the wine, for wine is made of many grapes which are crushed in the winepress and then flow together and become wine, and one cannot recognize which grape it comes from. ◆

Chiara Lubich

I F WE ARE UNITED, Jesus is among us. And this has value. It is worth more than any other treasure that our heart may possess, more than mother, father, brothers, sisters, children. It is worth more than our house, our work, or our property; more than the works of art in a great city like Rome; more than our business deals; more than nature which surrounds us with flowers and fields, the sea and the stars; more than our own soul.

It is Jesus who, inspiring his saints with his eternal truths, leaves his mark upon every age. This too is his hour. Not so much the hour of a saint but of him, of *him among us,* of him living in us as we build up – in the unity of love – his mystical body, the Christian community.

But we must enlarge Christ, make him grow in other members, become like him bearers of fire. Make one of all and in all, the One. It is then that we live the life that he gives us, moment by moment, in charity.

The basic commandment is brotherly love. Everything is of value if it expresses sincere fraternal charity. Nothing we do is of value if there is not the feeling of love for our brothers and sisters in it. For God is a father and in his heart he has always and only his children.

◆ ◆ ◆ ◆ ◆

HOWEVER MANY NEIGHBORS YOU MEET throughout your day, from morning to night, in all of them see Jesus. If your eye is simple, the one who looks through it is God. God is love, and love seeks to unite by winning over.

How many people, in error, look at creatures and things in order to possess them! It may be a look of selfishness or of envy, but whatever the case, it is one of sin. Or people may look within their own selves, and be possessive of their own souls, their faces lifeless because they are bored or worried. The soul, because it is an image of God, is love, and love that turns in on itself is like a flame that, because it is not fed, dies out.

Look outside yourself, not in yourself, not at things, not at persons; look at God outside yourself and unite yourself to him. He lives in the depths of every soul that is alive; and if the soul is not alive, it is still the tabernacle of God that awaits him as the joy and expression of its own existence.

Look at every neighbor, then, with love. To love means to give. A gift, moreover, calls for a gift, and you will be loved in return. Understood in this way, love is to love and be loved, as in the Trinity. God in you will ravish hearts, igniting the life of the Trinity in them, which may already rest in them through grace, although extinguished.

You cannot light up a space, even if electricity is available, until the current's two poles are brought together. The life of God in us is similar. It must circulate in order to radiate outside of us and give witness to Christ, the one who links heaven to earth, and people with one another.

Look, therefore, at every one of your neighbors. Give yourself to them in order to give yourself to Jesus, and Jesus will give himself back to you. It is the law of love: "Give, and it will be given to you" (Luke 6:38).

Out of love for Jesus, let your neighbors possess you. Like another Eucharist, let yourself "be eaten" by your neighbors. Put your entire self at their service, which is service to God, and your neighbors will come to you and love you. The fulfillment of God's every desire lies in fraternal love, which is found in his commandment: "I give you a new commandment, that you love one another" (John 13:34). ◆

Stephen B. Clark

THE LORD DESIRES each body of Christians to be one, even as he and the Father are one. He offers Christians oneness which manifests his glory and the Father's love to the world (John 17:20–23). Without that unity Christians cannot witness to the world with full power. With that unity, they can already realize the power and victory of the Lord in their midst (Acts 4:32–33).

The bond of peace, that is, of good, loving relationships, preserves the unity of the Spirit (Eph. 4:3). When there is mutual love in a body of Christians, that body can be one. Service, obedience, self-sacrifice, and care build unity in a body of Christians. Unity involves more than an absence of division and conflict. Christian unity means loving one another as the Father loves the Son and the Son loves the Father. As Christians learn how to love one another with the love of the Father and Son, they will forge bonds among them that will resist all the attacks of the enemy. . . .

Members of a Christian community could choose to approach discussion and disagreement in a spirit of conflict or in a spirit of meekness. When a spirit of conflict prevails, disunity results and love ebbs away. When a spirit of meekness prevails, unity grows and love thrives. Christians cannot approach disagreement in a spirit that comes from the world, the flesh, and Satan and still expect to be a body of people who love one another.

Those who approach discussion and disagreement in a spirit of conflict attempt to influence direction by applying pressure. . . . Sometimes the conflict and hostility simply come out of the willfulness that is rooted in the flesh. Sometimes they come from a conviction that conflict is the best way to raise issues and get action. Underlying such a conviction is the view that power, at least in the form of resistance, whether physical or verbal, is needed to see that the affairs of the body are directed in the right way.

Those who approach questions about the direction of the body in a spirit of conflict often believe that everyone has the same responsibility for the direction of the body, and that the body as a whole is the proper forum for discussion. They feel entitled to advocate whatever they judge to be proper, and to make their opinions heard whenever it seems good to them. While they may recognize the need to entrust final decision-making to another body, they will not accept a limitation on discussion or enter into any submission to the judgment of the body responsible for direction.

The spirit that prevails in a Christian community should be a spirit of meekness, the spirit of those who know that they are servants of the Lord and of one another (Phil. 2:1–12). A Christian community should be free of hostility, protest, factions, and party spirit. Christians should enter discussion in good faith, trusting that their brothers and sisters will give their words a good hearing and will want to know the truth and follow it. They should also have a trust that the Lord will lead his people. Therefore, they can rely on directly and peacefully speaking the truth rather than on using pressure or conflict to further their own views.

In a Christian community, concern for the direction of the community should also be based upon an acceptance of the authority of the elders in the community for decision-making. Thus, the spirit of meekness also manifests itself in a cooperative and submissive spirit. Christians should be willing to receive and to accept a decision that differs from their own. The spirit of meekness and cooperativeness, however, should not lead to reticence and unwillingness to be open in discussion. Peacefulness and brotherly love should lead to a greater mutual trust and a greater ability to speak freely. Christians should be able to give their opinions directly and firmly to those responsible for the matters that they are concerned about. Those in authority should be all the more ready to listen because they know that the Lord can speak through any member of the body. . . .

God is love, and love is essential to a Christian community. Many in modern society put the highest value on opinions, policies, and approaches. But in a Christian community the highest value is placed upon a loving relationship to God and to the brothers and sisters. To love God we must be faithful to his truth, and our love for one another must be based on our faithfulness to God. Nonetheless, more effort should go into building one another up and serving the Lord than into discussing issues, debating policies, and evaluating performance. When love is valued rightly, many of the causes of disunity disappear. ◆

Dialogue

• • • • •

Elizabeth O'Connor

I N O U R O W N C O M M U N I T Y we have hurt each other most when we rushed by one another without taking time either to share ourselves or to listen. We were always able to explain our failure away – at least in our own eyes – by saying that "we have too many groups for us to stay in communication"; "nothing gets done, if we all have to participate"; "these conversations drag on and on"; "we can't talk while people are shivering in the cold." These statements will have a familiar ring to anyone who is living in community where there is wide diversity of mind and temperament. They are anti-dialogue statements, but they are hard to confront because they are full of truth; we find them in our own hearts and on our own lips at times when we are longing to move on and the group seems to be covering the same ground over and over again, or resisting the making of a decision.

Groups are often paralyzed and fail to move in any constructive way because of the few members who want to hammer
through every detail in advance, to know exactly what the
future will be, to map out every step, and to be certain that
everyone is equally committed to picking up the pieces and
bearing the cost in the eventuality of failure. In such a case,
commitment to dialogue does not mean that those who are
positive, willing to take risks and embrace an unknown future,
must always be asked to wait until everyone arrives at the same
place. That will never happen. At the same time, the fearless
ones cannot forge ahead as though justice and righteousness
were forever on their side. If they do, they will only appear to
be getting things done. In actuality they will be building structures all new on the outside and full of rotting bones inside.

When important issues have to be decided, to ensure true
dialogue communities and groups must learn to conduct that
dialogue within the context of a passionate waiting on God.
This does not mean merely beginning meetings with a time of
silence, but allowing a period of silence after each one speaks
so that there is opportunity to reflect on what has been said.
If this seems too burdensome of a way for some, then I would
suggest that discussion at least be interspersed with periods of
silence, so that a deeper level may be attained from which to
speak and to listen.

   Dialogue demands of each participant that we try to live
into the other's world, try to see things as another sees them.
We do not enter into dialogue in order to persuade another
to see things our way. We enter into dialogue because we are
open to change and are aware that our lives need correcting.
Dialogue requires a clear, radical, and arduous commitment to
listening. Essential to that listening is knowing in the deepest

recesses of our being that we really know very little about most things, and that the truth may rest with some unlikely soul. God says to the most gifted among us, "For my thoughts are not your thoughts, and your ways are not my ways" (Isa. 55:8). When we know that, when we are truly seeking God's will, we have to be persons of dialogue. The person of dialogue knows that no matter how mean, or hurt, or angry a person may be, he has something important to contribute to the dialogue. Each person in the recesses of his heart knows this about himself. He wants to speak his word and when he is not allowed to do that he feels in his being that a violence has been done to him. True listening requires that we not only listen to words, but also pay heed to feelings and acts. . . .

True dialogue is difficult for everyone. They listen well who know they have been listened to, but few of us feel really heard. I think that I can let the other go when I believe that he has truly heard my story, or point of view, or opinion. If I think he hasn't heard me, I am apt to hold him with my "glittering eye," and tell my tale over and over. The ache caused by the inability to communicate can become a kind of throbbing pain that finds expression in too many words or conversely in the silence that locks oneself in and others out, or, even more unacceptably, in the outrageous deed. . . .

We can too easily become identified with goodness – feel that we are "the enlightened ones." We cease to ask questions about what we are doing, how we are doing it, and whether it might better be done another way. Not only must we question ourselves; we must create the kind of atmosphere that invites others to question us and to give us feedback on how they perceive and hear and experience us.

We all flower in the company of those who confirm and accept us, but sometimes the way to deeper relatedness and increased consciousness is along a more painful path. We each have characteristics and ways of responding that hurt our relationships with others – that make dialogue and community difficult – but we have no deep understanding of these failings. We have been given very little help and practice in the creative giving and receiving of feedback. We have not faced in any decisive way the fact that others have information about us that we do not have about ourselves, and that our blindness might be healed if we had the courage or ego strength to ask for it. Until we have become experienced in the giving and the receiving of constructive criticism it will remain extraordinarily difficult work. ◆

C. Christopher Smith

A S WE BEGIN to practice conversation in our churches, a crucial question arises: What do we talk about? ... While some conversations may be more helpful than others in building up our body, there are no wrong conversations, and we can always move on if we find that a specific conversation is not moving us in the direction of being a healthy embodiment of Christ. . . .

As a congregation begins to talk together, two types of conversations are decidedly unhelpful: abstract matters and highly charged topics. A time will come when we will indeed need to talk about both of these things, but neither is an especially fruitful place to begin a practice of conversation. Our call is to be a body, a tangible presence of Christ in our particular place, and our conversations should be moving us ever deeper into this calling.

As we talk together and seek God's presence with us, we recognize that although we will have disagreements that threaten to divide us, we will work through these disagreements in love and with patience, as we also recognize that we are united in Christ. God desires to heal the fractures in our body, but this healing will come in God's way, not ours – and it will come according to God's timing. Praying and talking together in a way that acknowledges both our unity and our disagreement is a means by which we learn patience. We are powerfully tempted to resolve this tension by either fleeing and pretending it doesn't exist or by fighting it, manipulating or forcing one another toward the unity we proclaim. Patience is a third way that is neither fighting nor fleeing. Nouwen says that "patience means overcoming the fear of a controversial subject.... It means welcoming sincere criticism and evaluating changing conditions. In short, patience is a willingness to be influenced even when this requires giving up control and entering into unknow territory."

In our conversations together, we confess our fragmentation and live patiently in the tension of being both unified and divided. We also, however, live in expectation that God's presence with us will heal our wounds and divisions. One way God begins the work of healing in us is through our human presence with one another. As we are present with one another, and particularly with those who differ substantially from us, we come to see them not as members of some opposing group

(Democrats, if we are Republicans; the older generations, if we are young, and so on) but rather as fellow humans beings and fellow sisters and brothers in Christ, with whom we share abundant common ground.

Indeed, some of the deepest public struggles of the twenty-first century stem from our inability to see those who are different from us as humans created in the image of God and to abide with them in a prayerful sort of relationship that recognizes God's presence with and among us. . . . In learning to trust others in these prayerful sorts of relationships, we also cultivate trust in God, particularly trust that God is at work in the relationship, healing and reconciling, and trust that God will continue to guide us together in the just, loving, and peaceable way of Jesus. ◆

33

Leadership

◆ ◆ ◆ ◆ ◆

J. Heinrich Arnold

A TRUE CHRISTIAN CHURCH cannot be a living organism unless there is clear leadership. The ship of community needs a helmsman to guide it, who must be guided from above in deep humility and must honor and respect the community. Being led from above means listening to the voice of the Holy Spirit as it speaks to the church as a whole. A leader must not become isolated. Through close cooperation with all members, a perfectly clear direction in all matters can be found. This is true for all matters of faith, all practical things, and for the overall inner attitude of the church.

◆ ◆ ◆ ◆ ◆

ANY TRUE SERVICE done for the church – including the service of leadership – is done as by an organ of the body, and it must therefore be done lovingly, sincerely, honestly, and in a childlike way. Someone who carries a responsibility is no higher than someone who does not: no one is higher, and no one is lower. We are all members of one body.

◆ ◆ ◆ ◆ ◆

TRUE LEADERSHIP means service, so it is a terrible thing to use it as a position of power over others. When such abuse of leadership takes place in a church community, it is especially devilish, because brothers and sisters give themselves voluntarily, trustingly, and openheartedly to the church. In a dictatorial state, people might yield to a greater power even though their souls reject it as evil. But in a community of believers, where members trust their leaders, the misuse of power is real soul-murder.

◆ ◆ ◆ ◆ ◆

WHEN WE ASK different ones to lead the church, we must ask God that much is given to them. But we must also let them be themselves – as God made them. They should not be presumptuous; they should express only what is given them by God. We do not expect more. It would be disastrous if anyone were to feel pushed into a role that was not genuinely his or hers. We do not expect someone who is meant to be an ear to be an eye.

◆ ◆ ◆ ◆ ◆

WHEN WE SPEAK about the authority of leaders in the church, it should be very clear that we never mean authority over people. Jesus gave his disciples authority, but he gave them authority over spirits – not people. In the same way, those of us asked to lead the church are given authority, but not over people. It is all too easy to forget this. We must seek for humility again and again.

◆ ◆ ◆ ◆ ◆

A LEADER OF THE CHURCH should certainly be admonished if someone feels he has done wrong. I remember how thankful I was years ago when a brother took me aside after a members' meeting – I had exploded at someone – and asked me, "Are you really sure your anger was of the Holy Spirit?" I had to admit that it was not, and so I called the meeting together again and set it straight. If you feel that I or anyone is misusing his position of authority, please do me the favor of pointing it out.

◆ ◆ ◆ ◆ ◆

WE DO NOT WANT a community that is bound to a leader. I fear nothing more than a service in the church – whether teaching, counseling, or whatever – that binds someone emotionally to another person. It is terrible, and I want to have nothing to do with it. We must be bound together in Christ.

◆ ◆ ◆ ◆ ◆

THERE IS NOTHING I hate more than human beings having power over the souls and bodies of others, especially in Christian community. I have vowed to myself to fight this evil until the end of my life, and if anyone can point out to me where I have used power over a human being – even without my knowledge – I want to repent deeply for it. Personal power is the greatest enemy of a living church.

◆ ◆ ◆ ◆ ◆

JESUS PUT A CHILD into his disciples' midst and said, "Unless you change and become like little children, you will never enter the kingdom of heaven. Therefore, whoever humbles himself like this child is the greatest in the kingdom of heaven" (Matt. 18:3–4). Here we see that Jesus loves the childlike spirit. This should also be true among us. In a marriage, both husband and wife must want to be the least. And in church community, each member must also want to be the least. That is our goal.

◆ ◆ ◆ ◆ ◆

SPEAKING THE TRUTH, which is a task of a leader of the church, is not a gift given only to especially clever and superior individuals. If it were, most people would have reason to fear being a disciple of Jesus or a leader in the church. It is not the intellect that is receptive to the truth; it is the childlike spirit. Jesus says, "Become like a child – only then will you be able to enter God's kingdom." The childlike spirit is and remains spirit, and because of that it is authority and revelation. The realization – that the truth is revealed only to children and to the simple-hearted – is crucial in the discipleship of Jesus.

◆ ◆ ◆ ◆ ◆

THERE IS AN INCLINATION in each of us to want to be great. And even if it is a small inclination – perhaps someone tends to be a bit bossy – it is the beginning of a much greater evil that will in the end bring much suffering. It is unbelievable what heartache can result when someone in a position of responsibility lets his authority be felt and treats his brothers and sisters as subjects. If a leader is bossy, it takes a certain courage to risk something and protest. But I wish everyone that courage. No one but Jesus is our master, and we are all brothers and sisters.

◆ ◆ ◆ ◆ ◆

WE REJECT THE IDEA of human greatness, which is foolishness before God. We long deeply for all other powers and spirits to yield, and for our beloved Jesus to lay his pierced hands over each of us. We long for him to be with us all, and we long to be ready to serve him. We ask for everything superficial in us and everything that might hinder or frighten us to melt away. We want to acknowledge the rulership of Jesus alone. Yes, everything is in his hands: he is the ruler over all powers and principalities, the head of the church, and the vine of which we are only branches.

◆ ◆ ◆ ◆ ◆

THE REVELATION OF CHRIST does not tolerate any human light next to it. If there is human light – pride and presumption – in any leader, it must be extinguished. Only the light of Jesus should rule in the church. God does not need human light. He needs men and women who wait in the darkness for his light, who hunger for truth and thirst for living water. If someone preaches the gospel to his own credit and does not acknowledge that without God he can do nothing, he

228

is a thief (Jn. 15:4). He steals the words of Jesus and uses them for his own glory.

◆ ◆ ◆ ◆ ◆

THE PARABLE OF THE TALENTS is perhaps best understood in the context of the church: the talents are gifts given to different brothers and sisters. One person receives the gift of wisdom, another knowledge, another faith, healing, prophecy, discernment, speaking in tongues, or interpretation (1 Cor. 12:8–10). These gifts are all required for the various tasks of the church, from leadership to any other. There is no difference in their importance; they all are parts of one body. The eye is no more important than the ear – they simply are two different organs.

Some people would like to see no differences. They think that if everyone were the same no one would know who was who, and then true justice would be established. But that is not the gospel of Jesus. In Matthew 25, we read of a man who was given only one talent. This man felt he had not been given his fair share, and so he hated his master. He did nothing with his talent but hardened his heart. He not only lacked love, he was filled with hatred. He said, "Master, I knew you to be a hard man." That is the worst thing that can happen to us: to feel we have not been given our fair share; to feel that others have received more from God; and then to become so envious and loveless – so separated from the body – that we do not contribute to it in any way at all. The master in the parable said, "You should have at least put the money in the bank." He meant, "Do at least the little you are able to do."

◆ ◆ ◆ ◆ ◆

ONE PERSON IS BRILLIANT, another deft with his hands, another very musical. These are natural gifts, and they should not be buried, though for the common good of the church they often have to be sacrificed. It would be wrong if someone with intellectual gifts thought he could do only intellectual work – otherwise he would be "burying his talents"– or if a very musical person thought she was wasting her talent by doing menial work. We must be willing to sacrifice our natural talents for the sake of the whole body. ✦

34

Submission

• • • • •

Richard J. Foster

EVERY DISCIPLINE has its corresponding freedom.
What freedom corresponds to submission? It is the
ability to lay down the terrible burden of always
needing to get our own way. The obsession to demand that
things go the way we want them to go is one of the great bond-
ages in human society today. People will spend weeks, months,
even years in a perpetual stew because some little thing did not
go as they wished. They will fuss and fume. They will get mad
about it. They will act as if their very life hangs on the issue.
They may even get an ulcer over it.

In the discipline of submission we are released to drop the
matter, to forget it. Frankly, most things in life are not nearly
as important as we think they are. Our lives will not come to
an end if this or that does not happen.

If you will watch these things, you will see, for example, that
almost all church fights and splits occur because people do

not have the freedom to give in to each other. We insist that a critical issue is at stake; we are fighting for a sacred principle. Perhaps this is the case. Usually it is not. Often we cannot stand to give in simply because it means that we will not get our own way. Only in submission are we enabled to bring this spirit to a place where it no longer controls us. Only submission can free us sufficiently to enable us to distinguish between genuine issues and stubborn self-will.

If we could only come to see that most things in life are not major issues, then we could hold them lightly. We discover that they are no "big deal." So often we say, "Well, I don't care," when what we really mean (and what we convey to others) is that we care a great deal. It is precisely here that silence fits in so well with all other disciplines. Usually the best way to handle most matters of submission is to say nothing. There is the need for an all-encompassing spirit of grace beyond any kind of language or action which sets others and ourselves free.

The biblical teaching on submission focuses primarily on the spirit with which we view one another. Scripture does not attempt to set forth a series of hierarchical relationships but to communicate to us an inner attitude of mutual subordination. Peter, for example, called upon the slaves of his day to live in submission to their masters (1 Pet. 2:18). The counsel seems unnecessary until we realize that it is quite possible for servants to obey their masters without living in a spirit of submission to them. Outwardly we can do what people ask and inwardly be in rebellion against them. This concern for a spirit of consideration toward one another pervades the entire New Testament. The old covenant stipulated that we must not murder. Jesus, however, stressed that the real issue was the inner spirit of murder with which we view people. In the matter of submission the same is true; the real issue is the spirit of consideration and respect we have for each other.

In submission we are at last free to value others. Their dreams and plans become important to us. We have entered into a new, wonderful, glorious freedom – the freedom to give up our own rights for the good of others. For the first time we can love people unconditionally. We have given up the right to demand that they return our love. No longer do we feel that we have to be treated in a certain way. We rejoice in their successes. We feel genuine sorrow in their failures. It is of little consequence that our plans are frustrated if their plans succeed. We discover that it is far better to serve than to have our own way. . . .

The touchstone for the biblical understanding of submission is Jesus' astonishing statement, "If any person would come after me, let him deny himself and take up the cross and follow me" (Mark 8:34). Almost instinctively we draw back from these words. We are much more comfortable with words like "self-fulfillment" and "self-actualization" than we are with the thought of "self-denial." (In reality, Jesus' teaching on self-denial is the only thing that will bring genuine self-fulfillment and self-actualization.) Self-denial conjures up in our minds all sorts of images of groveling and self-hatred. We imagine that it most certainly means the rejection of our individuality and will probably lead to various forms of self-mortification.

On the contrary, Jesus calls us to self-denial without self-hatred. Self-denial is simply a way of coming to understand that we do not have to have our own way. Our happiness is not dependent upon getting what we want. . . .

Again, we must underscore that self-denial means the freedom to give way to one another. It means to hold another's interests above our interests. In this way self-denial releases us from self-pity. When we live outside of self-denial, we demand that things go our way. When they do not, we revert to self-pity – "Poor me!" Outwardly we may submit but we do so in a spirit of martyrdom. This spirit of self-pity, of martyrdom, is a sure sign that submission has gone to seed. This is why self-denial is the foundation of submission; it saves us from self-indulgence. ◆

John F. Alexander

SUBMISSION MEANS KNOWING you don't know everything. It means knowing that the people of God gathered know more than you do by yourself. It means being willing to listen with an open heart when the body has the audacity to differ with your views. It means being willing pretty often to try out others' views for a while to see if maybe you're the one that's confused. . . .

That's all submission is – rejoicing that someone is wiser than us, that there are others whom we can respect. That frees us to rejoice that we don't have to know everything ourselves – betting that others know something too. It's a spirit, an attitude. Out of which grow unity and wisdom. . . .

Be clear: blind following of leaders is a terrible thing. But so is blind rejection of leaders. Passive acceptance of the way things are destroys, and so does aggressive destruction of everything established. It's a question of spirit. A spirit of passivity destroys as does a spirit of rejection. Maybe the only thing as deadly as conventional thinking is the need to debunk.

In my experience, more people have a need to debunk and complain than have a need to follow blindly. I know lots of complaining rebels, few blind followers. In my experience, a lot of people in our culture know how to question authority. Not so many know how to cooperate on a deep level. Not many know how to watch and listen till they know what's going on before they start rejecting and fighting.

We all know people who have a counterproposal for every proposal, whether it's about which restaurant to go to or which God to serve. And we all know people for whom most things are wrong most of the time. (Me, for instance.) People whose complaints are as extensive as the children of Israel's. People who are always testing authority, trying to prove that their wisdom is great, greater than God's. Life among those people becomes wearing and wearying.

In any case, blind following and blind rejecting isn't the full range of options. And I don't mean some moderating position between the two. On another continuum altogether is active, hopeful listening, where you aren't blaming and debunking but cheerfully cooperating while still asking friendly, pointed questions. . . . Instead of being passive followers or angry rebels, we can become people who are filled with the Spirit, singing psalms and hymns and spiritual songs among ourselves, making melody to the Lord in our hearts, while being enthusiastically cooperative with one another out of reverence for Christ. ◆

Money

♦ ♦ ♦ ♦ ♦

Jodi Garbison

THERE'S NOTHING COMMON about sharing money. It's quite unnatural. We each bring our own history, inherited perspectives, and entanglements when it comes to money and spending. In fact, when Eric and I got married, people warned us that most of our arguments would center around money. If this is true, and for many people it is, why would we take the risk of including five other people in something that can be difficult for even two people to navigate?

Our common purse started as an experiment to deepen our commitments to each other, by living simply and by practicing solidarity. We wanted to live lives that more closely resemble Acts chapter 2, which states, "Because believers shared all in common, no one was in need and all had enough." The idea of sharing each other's burdens – even financially – seemed scary, but we felt ready for the challenge. The idea was to live with a personal sacrifice and continue the downward mobility the gospel speaks of.

To do this, we needed something besides our own perspective and limited vision. We first sought advice from different communities we knew that had some form of common purse.... After much discussion and prayer we decided to combine things we had learned and tailor them to fit our needs.

As a first step, each of us submitted a personal budget, which included fixed bills, monthly income, and "wants." From that we tried to work through the differences between "wants" and "needs" and how to simplify the bills we had. We tried to imagine life without so many things and how we could cut back on things we had grown accustomed to. What could we potentially do without? This is where the ideal of common purse met the practical reality of day-to-day living. How were we going to actually implement our plan?

We agreed to find part-time jobs that would not require us to work more than twenty hours a week outside the community. This is important since we all understand our first call and commitment to be the work we share in common ... the works of mercy, peacemaking, and building community. We need money, however, for personal bills. These are bills that wouldn't be covered by donations, such as bills for cell phones, cars, and kids' activities. The money made from these part-time jobs would be our common purse – all of us would decide how to use it. It makes no difference whether you make $900 a month or $300 a month. We all have equal voice in the decisions, even though we all have jobs with different pay.

Once we worked through the bills we tried to determine a monthly stipend for each person. It's obvious that we are all at different places socially and what we do with our time and money for entertainment varies from person to person. I might go to a movie for rejuvenation, Eric might buy a book, and Nick might go to a concert. We came up with $100 for personal monthly stipend. The way this money is spent is discretionary. The purpose of the stipend is not solely for entertainment. It is also to be saved for trips or for vacations throughout the year. Any need that arises beyond the bills is brought to the community to discuss. If anyone needs something like clothes or shoes or hygiene items, we first look through donations. Many times, exactly what we need is given or, if we are patient, it might arrive soon. If we are unable to find what we need, then we discuss it as a group. The rub comes when not everyone agrees.

Is it working? It certainly isn't easy. We have struggled through many difficult conversations and we have all learned and grown from each one of them. Sharing money challenges the false sense of power and security we often place on money. We continue to need one another for accountability in order to move beyond selfish and careless spending. By releasing our tight grip on our money we hope to undo the culture's influence of consumerism and individualism. We have learned a lot from each other about how to challenge deep-seated practices of spending and yet still love one another.

Sounds like a miracle? Yes, you are right – it is a miracle! Several times throughout the last couple of years I've wanted to bail – gather "my" money, count the losses, and go my own way. It's certainly easier and cleaner to make decisions on my own. But is it healthier? Is it healing? Is it promoting the kingdom of God and restoring possessions and ownership to their right order? When I'm tempted to run, I'm gently reminded that this common purse isn't just for us, the seven who share it. Our common purse is for the good of everyone, the good of others who read about it or hear about it. It's for anyone who

is challenged by it and is inspired to try something similar. It's
for the good of others who benefit because we have realigned
our hearts to be sharers and not hoarders and to live in trust of
God instead of fear. Our hope is to have more in common with
no one in need. ◆

Jenny Duckworth

I N T H E E A R L Y D A Y S my husband, Justin, and I met
some inspiring types in the Catholic Worker world in
Brisbane. As we began to recognize the destructive cycles
of consumerism on our planet, a friend of ours asked, "If you
were to help a group of young adults like these guys know how
to start consuming in a better way, what would your advice
be?" With a deadpan face, the Catholic Worker guy said,
"Don't consume." An awkward silence followed. "Yes, sure, but
if you were going to help us find a place to start . . . ?" Again, a
pause. "No, just don't consume!" It did our heads in.

So, because we were disturbed, we were passionate to start
living the alternative somehow. We started along, eating less
meat, shopping at thrift stores, using recycled shopping bags.
Like all the justice issues, we needed to start somewhere, and
we enjoyed the challenge.

As we talked about justice and simplicity, in seeped our
pride and competitiveness (who could eat more chick peas in
a week), along with our judgment. Life began to lose joy as we
sacrificed everything for the sake of simplicity. We laughed
when we were accused by a friend (who was embarrassed of

us) at a social event of "dressing down for the poor"! But what did we actually mean by "for the poor"? Was all our talk and justice giving anything to others? Our antidote came in finding the missing piece of the puzzle: generosity.

We changed our language from a "simple lifestyle" to a "generous lifestyle." We went with less *in order that* others could have more. It was a significant shift. We didn't want to be known for what we went without or what we weren't allowed. We didn't want a culture where everyone focused on what they were doing without. That felt like a stingy life. We wanted to be known for our generosity, for what we gave away, for where we helped. We wanted to be generous with all our lives.

Spending less money allows us to have more money to give away. It allows us to share what we have materially with others. We are learning to look after what we have, to reuse and recycle. We are learning to be more responsible with the planet, taking less of the resources and adding less to the rubbish pile. In fact we have learned that we can survive with so much less than we thought. Even the simple discipline of really thinking before we buy anything has slowed the cash flow significantly. I try to have a gap between when I think I need something and when I buy it, in case during the gap, I think up an alternative. Sometimes I can borrow something from someone or can actually do without it. Sometimes the "need" fades quite fast. . . .

But the danger of getting good at recycling is hoarding, which is particularly rife among those drawn to the crazy life of community. . . . We had a young woman who used to hide stuff under her bed – clothing, games, leftover food. It did take me a few months to track down the smell in her room.

You can imagine the tensions when the "hoarders" share life with the "chuckers." The "chuckers" can include those who can confuse personal peace of mind with clean and tidy external spaces or those who have a power issue and find an arena to take some control. But in favor of the chuckers (okay, I myself am one of these), simplicity is not just about cheaper or not spending; it's about less. . . .

It frustrates me when I watch people become passionate about the Jesus lifestyle but who can't actually relocate to get involved because they have too much stuff. This has actually happened around us many times.

We had a young woman doing well in her early discipleship. She had faced some major challenges in her life and things were still tough. Her mum loved her dearly, so when she announced she was considering moving back in with us as part of our community, her mum went out and bought her a king-sized bed. The young woman then had to continue the payments on it herself, until it was paid off. Living in the inner city, this was problematic since space was tight; we had to share rooms to afford rent. Suddenly the whole discussion around whether she should move in and where God was calling her to became centered on what could work best for her bed! Bravely she moved in, bed and all. More brave still was the woman who offered to share a room with her. There was literally a few spare centimeters of floor space in that room, which allowed for the bucket to catch the leaks.

There is a time to nest in life, to know where we come from, where we belong, to establish a good sense of healthy home. . . . But what a gift it is when someone is free to move in response to the needs of those on the margins. How wonderful it is when someone can swap houses to take on a certain role or serve the community needs. Travelling light is a gift to others and a freedom to ourselves. ◆

36

Children

◆ ◆ ◆ ◆ ◆

Charles E. Moore

KYLE WAS THE YOUTH PASTOR of the church
at which I was interning. He was passionate about
serving Jesus, especially among the poor. I was
passionate about community, living out Jesus' teachings
together with like-minded believers. Along with several
others, we decided to move together to Denver's Capitol Hill
district – the area with the most homeless – and start living in
community. It was our way of trying to demonstrate the breaking in of God's kingdom.

Kyle and his wife Katie already had a child. Then another
came along. Our downtown community was growing. A
steady stream of twenty-somethings, some single and some
newly married, started joining us. Our one duplex eventually
extended to several houses along the same street. We shared
housing, vehicles, food. During this vibrant beginning, we
faced many unknowns that stretched our faith and our hearts.

We were learning how to live together and how to bring the transforming love of Christ to those who had been discarded by society.

A couple of years later, Kyle and Katie left the community. Among other reasons, they were now expecting a third child. As the only family with children, they felt out of place. Then Rick and Heather, expecting their first child, also wanted out, to be closer to Rick's family. We were saddened, but understood – it was kind of natural, we thought. In the meantime, more singles joined us. Then Jay got married and moved to a suburban neighborhood better suited for raising a family. Before long, our community dissipated. Somehow community and family didn't mix. We eventually disbanded.

I've now lived in community for over thirty years. What I experienced in Denver is not unique. Since that time, I've encountered others who tried living in community but, when children came along, became frustrated and left. Community and family life simply didn't mesh. Schedules conflicted, childcare was in short supply, priorities shifted, and the radical Christian life was somehow no longer possible.

Many years later, my wife and I found ourselves living in Albany, New York, in a setting similar to the one in Denver. Our big Victorian house was right along one of the busiest thoroughfares in the city, in one of the seediest neighborhoods. But this time our community was a mix of elderly, middle-aged, and young; married and single; and children of all ages. The household was bustling with life and chaos but also committed to a life of complete discipleship. Some of us worked in our community sign business while others worked at the nearby hospital, went to school, or volunteered at nearby Christian missions.

Life was intense. Even so, this time our life in community didn't conflict with family. I had learned something I didn't know back in Denver: what is good for children is good for the community.

Looking back, I think one reason our community in Denver fell apart was that we were just too "top heavy" with adult sophistication. We suffered from an unfreedom born of pride, over-analyzing our problems, and trying to be avant-garde and hip in the name of being relevant. Being childlike was not cool. Being "radical" was.

Had there been more children in our midst, and had we been committed to learning from them, our complex scruples might have evaporated. I experienced the truth of this first-hand in Albany. Instead of holding long, arduous meetings to process one another's junk and consider every possible angle on a decision, we adults did lots of singing, dancing, playing games, doing pranks, reading stories, and going on hikes that everyone could manage. By keeping it simple, the children in our household pointed us to Jesus. Our encounters with neighbors and strangers took on a different feeling as well: they were simpler and gentler, more mutual and participatory. Often, the children managed to draw out of even the most despondent the childlike gem buried within them.

The more we involved the children in our community, the more joy we had. They wanted to play run-around-the-house, or play kickball in the park across the street, or chase the Easter Bunny. It didn't matter if their play was in full view of commuters, or of the drunks and the mentally ill who regularly passed along the sidewalk outside our house. After all, weren't they all just people whom God loved?

This doesn't mean life was stress-free. There were safety issues, and childcare was a huge commitment. Couples needed time alone. College students sometimes didn't get home until late. There were also heavy needs in the neighborhood that demanded our attention. But if one thing kept us centered, and kept our faith simple and focused, it was the children. And, at least in my experience, a community in which children and families come first more readily and freely serves others.

"It is the child who leads us to the gospel," writes Eberhard Arnold. In children's generosity and helpfulness, in their natural happiness, and even in their naughtiness, we can experience a freedom to be ourselves. And children often possess an unshakable faith. Jesus is quite forthright about the role children play in his kingdom: "Unless you become like a child, you cannot enter the kingdom" (Matt. 18:3). We too easily forget this, or worse, resist it. The disciples got upset that so many children were being brought to Jesus. If we're honest, we too, under the guise of serving Christ's cause, often make ourselves too busy to pay attention to children.

A community centered on the kingdom will not just include but also nurture families. Again, this takes work. Sometimes a lot of work! The community I live in now is located in a former Catholic seminary. The building is huge, and the hallways are long and loud. Accommodations are such that living quarters are right off the main hallway, except for the corner apartments. Recently, we decided to do a big move-around. Quite honestly, it was a hassle. Families with small children, however, were able to move to the larger corner apartments, where the children were not so easily disturbed. That simple change has helped our children to be more peaceful and, oddly enough, more outgoing. The space they and their parents now have enables them to flourish.

When children are properly tended to, they give joy to those around them. When children are welcomed, when they are given opportunities to bring their natural wonder to the community – sharing about a special experience, for example, or singing a song they've learned – their happiness is infectious. This is something many intentional communities lack. Their members work hard, minister to others, live by lofty principles, take great risks, and make great sacrifices but still never experience fully the joy of sharing life together.

When we fail to find space and time for children, when we forget to consider the needs of families, we risk losing sight of how God reigns on earth. In God's kingdom, the "least of these" are the greatest. Jesus' warning about anyone who causes one of these little ones to stumble (Matt. 18:6–9) is a serious one. He goes on to say that the angels sent to protect children "always see the face of my Father in heaven." That's how much God cares about each child and whether they are truly welcomed and loved. A community must do everything in its power to protect and nurture an atmosphere in which children can grow in faith. Otherwise, God's kingdom is thwarted.

A Christ-centered community depends on a childlike spirit. What is good for children is indeed good for the community. Anything that threatens a childlike spirit – be it our conversation, the music we listen to, the films we watch, the rituals we observe – is corruption. If we want to demonstrate the kingdom of God on earth, we will not only welcome children, we will cherish and learn from them. For in them the pure love of God is revealed. ◆

37

Family Values

• • • • •

Andy Crouch

CHRISTIAN COMMUNITY made my years as an
unmarried person very rich – so rich that marriage
snuck up on me. I lived for four years in a household
on Mount Auburn Street in the heart of Cambridge's Harvard
Square. Depending on the year, four to six post-college
twenty-somethings ate together, prayed together, and enter-
tained friends together. For several years, the members of the
household shared one bank account, which soared and dipped
dramatically along with our career fortunes.

Guided by a covenant that we reaffirmed each year, we
sought to live out Luke's description of the early church in
Acts 2, the one so often quoted and so little practiced: "All
who believed were together and had all things in common;
they would sell their possessions and goods and distribute
the proceeds to all, as any had need." (Quite true – one year
Steve lost his job and spent the next nine months unemployed,

on us.) "Day by day, as they spent much time together in the temple" (historical circumstances prevented us from doing that part), "they broke bread at home and ate their food with glad and generous hearts" (creative amateur chefs are integral to the success of any Christian community, and ours was no exception), "praising God and having the goodwill of all the people." (I don't know what all the people thought of us, but our neighbors liked us well enough.) "And the Lord added to their number daily those who were being saved." (Not daily. But regularly.)

It is possible to be lonely anywhere, of course. But in that household I could go for weeks with only a vague awareness of my aloneness. My life, in its mundane and profound aspects, was full. Christian community is a powerful antidote to loneliness.

In the fourth year of living on Mount Auburn Street, however, I found myself, as Walter Wangerin memorably describes, "pitched headlong into a crisis wherein I suffered a blindness, from which I arose – married." In God's inscrutable providence, so did two other men from my household. In the course of a summer, like some highly unstable molecule, our community had split into three marriages and two free radicals.

It is at this point – the beginning of marriage and family – that most North Americans begin the long retreat into the nuclear isolation so celebrated by proponents of "family values." Experiments like the household at Mount Auburn Street may be tolerable, even enviable, holding patterns for single persons, but once those persons marry, powerful internal and external forces discourage them from pursuing more lasting forms of day-in, day-out relationship with other Christians. Housing, especially outside of urban areas, is constructed to serve the nuclear family. The real needs of a marriage for privacy – and the false needs conjured up by our atomized American conception of liberty – make any sort of "extended family" seem unrealistic at best, suffocating at worst. Sharing living space seems like an impossible intrusion to people who balk at sharing a lawnmower.

Even at the simpler level of friendship, married persons quickly find themselves socializing primarily with other couples. Churches provide a lifetime's worth of fellowship opportunities that trade on marital status – the young marrieds' Sunday school class, the parents' club, and so forth. With so many opportunities, small wonder that some newlyweds behave like former slum residents who have hit the lottery jackpot – moving out and leaving their single friends behind. Is it any wonder that singles are obsessed with getting married or, at least, finding a companion?

Here, again, the biblical world offers something different. The early Christians lived in a world, not of nuclear families, but "households." These complex assemblies of an extended family, slaves, freedmen, business associates, and tenants were the basic building block of Greco-Roman society. And when the gospel touched people's lives, it touched their households. Priscilla and Aquila, Philemon, and Stephanas all opened their homes to the Christian community. Paul wrote his letters largely to "household churches," which shared many of the characteristics of actual households, from regular meals to the holy kiss of affection. The ubiquitous Pauline forms of address, "brothers" or "beloved," underlined what Paul made explicit in his letters: we are all part of the "household of God" (Eph. 2:19), which is not so much a cozy Trinity-plus-two-kids arrangement as a multifaceted extended family from all walks of life.

What would it mean to recapture this sort of household church today? This has been a driving question in my own marriage since Catherine and I committed, during our engagement, to resist the cultural forces that would tend to isolate us from our still-single friends. Our pre-marriage experiences with community and the convictions that were formed there have led us, in each year of our marriage, into a household with others – our first year, with one other single person, and then for several years, with another married couple and two single persons. We are not alone in extending our family in this way – we count among our friends several similar households in Boston, as well as in California, Mississippi, Wisconsin, and elsewhere. Though their form varies, these households all have something in common: married couples, children, and single people making a common life of prayer, fellowship, and ministry in one home. This common life brings gifts and challenges. (Usually the gifts are the challenges.) In particular, life in a household has everything to do with making both singleness and marriage into true and livable Christian callings.

In community we receive the gift of companionship – the day-to-day intimacy that makes these friendships different from those carried on within defined and relatively public spaces. This is a tremendous gift to single persons, who not only gain brothers and sisters but, when children are present, nephews and nieces too. It is also a gift to married couples and families, as we invite others into our day-to-day life and receive their prayers, counsel, and often mediation!

However, the challenge to privacy is real, especially when the two partners in marriage have different expectations for personal space. Our first year of marriage, already difficult in the ways such years are, was harder – much harder – because we were living in community. One couple we know, who have extended their family for seventeen of the past twenty-four years, acknowledge that their first year living with others almost cost them their marriage. The intimacy of a household brings everyone's needs, fears, and sin to the surface very quickly, where they can be healed or turn toxic. Most households experience some of both.

This double-edged effect of community is evident in the area of sexuality. A major reason that couples tend to socialize with other couples may be that we subconsciously feel that such friendships are more stable (even though countless adulteries have arisen out of such friendships). Household living offers no such stability. The opportunities for temptation are many. But as one friend said, where else could a married person become close friends with someone of the other sex except in a context where all such friendships are kept relentlessly accountable to one another and to God? Life in household community restores the possibility of deep brother-sister relationships that many leave at the door of the single-family home.

Household life, indeed, both heightens and confronts one of our most persistent and common sins: the belief that if our circumstances were different, we would be happy. For a single person, life in a household can heighten the already-intense awareness that, as one friend said, "Some people don't have to sleep alone at night." But if household life brings marriage and its joys into acute focus, it also makes it impossible to idealize marriage. Our housemates see Catherine and me for what we are – real people who hurt each other in spite of, and sometimes because of, our commitment to one another.

And again, the gift and challenge go the other way. How many marriages have been ended by one or both partners' fantasy of regaining the freedoms that come with singleness?

In our household we do not have the luxury of idealizing the single life. Our friends live it. We try to ease their times of loneliness, acutely aware of our inability to fully comfort them. Yet if we suffer faithfully together, eventually we see that what is true of marriage is true of singleness too: it is a gift that, like all God's best gifts, brings suffering that – with the help of the Holy Spirit – can produce endurance, character, hope, and love.

This is perhaps the greatest blessing of life in a household: it confirms that each of our lives is a gift. Neither marriage nor singleness is ideal. Neither one will make us happy. Both are gifts from God, and only as we receive them from God, and live them in God, will we find joy. Indeed, in the household we find that our true joy is not in anything but the church, the body of Christ, the household of God.

Household life is consequently subversive of what is usually meant by "family values." Life in a household undermines any idealization of marriage even while it enables both married and single people to live joyfully and faithfully together. Household life, you might say, dethrones the family, but it also elevates the church, the great family in which all, no matter their situation or calling, are welcomed and loved. Perhaps that is what Christian family values should be all about. ◆

Solitude

♦ ♦ ♦ ♦ ♦

Henri J. M. Nouwen

SOLITUDE IS THE PLACE where we can reach the profound bond that is deeper than the emergency bonds of fear and anger. Although fear and anger can indeed drive us together, they cannot give rise to a common witness. In solitude we can come to the realization that we are not driven together but brought together. In solitude we come to know our fellow human beings not as partners who can satisfy our deepest needs, but as brothers and sisters with whom we are called to give visibility to God's all-embracing love. In solitude we discover that community is not a common ideology, but a response to a common call. In solitude we indeed realize that community is not made but given.

Solitude, then, is not private time in contrast to time together, nor a time to restore our tired minds. Solitude is very different from a time-out from community life. Solitude is the ground from which community grows. When we pray alone, study, read, write, or simply spend quiet time away from the places where we interact with each other directly, we enter into a deeper intimacy with each other. It is a fallacy to think that we grow closer to each other only when we talk, play, or work together. Much growth certainly occurs in such human interactions, but these interactions derive their fruit from solitude, because in solitude our intimacy with each other is deepened. In solitude we discover each other in a way that physical presence makes difficult if not impossible. There we recognize a bond with each other that does not depend on words, gestures, or actions, a bond much deeper than our own efforts can create.

If we base our life together on our physical proximity, on our ability to spend time together, speak with each other, eat together, and worship together, community life quickly starts fluctuating according to moods, personal attractiveness, and mutual compatibility, and thus will become very demanding and tiring. Solitude is essential for community life because there we begin to discover a unity that is prior to all unifying actions. In solitude we become aware that we were together before we came together and that community life is not a creation of our will but an obedient response to the reality of our being united. Whenever we enter into solitude, we witness to a love that transcends our interpersonal communications and proclaims that we love each other because we have been loved first (1 John 4:19). Solitude keeps us in touch with the sustaining love from which community draws its strength. It sets us free from the compulsions of fear and anger and allows us to be in the midst of an anxious and violent world as a sign of hope and a source of courage. In short, solitude creates that free community that makes bystanders say, "See how they love each other."

This view of solitude as the fertile ground of community has very practical implications. It means that time for silence, individual study, personal prayer, and meditation must be seen to be as important to all the members of the community as acting together, working together, playing together, and worshiping together.

I am deeply convinced that gentleness, tenderness, peacefulness, and the inner freedom to move closer to one another, or to withdraw from one another, are nurtured in solitude. Without solitude we begin to cling to each other; we begin to worry about what we think and feel about each other; we quickly become suspicious of one another or irritated with each other; and we begin, often in unconscious ways, to scrutinize each other with a tiring hypersensitivity. Without solitude shallow conflicts easily grow deep and cause painful wounds. Then "talking things out" can become a burdensome obligation and daily life becomes so self-conscious that long-term living together is virtually impossible. . . .

With solitude, however, we learn to depend on God, by whom we are called together in love, in whom we can rest, and through whom we can enjoy and trust one another even when our ability to express ourselves to each other is limited. With solitude we are protected against the harmful effects of mutual suspicions, and our words and actions can become joyful expressions of an already existing trust rather than a subtle way of asking for proof of trustworthiness. With solitude we can experience each other as different manifestations of a love that transcends all of us. ◆

Eberhard Arnold

WHAT IS THE RELATIONSHIP between togetherness and solitude in community life, between our need to be *alone* with God and our need for *fellowship* in him?

We are not almighty; our strength and power are limited. One writer speaks about the breathing of the soul, the breathing in and the breathing out of the inner person. He uses the expression "the creative pause."

Living together with others means receiving and giving. In every encounter between people there is giving and taking, breathing in and breathing out. We cannot be in the presence of others without giving something. Nor can a childlike, reverent person be in the company of others without receiving something from them.

This reverence and gratefulness in which we give and take are signs of true community. Community is impossible for those who think they are only giving. The opposite is also true – people who try to convince themselves that they only receive and have nothing to give render themselves unfit for community. The secret that makes us all brothers and sisters is that we both give and receive service. We not only live *with* one another but also *from* one another. And if the body of Christ receives the Spirit in all its members and the whole body is of one soul, then all members serve one another. No one can do without the other. Each one lives for the others, and all live together for the one united body. That is the secret of life in community.

But we are weak human beings; we cannot constantly give and take, breathe in and out. This is where the creative pause comes in. We cannot live without it. The day is spent in a rhythm of wakefulness and sleep, and the life of the soul needs creative quiet, an inner resting point, a gathering of our innermost thoughts before God in solitude. To be sure, a believing heart is never completely alone; God is always close. That is why common silence is of such importance.

. . . The secret of common silence between souls is the secret of the creative pause, a silence in which we are attentive to what God is accomplishing in us. That is why there can never be total solitude for us, for people who believe and love. But we do need silence, a time when we neither take nor give but rest close to the source of life.

If our community life is so bustling with activity that we have too little time for sleep and for this creative pause, then our spiritual life is in great danger. A soul requires quiet – God created it that way. Without quiet we feel exhausted and burned-out, and an unnecessary crisis follows. We are spiritually unfruitful when we are deprived of the creative pause. We are incapable of a constant love when we do not know moments of quiet. Such moments are essential in human relationships. We must not forget this. We are not fanatics about community, saying we should never be alone. That would be inhuman and ungodly. We know we are weak people, and sin follows hard on the heels of overstrained nerves. . . .

Instead, we need to ask God for the right rhythm – the rhythm that allows us to draw strength in quiet; new strength to love, to give, and to receive. We must never seek solitude just because living together with so many people is a strain on our nerves. Such loneliness would be unbearable after having once known the gift of voluntary community. We should watch out when the temptation to get away from it all comes over us. It is a signal for us to turn once more to God so that we can love again. For a short time we should enter the lonely cave of solitude so that we can return to people with renewed love – a love poured into our hearts by the Holy Spirit.

Let us also sometimes be silent together. Then both will be given to us – the creative pause, in which God speaks to the heart of each one, and the awareness that in our common silence he speaks to the hearts of all who are united here. ♦

39

Transparency

♦ ♦ ♦ ♦ ♦

Roy Hession

THE WORK OF THE LORD JESUS CHRIST on the cross was not only to bring us back into fellowship with God, but also into fellowship with one another. Indeed it cannot do one without the other. As the spokes get nearer the center of the wheel, they get nearer to one another. But if we have not been brought into vital fellowship with our brother, it is a proof that to that extent we have not been brought into vital fellowship with God. . . .

Everything that comes as a barrier between us and another, be it ever so small, comes as a barrier between us and God. We have found that where these barriers are not put right immediately, they get thicker and thicker until we find ourselves shut off from God and our brother by what seem to be veritable brick walls. Quite obviously, if we allow new life to come to us, it will have to manifest itself by a walk of oneness with God and our brother, with nothing between.

On what basis can we have real fellowship with God and our brother? *"If we walk in the light, as he is in the light,* we have fellowship one with another, and the blood of Jesus Christ his Son cleanseth us from all sin" (1 John 1:7). What is meant by light and darkness is that light reveals, darkness hides. When anything reproves us, shows us up as we really are – that is light. "Whatsoever doth make manifest is light" (Eph. 5:13). But whenever we do anything or say anything (or don't say anything) to hide what we are or what we've done – that is darkness.

Now the first effect of sin in our lives is always to make us try and hide what we are. Sin made our first parents hide behind the trees of the garden and it has had the same effect on us ever since. Sin always involves us in being unreal, pretending, duplicity, window dressing, excusing ourselves and blaming others – and we can do all that as much by our silence as by saying or doing something. . . .

"God is light," that is, God is the all-revealing one, who shows up every person as he or she really is. And John goes on to say, "In him is no darkness at all," that is, there is absolutely nothing in God which can be one with the tiniest bit of darkness or hiding in us. Quite obviously, then, it is utterly impossible for us to be walking in any degree of darkness and have fellowship with God. While we are in that condition of darkness, we cannot have true fellowship with our brother either – for we are not real with him, and no one can have fellowship with an unreal person. A wall of reserve separates him and us.

The only basis for real fellowship with God and with one another is to live out in the open with both. "But if we walk in the light, as he is in the light, we have fellowship one with another." To walk in the light is the opposite of walking in darkness. Spurgeon defines it in one of his sermons as "the willingness to know and be known." As far as God is concerned, this means that we are willing to know the whole truth about ourselves, we are open to conviction. We will bend the neck to the first twinges of conscience. Everything he shows us to be sin, we will deal with as sin – we will hide or excuse nothing. . . .

But the fellowship promised us here is not only with God, but "one with another"; and that involves us in walking in the light with our brother too. In any case, we cannot be "in the open" with God and "in the dark" with our brother. This means that we must be as willing to know the truth about ourselves from our brother as to know it from God. We must be prepared for our brother to hold the light to us (and we must be willing to do the same service for him) and challenge us in love about anything he sees in our lives which is not the highest. We must be willing not only to know, but to be known by him for what we really are.

That means we are not going to hide our inner selves from those with whom we ought to be in fellowship; we are not going to window dress and put on appearances; nor are we going to whitewash and excuse ourselves. We are going to be honest about ourselves with them. We are willing to give up our spiritual privacy, pocket our pride, and risk our reputations for the sake of being open and transparent with our brothers and sisters in Christ. It means, too, that we are not going to cherish any wrong feeling in our hearts about another, but we are first going to claim deliverance from it from God and put it right with the one concerned. As we walk this way, we shall find that we shall have fellowship with one another at an altogether new level, and we shall not love one another less, but infinitely more.

Walking in the light is simply walking with Jesus. Therefore there need be no bondage about it. We have not necessarily got to tell everybody everything about ourselves. The fundamental thing is our *attitude* of walking in the light, rather than the *act*. Are we willing to be in the open with our brother – and be so in word when God tells us to? That is the "armor of light" – true transparency. This may sometimes be humbling, but it will help us to a new reality with Christ, and to a new self-knowledge. . . . This is the reason why James tells us to put ourselves under the discipline of "confessing our faults one to another."

Of course, the purpose of "walking in the light" is that we might "have fellowship one with another." And what fellowship it is when we walk this way together! Obviously, love will flow from one to another, when each is prepared to be known as the repentant sinner he or she is at the cross of Jesus. When the barriers are down and the masks are off, God has a chance of making us really one. But there is also the added joy of knowing that in such a fellowship we are "safe." There is no fear now that others may be thinking thoughts about us or having reactions toward us, which they are hiding from us. In a fellowship which is committed to walk in the light beneath the cross, we know that if there is any thought about us, it will quickly be brought into the light, either in brokenness and confession (where there has been wrong and unlove), or else as a loving challenge, as something that we ought to know about ourselves. ◆

Dietrich Bonhoeffer

G OD HAS COME TO YOU to save the sinner. Be glad! This message is liberation through truth. You can hide nothing from God. The mask you wear before others will do you no good before him. He wants to see you as you are; he wants to be gracious to you. You do not have to go on lying to yourself and your brothers, as if you were without sin; you can dare to be a sinner. Thank God for that; he loves the sinner but he hates the sin.

Christ became our Brother in the flesh in order that we might believe in him. In him the love of God came to the sinner. Through him we could be sinners and only so could we be helped. All sham was ended in the presence of Christ. The misery of the sinner and the mercy of God – this was the truth of the gospel in Jesus Christ. It was in this truth that his church was to live. Therefore, he gave his followers the author- ity to hear the confession of sin and to forgive sin in his name. "Whose soever sins ye remit, they are remitted unto them; and whose soever sins ye retain, they are retained" (John 20:23).

When he did that, Christ made the church, and in it our brother, a blessing to us. Now our brother stands in Christ's stead. Before him I need no longer to dissemble. Before him alone in the whole world I dare to be the sinner that I am; here the truth of Jesus Christ and his mercy rules. Christ became our Brother in order to help us. Through him our brother has become Christ for us in the power and authority of the commission Christ has given to him. Our brother stands before us as the sign of the truth and the grace of God. He has been given to us to help us. He hears the confession of our sins in Christ's stead and he forgives our sins in Christ's name. He keeps the secret of our confession as God keeps it. When I go to my brother to confess, I am going to God.

So in the Christian community when the call to brotherly confession and forgiveness goes forth it is a call to the great grace of God in the church. ◆

40

Repentance

• • • • •

Benedict of Nursia

THE COMMUNITY'S LEADERS must pour out all their energy, and exercise their best pastoral gifts to care for the wayward member, because "it is not the healthy who need a doctor, but the sick" (Matt. 9:12). They should use every skill of a wise doctor and send in "specialists" – that is, wise and mature members who can support the wavering member, even as he continues to face the harsh possibility of a life cut off from those who love him the most. These specialists should urge him to be humble, as a way of working toward reconciliation, and they should console him "lest he be overwhelmed by excessive sorrow" (2 Cor. 2:7). For Paul also says: "Let love for him be reaffirmed" (2 Cor. 2:8). So everyone should pray for him. . . .

If a member has been confronted time and again for the same fault, or if he has even been cut off for a time, but still hasn't changed his ways, then he needs something else – a form of discipline that can shake him from his sleep. Every good doctor knows that the best treatment can sometimes hurt the worst. Still, there's no guarantee that the treatment will work.

If, God forbid, the patient gets worse – if he becomes proud and tries to defend his actions – the good doctor must go through the whole course, applying compresses, the ointment of encouragement, the medicine of the Holy Scripture, and finally the cauterizing iron of discipline.

But if, even after all of this, the good doctor can see that his efforts are not working, he should resort to an even better remedy: he and the whole community should pray for the wayward member so that the Lord, who can do all things, may miraculously send healing.

If even this procedure does not work, then finally the good doctor must use his knife and amputate. For Paul does say: "Banish the evil one from among you" (1 Cor. 5:13), and again: "If the unbeliever departs, let him depart" (1 Cor. 7:15), so that one diseased sheep might not infect the whole flock. ◆

Johann Christoph Arnold

To FORGIVE ON A PERSONAL BASIS is one thing; for a fellowship to pronounce forgiveness is quite another. Is it even necessary? Granted, in many instances a wrong committed can be put right by a simple apology. In community this should be a daily experience. But grave sins may need to be brought before the community or at least before a small group of trustworthy brothers and sisters. To use the New Testament analogy of the church as a body, it would be unthinkable for an injury to one part to go unnoticed by the whole: the defenses of the entire body are mustered. So too the sin of one person in a church will affect every member.

As Stanley Hauerwas writes, "A community cannot afford to 'overlook' one another's sins because they have learned that sins are a threat to being a community of peace." Members of a united community will "no longer regard their lives as their own" or harbor their grievances as merely theirs. "When we think our brother or sister has sinned against us, such an affront is not just against us but against the whole community."

Most churches today shy away from practicing discipline. Unfortunately, because of this, members who stumble and fall have little chance for repentance, let alone a new beginning. Mark and Debbie, members of the community I belong to, experienced this firsthand before coming to join us:

> Over the years we witnessed the disastrous results of ignoring sin or secretly hiding it. We lived in a small urban community with several people, one of whom was a single man who had fallen in love with a married woman in our group. Some of us tried to tackle their affair by talking with them separately about it. Yet there was no way to really "bring it out in the open" – we had no mutual understanding or covenant, and no grasp of the authority Jesus had given to his church to expose and rid itself of sin – and so there was no way to experience clarity or victory.
>
> Under the excuse that church discipline was too harsh or fundamentalistic, too legalistic, and too judgmental, we opted for the lie that this sin wasn't a very serious matter, at least not serious enough to bring it out into the open. Didn't

we all sin? Who were we to judge? Anyway, as the modern myth goes, we thought that what people needed most was loving acceptance and space to fail, not confrontation. We were under the illusion that confrontation not only added to the pain of personal shame and self-condemnation but perpetuated the cycle of failure. So we avoided it like the plague. Now we see that it was our so-called compassion that did the perpetuating.

Tragically, the man eventually left. Two years later the woman also left the community – and divorced her husband.

Naturally I cannot advise others on how – or even whether – to practice church discipline. There is some guidance in the New Testament (e.g., 1 Cor. 5), but every situation calls for discernment. Clearly, we must reject the practice of "shunning," which is used in some denominations to separate the "righteous" from the "evildoer" – the emphasis on punishment rather than hope for redemption and reconciliation has devastating consequences. A great deal depends on the level of commitment and accountability a community has. In a united church community whose members are accountable and committed to one another, discipline is a great gift: in rooting out sin, it can bring clarity to the most clouded situations; and by restoring those who fall, it can cleanse and enliven the body by purifying its members and giving them new faith and joy.

There are, I feel, a few basic aspects of communal discipline that must be considered if it is to be practiced redemptively. First, it must be voluntary; otherwise it will only harm the person who needs to be helped by it. Second, it must be practiced with love, sensitivity, and respect – not overzealously, not judgmentally, and certainly never with gossip. Instead of holding ourselves above the disciplined member, we need to repent with him and see where our own sin might have caused him to stumble. Our goal should never be punishment, but restoration.

Finally, discipline must be followed by complete forgiveness. Once the member shows himself to be repentant, he should be joyfully reaccepted, and the reason for his discipline should never be mentioned again. There are few joys as great as accepting a brother and sister who has undergone discipline back into the life of the fellowship. Repentance is a gift which we should actually all ask for again and again. ◆

J. Heinrich Arnold

I N MY CHURCH COMMUNITY, each member makes a covenant with God at baptism and promises never again to sin willfully against him. If after baptism someone does sin willfully against God, he must undergo church discipline in order to make a completely new beginning.

The small sins we all commit every day can be forgiven through our daily prayer. If the sins are worse, they can be forgiven through confession. James says, "Confess your sins to one another, and pray for one another, and then you will be healed" (5:16). For more serious sins, church discipline is necessary.

Discipline is offered only at the request of the person concerned. In some cases a person may be asked to refrain from common prayer and from members' meetings until he has repented and is forgiven. If an even graver sin is committed, a person may be asked to not take part in the communal life of the church until he has found a repentant heart.

We believe – and have experienced it – that through discipline people who have sinned can find full repentance and full forgiveness and can become true brothers and sisters again.

The writer of Hebrews warned the early church to let no bitter weed grow up to poison the whole (12:15). If this warning was given to the earliest believers, then it surely applies to us too. That is one reason we use church discipline: so that no poison may destroy the church. Another reason is to give the person who is disciplined a chance to begin anew, to find forgiveness of sins, and to purify his or her life.

We can discipline a brother or sister only if we recognize that the sin in our own hearts must be judged as well. The purpose of church discipline is not to judge a person, but to separate the evil in a person from the church. This has to happen again and again in our own hearts.

When brothers and sisters accept church discipline, it should remind us of the grace of repentance. If they really repent, they do something for the whole church – in fact, for the whole world – because evil is overcome by Jesus. In this sense we must have deep respect and reverence for those who are disciplined, because we know that we need God's mercy and compassion ourselves.

We must be very careful not to load onto a person even one milligram more than his actual guilt. We should be thankful that repentance and reconciliation with God is possible for those accepting church discipline, for us, and for all humankind.

Church discipline is a victory of light over darkness; it is the beginning of healing in a person. If it is accepted in this sense – the only true sense – it is a grace.

When something is not right in a brother or sister, we must speak to him or her about it out of love. And if someone speaks plainly to us, we must not be touchy. I can assure you that those who lived with Jesus heard plenty of straight talking. In comparison to Jesus, we are perhaps still much too polite. Jesus honored his mother, but he also said to her, "What have I to do with you, woman?" (John. 2:4). His way of love is not a way of politeness.

In the Letter to the Hebrews it says that the spirit of God is as sharp as a two-edged sword (4:12). We should apply this sharpness to ourselves first of all. But the New Testament also speaks of the great compassion, love, and warmth that come from the Spirit, and we should always show this love to others, especially to sinners. . . . God wants us to become clearer in discernment, but he also wants us to become more loving, more understanding, and more merciful. ◆

Forgiveness

• • • • •

Johann Christoph Arnold

MILLIONS OF CHRISTIANS recite the Lord's Prayer every day. We ask God to "forgive us as we forgive our debtors," but do we really mean what we say? Many of us will never be faced with forgiving a murderer. But all of us are faced daily with the need to forgive husband or wife, children, colleagues, fellow community members. And this task is no less important.

In his poem "A Poison Tree," William Blake shows us how the smallest resentment can blossom and bear deadly fruit:

> I was angry with my friend:
> I told my wrath, my wrath did end.
> I was angry with my foe:
> I told it not, my wrath did grow.
>
> And I water'd it in fears,
> Night and morning with my tears;

And I sunned it with smiles,
And with soft deceitful wiles.

And it grew both day and night,
Till it bore an apple bright;
And my foe beheld it shine,
And he knew that it was mine,

And into my garden stole
When the night had veil'd the pole:
In the morning glad I see
My foe outstretched beneath the tree.

The petty grudges of everyday life are the seeds to Blake's tree. If they fall into fertile hearts, they will grow, and if they are tended and nurtured they will take on a life of their own. They may be small, seemingly insignificant, even hardly noticeable at first, but they must nonetheless be overcome. Blake shows us in the first two lines how easily this can be done: we must face our anger immediately and root it out before it grows.

Human nature being what it is, the ability to forgive doesn't come naturally; it is a grace. Even our relationships with those who are closest to us are clouded now and then. True peace with others requires effort. Sometimes it demands the readiness to yield; at other times, the willingness to be frank. Today we may need humility to remain silent; tomorrow, courage to confront or speak out. One thing remains constant, however: if we seek peace in our relationships, we must be willing to forgive over and over.

Each of us has been hurt at one time or another, and each of us has hurt others. Therefore, just as all of us must forgive, so all of us need to be forgiven. Without forgiveness, we will not find peace.

What is forgiveness? Forgiving has nothing to do with being fair, or with excusing wrongdoing; in fact, it may mean pardoning someone for something inexcusable. When we excuse someone, we brush his mistake aside. When we forgive someone, there may be good reason to hold onto our hurt, but we let go of it anyway. We refuse to seek revenge. Our forgiveness may not always be accepted, yet the act of reaching out our hand in reconciliation saves us from anger and indignation. Even if we remain wounded, a forgiving attitude will prevent us from lashing back at someone who has caused us pain. And it can strengthen our resolve to forgive again the next time we are hurt.

It is less difficult to forgive a stranger than to forgive a person we know and trust. This is why it is so hard to overcome betrayal by close friends or colleagues. They know our deepest thoughts, our frailties, our quirks – and when they fail us or turn on us, we are left reeling. As a pastor of a Christian community, the Bruderhof, I've certainly experienced this.

In 1980 my church community suddenly asked me to step down from my work as assistant pastor to my father, a task I had been appointed to almost ten years earlier. To this day I am not completely sure why it happened. But all of a sudden, the very same people who had always praised and encouraged me began to find fault with everything I had ever done.

Confused and angry, I was tempted to fight back. My father needed me more than ever; only weeks before, my mother had died of cancer. I desperately wanted to set my record straight and reestablish my "rightful" place.

My father, however, refused to support me in fighting back. Instead he pointed me to the Sermon on the Mount, where Jesus speaks of forgiving others for their trespasses so that we, too, may be forgiven. He reminded me that in the end we won't have to answer for what others do to us – only for what we do to them.

Suddenly I realized I wasn't as good as I had thought I was. I began to see that deep down I held grudges against certain members of my community, and that instead of trying to justify myself, I needed to get down on my knees and ask God to forgive me. Then I would find strength to forgive. As soon as I did this, my struggle took on a wholly new meaning. I felt as if a dam had burst open somewhere deep inside my heart. Before, I had felt the pain of hurt pride; now I could ask myself: What does it matter in God's eyes?

With a new determination to set things straight and to take the blame for whatever tensions existed, I went with my wife to people we felt we had hurt in the past and asked them to forgive us. As we went from one to another, we felt God at work, and our hearts became lighter.

That year was a very painful one for me and my wife, but it was also an important one. It prepared us for the respon-sibilities we would carry later by giving us a greater sense of compassion for others. And it taught us some lessons we will never forget. First, it does not matter if people misunderstand you or accuse you unjustly; ultimately, what matters is that your heart is right before God. Second, though the decision to forgive must always come from within, we cannot change in our own strength. The power of forgiveness comes not from us, but from God. He can work in us only when we turn to him in prayer, trust, and humble recognition of our weaknesses.

This does not mean we should just swallow our hurts. To the contrary, when we push our grievances down into our subcon-scious in an attempt to forget them we only cripple ourselves.

Before we can forgive a hurt, we must be able to name it. Once we have done this, however, we must forgive and let go.

When we get hurt, we must guard against the temptation to drop comments or to gossip. When we complain to others about our hurts in order to gain sympathy, we add fuel to the fire and spread our resentments further. Difficult as it may be, direct speaking is usually the best way to rid ourselves of anger and pent-up feelings in an honest and straightforward manner.

At other times, however, it may be best to forgo direct confrontation and simply forgive, especially when our resentment has no proven cause – if, for example, it is based on a second-hand remark. Otherwise we may remain sullen and mistrustful forever, waiting for an apology that can never be made.

All of us have wronged (and have been wronged by) others at some point in our lives. Yet to dwell on human failings is to deny the power of love and forgiveness. The Spirit can move in our lives if we only open our hearts to it. Love is greater than hatred, faith is greater than doubt, and hope is greater than despair.

Five hundred years ago Thomas à Kempis advised fellow monks that "our peace in this life should depend on humble forbearance rather than on the absence of adversity." This forbearance, which is willingness to forgive, is the secret of a truly happy life. Without forgiveness we will never experience real community with God, nor lasting relationships with each other. With it, our lives will be more richly blessed than we can ever imagine. ◆

42

At Table

• • • • •

Leonardo Boff

TABLE FELLOWSHIP means eating and drinking together around the same table. This is one of the most ancient signs of human intimacy, since the relationships that sustain the family are built and rebuilt continuously through it.

The table, before being a piece of furniture, marks an existential experience and a rite. It is the foremost place of the family, of communion and kinship. Meals are shared; there is the joy of gathering, of well-being without pretense, and of direct communion, which translates into uncensored commentary on daily activities and local, national, and international news.

A meal is more than just something material. It is the sacrament of reunion and communion. The food is appreciated and is the object of praise. The greatest joy of the cook is to note the satisfaction of the diners.

But we should recognize that the table is also a place of tensions and conflicts, where matters are debated openly, where differences are spelled out and agreements can be established, where disturbing silences also exist that reveal a collective malaise. Contemporary culture has so changed the sense of daily time as a result of work and productivity that it has weakened the symbolic sense of the table. This has been set aside for Sundays or special moments such as birthdays or anniversaries when family members and friends get together. But, as a general rule, it has ceased to be the fixed point of convergence of the family. Unfortunately, the table has been substituted by fast food, a quick meal that makes nutrition possible but not table fellowship.

Table fellowship is so crucial that it is linked to the very essence of the human being as human. . . . Ethno-biologists and archeologists call our attention to an interesting fact: when our anthropoid ancestors went out to gather fruit and seeds, to hunt and to fish, they did not eat individually what they were able to collect. They took the food and brought it to the group. And thus they practiced table fellowship – distributing the food among themselves and eating communally as a group.

Therefore, table fellowship, which assumes solidarity and cooperation with one another, enabled the first leap from animality to humanity. It was only a beginning step, but a decisive one, because it initiated a basic characteristic of the human species that sets it apart from most other species – table fellowship, solidarity, and cooperation in the act of eating. And that small distinction makes all the difference.

That table fellowship that made us human yesterday continues to renew us as human beings today. Therefore it is important to set aside time for the meal in its full meaning of table fellowship and free and disinterested conversation. It is one of the permanent sources of renewal for humanity, which is totally anemic today. ◆

Dietrich Bonhoeffer

THE CONGREGATION OF JESUS believes that its Lord wants to be present when it prays for his presence. So it prays: "Come, Lord Jesus, be our guest" – and thereby confesses the gracious omnipresence of Jesus Christ. Every mealtime fills Christians with gratitude for the living, present Lord and God, Jesus Christ. Not that they seek any morbid spiritualization of material gifts; on the contrary, Christians, in their wholehearted joy in the good gifts of this physical life, acknowledge their Lord as the true giver of all good gifts; and beyond this, as the true gift, the true bread of life itself; and finally, as the one who is calling them to the banquet of the kingdom of God. So in a singular way, the daily table fellowship binds the Christians to their Lord and one another. At table they know their Lord as the one who breaks bread for them; the eyes of their faith are opened.

The fellowship of the table has a festive quality. It is a constantly recurring reminder in the midst of our everyday work of God's resting after his work, of the Sabbath as the meaning and goal of the week and its toil. Our life is not only travail and labor, it is also refreshment and joy in the goodness of God. We labor, but God nourishes and sustains us. And this is reason for celebrating. We should not eat the bread of sorrows (Ps. 127:2);

rather, "eat thy bread with joy" (Eccles. 9:7); "I commended mirth, because a man hath no better thing under the sun, than to eat, and to drink, and to be merry" (8:15); but, of course, "who can eat, or who can have enjoyment apart from him?" (2:25). It is said of the seventy elders of Israel who went up to Mount Sinai with Moses and Aaron that "they beheld God, and did eat and drink" (Exod. 24:11). God cannot endure that unfestive, mirthless attitude of ours in which we eat our bread in sorrow, with pretentious, busy haste, or even with shame. Through our daily meals he is calling us to rejoice, to keep holiday in the midst of our working day.

The table fellowship of Christians implies obligation. It is *our* daily bread that we eat, not my own. We share our bread. Thus we are firmly bound to one another not only in the Spirit but in our whole physical being. The *one* bread that is given to our fellowship links us together in a firm covenant. Now no one needs to go hungry as long as another has bread, and he who breaks this fellowship of the physical life also breaks the fellowship of the Spirit. "Deal thy bread to the hungry" (Isa. 58:7). "Make not an hungry soul sorrowful" (Ecclus. 4:2), for the Lord is meeting us in the hungry brother and sister (Matt. 25:37). "If a brother or sister be naked, and destitute of daily food, and one of you say unto them, Depart in peace, be ye warmed and filled; notwithstanding ye give them not those things which are needful to the body, what doth it profit?" (James 2:15–16). So long as we eat our bread together we shall have sufficient even with the least. Not until one person desires to keep his own bread for himself does hunger ensue. This is a strange divine law. May not the story of the miraculous feeding of the five thousand with two fishes and five loaves have, along with many others, this meaning also?

The fellowship of the table teaches Christians that here they still eat the perishable bread of the earthly pilgrimage. But if they share this bread with one another, they shall also one day receive the imperishable bread together in the Father's house. "Blessed is he that shall eat bread in the kingdom of God" (Luke 14:15). ◆

Celebration

• • • • •

Richard J. Foster

FAR AND AWAY the most important benefit of celebration is that it saves us from taking ourselves too seriously. This is a desperately needed grace.... It is an occupational hazard of devout folk to become stuffy bores. This should not be. Of all people, we should be the most free, alive, interesting. Celebration adds a note of gaiety, festivity, hilarity to our lives. After all, Jesus rejoiced so fully in life that he was accused of being a winebibber and a glutton. Many of us lead such sour lives that we cannot possibly be accused of such things.

Now I am not recommending a periodic romp in sin, but I am suggesting that we do need deeper, more earthy experiences of exhilaration. It is healing and refreshing to cultivate wide appreciation for life. Our spirit can become weary with straining after God just as our body can become weary with overwork. Celebration helps us relax and enjoy the good things of the earth.

Celebration also can be an effective antidote for the periodic sense of sadness that can constrict and oppress the heart. Depression is an epidemic today and celebration can help stem the tide. In his chapter titled "Helps in Sadness," François Fénelon counsels those who are bowed low with the burdens of life to encourage themselves "with good conversation, even by making merry."

Another benefit of celebration is its ability to give us perspective. We can laugh at ourselves. We come to see that the causes we champion are not nearly so monumental as we would like to believe. In celebration the high and the mighty regain their balance and the weak and lowly receive new stature. Who can be high or low at the festival of God? Together the rich and the poor, the powerful and the power-less all celebrate the glory and wonder of God. There is no leveler of caste systems like festivity.

Thus freed of an inflated view of our own importance, we are also freed of a judgmental spirit. Others do not look so awful, so unspiritual. Common joys can be shared without sanctimonious value judgments.

Finally, an interesting characteristic of celebration is that it tends toward more celebration. Joy begets joy. Laughter begets laughter. It is one of those few things in life that we multiply by giving. Kierkegaard says that "humor is always a concealed pair."

Celebration is primarily a corporate discipline, and if it brings such benefit to the people of God, how is it practiced? The question is a good one, for modern men and women have become so mechanized that we have snuffed out nearly all experiences of spontaneous joy. Most of our experiences of celebration are artificial, plastic.

One way to practice celebration is through singing, dancing, shouting. Because of the goodness of God, the heart breaks forth into psalms and hymns and spiritual songs. Worship, praise, adoration flow from the inner chambers. In Psalm 150 we see the celebration of the people of God with trumpet and lute and harp, with timbrel and dance, with strings and pipe and loud clashing cymbals.

What do little children do when they celebrate? They make noise, lots of noise. There is not a thing wrong with noise at the appropriate time, just as there is nothing wrong with silence when it is appropriate. Children dance when they celebrate. When the children of Israel had been snatched from the clutches of Pharaoh by the mighty power of God, Miriam the prophetess led the people in a great celebration dance (Exod. 15:20). David went leaping and dancing before the Lord with all his might (2 Sam. 6:14). The folk dance has always been a carrier of cultural values and has been used repeatedly in genuine celebration. Of course, dancing can have wrong and evil manifestations, but that is another matter entirely.

Singing, dancing, and noise-making are not required forms of celebration. They are examples only, to impress upon us that the earth indeed is the Lord's and the fullness thereof. Like Peter, we need to learn that nothing that comes from the gracious hand of God is inherently unclean (Acts 10). We are free to celebrate the goodness of God with all our viscera! ✦

Juan Mateos

THE FEAST EXPRESSES solidarity with the world, a holding to God's "very good." But here we come upon another difficulty: How can we approve a world so riddled with injustice and evil? The feast would seem a very partial affirmation; consequently, would it not be unreal and imaginary? Celebrating a feast together does not ignore the existence of evil, but it maintains that everything is basically good. In order to assert this fact, we are ready to die for it. We can celebrate the world, even when for a time it is disfigured by evil because we know this lies on superficial levels and is already doomed. In the feast we raise a flag of hope; when we affirm the triumph of life over death we assert that good is over evil.

The feast is a symbol of very high import; that is, a reality, in our case a shared and felt experience, that points to something much higher and in a certain way contains it. The human yearning for unconditional happiness comes to the surface and is partially realized in the feast. Contemplative intuition sees through the festive gifts of celebration that, fully accepted and shared, become symbols of higher realities. But such intuition does not isolate us, because it is precisely in enthusiastic participation that it discovers the mysterious presence of an unattained reality. The walls of the present fall down and let the winds of the future rush through. Festivity liberates,

putting us in contact with the great realities that make the
rest of life relative; it restores a healthy sense of humor, so that
while we take everything in earnest we can still smile over the
daily struggle. . . .

Festivity is a generous thing. The first condition for the one
who is at a feast is to be capable of giving and to be ready to do
so. It is a mutual gift, in which the words of Christ are carried
out: "It is better to give than to receive" (Acts 20:35). One's
own enrichment, although tangible, is not the main purpose
of the feasting, but rather self-giving through expression.
Festivity consists in mutual giving, not earning; there are no
fixed rates of exchange: everyone throws their wine freely into
the common cup from which all will drink happily.

The feast is the experience and loud affirmation of the
kingdom of God. Here the Christian gives substance to the
utopia of a human society bound together in brotherhood. The
elbow-to-elbow contact of the celebration, the human warmth
of acceptance and mutual appreciation and other people's
example, manifest Christ's presence within the group; we feel
and understand ourselves to be a part of the new creation, to
be living already in the new age. . . .

Celebration is not only a spur to fidelity to the Lord; it also
leads to quiet self-scrutiny. The ideal proclaimed and shared
and our profession of Christ's sovereignty stir us up to realize
the meanness of our actions and inward disposition, our
obstinate grudges and the envy and unacknowledged ambitions we carry within us. The more intense the atmosphere
of celebration and the more enthusiastic the gaiety, the
greater the detestation we shall feel for anything opposing
the kingdom. Thirst for honor, possessions, and power appear

incompatible with the unity we are seeking and already experiencing. Celebration purifies.

Festivity is so much the more needed as our daily life becomes more difficult. Precisely because so many are victims of oppression and injustice, we have more frequently to affirm and stir up our belief in life, to remind ourselves of our right to freedom and plenitude, and to avoid falling into resigned indifference. In itself celebration is already a protest against oppression and upholds the aspiration toward a more just life. The feast, with its enjoyment of true values, raises the standard of Christian intransigence. That this exists is certain, otherwise we should have no martyrs. ◆

Jeremiah Barker

THE FOUNDER OF Madonna House, Catherine Doherty, was a big believer in the restoration of all things in Christ (Eph. 1:10). For Catherine, a big part of what she saw as standing in need of restoration was the human capacity for simply *being,* and being *together.* This is why she was so insistent that in the midst of our work – which can indeed be holy in and of itself – we also take breaks. Breaks remind us what the work is for: work is for humanity; humanity is not for work. That is to say, as Pope Leo XIII explained in *Rerum novarum,* humanity is the end of work and not merely a means for its accomplishment. Humanity is not to be thought of as mere capital along with the other things that play a role in the process of production, or of amassing wealth. The goal of work is the well-being of humanity.

At Madonna House, the constant back-and-forth between the call to work and the call to refrain from work is an on-the-ground, nitty-gritty reminder of the tension between the importance and dignity of work on the one hand, and the need to keep work in its proper place on the other. We stop for tea time. We stop for daily Mass. We stop for meals. We stop for the Lord's Day. We stop for major feasts.

When I was a guest at Madonna House, I asked why there is such a high ratio of staff assigned to the main center in rural Ontario compared to the small field houses scattered across the globe. Susanne Stubbs, one of the directors at the time, replied: "Here in Combermere, we're all about feasting. We put a lot of energy into preparing for Christmas and for Easter. And to put on a good feast, you need a lot of people."

By feasting Susanne didn't simply mean putting on a fancy meal and eating a lot of food – though that can be an aspect of Christian feasting, and it is at Combermere. The feast is an external expression of a deeper mystery. "Where would you like us to prepare the feast?" the disciples asked our Lord prior to the Passover (Luke 22:7–13). And, speaking of the ongoing celebration of the Lord's Supper, Paul declares, "Christ our Passover is sacrificed for us. Therefore, let us keep the feast" (1 Cor. 5:7–8).

The practice of Christian feasting isn't contingent upon having fancy food, or having a lot of food, or even having food at all. Susanne's identification of the Christian feasting that sees the birth of Christ at Christmas and his death and resurrection at Easter as the center of our communal life points to a truth at the center of Christian life in general. "What is all this work for?" I began asking myself as I fixed leaky pipes or turned compost. The answer: We're doing all this work so that we can celebrate – together, and with whoever comes our way – the feast of Christ's birth and the feast of Christ's resurrection.

"Where would you like us to prepare the feast for you?" This question became my daily prayer to Christ as I began the day, performing whatever tasks I was asked to do as a guest, and later as a community member. At Madonna House we celebrate Mass every evening in our little Island Chapel in the woods. So, in addition to looking ahead to Christmas and Easter throughout the year, as we perform the tasks of raising food, maintaining our living space, or harvesting firewood to heat our buildings, we look ahead to celebrating the birth, death, and resurrection of Christ in this daily celebration of the Lord's Supper. The gifts of bread and wine – the fruits of the earth and the work of our hands, as the liturgy puts it – we offer to God the Father, who has generously bestowed all these gifts upon us.

And really, each our meals and, yes, each of our tea times is an opportunity to participate in fellowship with the newborn and risen Christ in our midst, and in fellowship with one another united in him. Each day's labor, then, is preparation for the feast of Easter and the feast of Christmas that lie months, weeks, or days ahead. And just as much, each day's labor is preparation for that day's opportunities to celebrate. ◆

PART IV

Beyond the Community

If we are no longer here for all people, if we can no longer concern ourselves with the need and suffering of the whole world, community life has lost its right to exist.

EBERHARD ARNOLD, God's Revolution

Revolution

• • • • •

Andreas Ehrenpreis

WHEN WE ARE filled with the spirit of community, we become simple and modest. We will be satisfied with what little food and clothing we have. . . . Any profits from our work should not be hoarded. The fruits of our work must be at the disposal of all our brothers and sisters in God. They are for the feeding, housing, and clothing of the poor, the hungry, and the old. It was through love that Jesus became poor and one of the lowliest on earth. . . .

Our love for our fellow human beings must be so great that it compels us to share all our possessions with them; anyone who does not have that love for his neighbor should not think that the blood of Christ frees him from sin. As love springs from faith, so works spring from love. The only true charity, consisting in acts of fervent love, is inseparable from true life and real freedom from sin. Active love will urge us to work for the overcoming of need and poverty rather than for our own benefit. Whoever does otherwise has not a spark or drop of divine love.

Whoever loves God must love all people who have their life from God. If we really believe that all people have one God and one Father, we cannot possibly seek to gain or maintain an advantage over one of our brothers or sisters. If we still seek our own advantage, then love is extinguished and cold in us. We see the need and poverty of God's children; we could help, but we do not do it, perhaps even saying, "Should I give bread to those I do not know?" So we become evil. We want to keep for ourselves what has been stolen from others. We are pleased we have succeeded in life. Those who have dropped behind on the way get nothing from us. Do they not need their share just as we do? This is how we lose our feeling for justice. It grows darker and darker around us because we cannot love our brother. The cries of the poor surround us like dark shadows; they have nothing and suffer privation while we have more than enough of the best.

God wants us to love the poor. Christian community is the best way to put this love into practice. Through hard and steady work, we can provide an adequate standard of living for the poor and homeless; we can provide food and spread the table for them at every mealtime. We can do this even while we own nothing ourselves. Through this service people are enabled to live who would otherwise have to beg from door to door or die of misery and starvation. This is done for love alone by all who live in community; purely for Christ's sake and the sake of the poor. It is a question of love and friendship and brotherhood; in the first place, love and friendship toward our brothers and sisters in the faith. Only in joyful dedication can this work be done. ◆

John M. Perkins

THE MOVEMENT of Christian community, where more and more Christians are seeking to share their lives and resources together at deeper and deeper levels, could very easily end up in groups of white, middle-class Christians talking themselves out of the loneliness and meaninglessness of the suburbs. It could end up as a new form of withdrawal from the realities of evil in our systems into a new form of communal materialism. Christian community is still a phenomenon enjoyed basically only by those people able to have the mobility and the leisure to "shop" around the country for a new life, a luxury which the poor and disenfranchised in our country have never been able to afford.

And the movement of church renewal could follow the institutional church's pattern of noninvolvement with victims in the poor, black communities of this country and result in the terrible stagnation that has been the fate of so many religious movements committed to inner growth without relevant outreach.

We need a quiet revolution.

But for me, hope and fear dwell together as I look out at the church today and see how what could be revolutionary might be just some more religious jive. Pope Paul VI said it for me.

He was hosting a conference in the Vatican on church spiritual renewal and in one address he said something like, "This movement for our church is like opening up the windows in an old house. The joy! The life! But I admonish you, there are those in the world who make up the majority – they are hungry, thirsty, naked, without shelter. They will demand more than your joy."

There is, I believe, one key issue, which if addressed by the church today, would give meaning to each of these movements. The issue is this: How do we as Christians relate our lives and our resources to the real needs of the human victims around us? This issue could take the form of some specific questions too, like: "How do we as Christians get rid of and replace the welfare system in America?" or "How do we as Christians preach the gospel in the Mississippi Delta?" or "How do we as Christians begin to minister in the Hill District of Pittsburgh?"

How can we be part of a quiet revolution?

To me, our legitimacy and our identity as the church of Jesus Christ is wrapped up in our response to the victim in our world. As Howard Snyder writes in his book *The Problem of Wineskins*, "The gospel to the poor and the concept of the church are inseparably linked. Failure to minister to the poor testifies to more than unfulfilled responsibility; it witnesses to a distorted view of the church."

If the church is to be the quiet revolution, it must face the poor in our society. . . .

We must relearn what it means to be a body and what it means to continue Christ's ministry of preaching the gospel to the poor. I believe there is a strategy to do this. We have seen three principles work that seem to be at the heart of how a local body of Christians can affect their neighborhood. We call them the three Rs of the quiet revolution: *relocation, reconciliation,* and *redistribution.*

First, *we must relocate the body of Christ among the poor and in the area of need.* I'm not talking about a group of people renting a storefront through which to provide services to the community. I'm talking about some of us people voluntarily and decisively relocating ourselves and families for worship and for living within the poor community itself. . . .

If we are going to be the body of Christ, shouldn't we be like he was when he came in history? He didn't commute daily from heaven to earth to minister to us poor sinners. He didn't set up his own nice mission compound. No, the Bible says that "the Word became flesh and *dwelt* among us, full of grace and truth" (John 1:14). That's how we were able to behold his glory, because he dwelt among us. . . .

Relocating myself makes me accountable to the real needs of the people because they become my needs. Ministering from within the neighborhood or community, I will know and be able to start with the real needs of those around me instead of forcing on the people what I have assumed their needs are. After meeting some real needs, I can begin to communicate through these "felt needs" to the deeper spiritual needs of a person.

When this happens the quiet revolution has begun.

Then *we must reconcile ourselves across racial and cultural barriers.* I hear people today talking about the black church and the white church. I do it too – it's reality. But it's not in Scripture. We should not settle for the reality our culture presents us with.

You see, the whole idea of the love of God was to draw people together in one body – reconciled to God. That's sup-

posed to be the glory of the church! But we aren't manifesting
the love of God today that can really move across racial and
cultural barriers. What we do is to go on preaching the gospel
within the limits of our own culture and tradition.

The test of the gospel in the early days of the church was
how was it going to affect Samaria. I believe the gospel is being
tested again today. To reconcile people across racial lines,
black people, white people, all people, is to stage a showdown
between the power of God and the depth of the damage in us
as human beings. It's been my experience that the power of
God wins and the result is a dynamic witness for Jesus Christ
that brings others to confront him in their lives.

When reconciliation is taking place across cultural lines –
between blacks and whites, between rich and poor, between
indigenous and those who are new in the community – the
quiet revolution is ready to spread.

The final result is redistribution. If the blood of injustice is economics, we must as Christians seek justice by coming up with
means of redistributing goods and wealth to those in need. . . .
A ministry in the poor community which has no plans to
create economic support systems in the community is no better
than the federal government's programs which last only as long
as outside funds are budgeted. The long-term goal must be to
develop a sense of self-determination and responsibility with
the neighborhood itself.

It's at the point of redistribution that I begin to see a possibility for structural change to take place. What we need is a
change, created by Jesus Christ, in our institutional behavior
equal to the change that can occur in the life of an individual.
And as we commit ourselves to just redistribution in terms
of creating a new economics in broken communities, we can

see how Jesus, through us, offers himself. The body of Christ becomes the corporate model through which we can live out creative alternatives that can break the cycles of wealth and poverty that oppress people.

When this happens, the quiet revolution is winning the battle for the community. . . .

If we as Christians can see the issues of our day – poverty, racism, war, and injustice – and if we can use the skills and resources that we get from our training at school or on the job, and if we can really be open to being equipped by the spirit of God, then we will be used. We must lie awake at night and wrestle with how we can individually and collectively bring our faith from talk to power, how we can bring our faith and works to bear on the real issues of human need. ◆

45

Comfort Zones

• • • • •

Eugene H. Peterson

SECTARIANISM is a common problem in Christian community. The boundaries and definitions are not fixed – it is more like a tendency, an ever-present pull to something smaller, a reduction that enables us to exercise control. Sectarianism involves deliberately and willfully leaving the large community, the "great congregation" that is featured so often in the Psalms, the whole company of heaven and earth, and embarking on a path of special interests with some others, whether few or many, who share similar tastes and concerns. But God's clear intent from the outset is to bless "all the families of the earth" (Gen. 12:3), and the anticipated hope is that "at the name of Jesus every knee should bend, in heaven and on earth and under the earth, and every tongue should confess that Jesus Christ is Lord, to the glory of God the Father" (Phil. 2:10–11).

Sectarianism is to the community what heresy is to theology, a willful removal of a part from the whole. The part is, of course, good – a work of God. But apart from the whole it is out of context and therefore diminished, disengaged from what it needs from the whole and from what the rest of the whole needs from it. We wouldn't tolerate someone marketing a Bible with some famous preacher's five favorite books selected from the complete sixty-six and bound in fine leather. We wouldn't put up with an art dealer cutting up a large Rembrandt canvas into two-inch squares and selling them off nicely framed. So why do we so often positively delight and celebrate the dividing up of the Jesus community into contentious and competitive groups? And why does Paul's rhetorical question, "Has Christ been divided?" (1 Cor. 1:13), continue to be ignored century after century after century? . . .

The impulse to sectarianism has its roots in "selfism," the conceit that I don't need others as they are but only for what they can do for me. Selfism reduces life to my appetites and needs and preferences. Selfism results in expulsion from the Garden. But once out there "on our own," east of Eden, we find that we can't quite make it without a little help, so we join forces with a few others out of necessity, meanwhile fiercely insisting on our independence and excluding all who don't suit our preferences. We become a sect. Sects are composed of men and women who reinforce their basic selfism by banding together with others who are pursuing similar brands of selfism, like the same foods, believing in the same idols, playing the same games, despising the same outsiders. Early on, selfism developed into sectarianism in order to build a tower to heaven without having to bother with the God of heaven. The attempt disintegrated into a snake pit of sects, each incomprehensible to the other. Babel is the mother city of sectarianism. With the call of Abraham, the long, slow, complex, and still continuing movement to pull all these selves into a people-of-God community began. The birthing of the Jesus community on the Day of Pentecost was an implicit but emphatic repudiation and then reversal of Babel sectarianism. . . .

The usual way in which we avoid the appearance of crass individualism is through sectarianism. A sect is a front for narcissism. We gather with other people in the name of Jesus, but we predefine them according to our own tastes and predispositions. This is just a cover for our individualism: we reduce the community to conditions congenial to the imperial self. The sectarian impulse is strong in all branches of the church because it provides such a convenient appearance of community without the difficulties of loving people we don't approve of, or letting Jesus pray us into relationship with the very men and women we've invested a good bit of time avoiding. A sect is accomplished by community reduction, getting rid of what does not please us, getting rid of what offends us, whether ideas or people. We construct religious clubs instead of entering resurrection communities. Sects are termites in the Father's house.

The attempt to reduce the community of the resurrection to a sect is a perpetual threat. This is not what God had in mind when he poured out his Spirit on the praying followers of Jesus that memorable day in Jerusalem. ◆

Elton Trueblood

NY CAREFUL READER of the Gospels is bound to
be struck by the obvious effort of Christ to make his
hearers understand the nature of his cause. The
effort was marked by the tireless use of a great many figures.
He told his little company that they were the salt of the earth,
that they were the light of the world, that he had turned over
the keys of the kingdom; he compared his own work to that
of bread and of water; he said the kingdom was like leaven; he
said he had come to cast fire on the earth. At first the variety of
these figures is bewildering, but a powerful insight comes when
we realize, suddenly, what they have in common. Each figure
represents some kind of penetration. The purpose of the salt is
to penetrate the meat and thus preserve it; the function of light
is to penetrate the darkness; the only use of the keys is to penetrate the lock; bread is worthless until it penetrates the body;
water penetrates the hard crust of earth; leaven penetrates the
dough to make it rise; fire continues only as it reaches new fuel,
and the best way to extinguish it is to contain it.

The cumulative effect of all of these figures is almost
overwhelming. In any case, they make absolutely clear what
the function of Christ's company is meant to be. The church is
never true to itself when it is living for itself, for if it is chiefly
concerned with saving its own life, it will lose it. The nature of
the church is such that it must always be engaged in finding
new ways by which to transcend itself. Its main responsibility

is always outside its own walls in the redemption of common life. That is why we call it a redemptive society. There are many kinds of religion, but redemptive religion, from the Christian point of view, is always that in which we are spent on those areas of existence that are located beyond ourselves and our own borders. ◆

Good Fences

• • • • •

Elizabeth Dede

WHEN I WAS IN HIGH SCHOOL, one of my English teacher required us to memorize one thousand lines of poetry. Being a somewhat lazy scholar, I decided to commit several of Robert Frost's poems to memory, because most of them had a regular rhyme scheme and meter. If I got the pattern down, I found it easy to fit the words in and to remember the whole poem. Consequently, I can recite one thousand lines of Robert Frost. At the time it was a chore, but I have since grown to love the poems. I suppose my favorite is "Mending Wall," which, incidentally, was more difficult to learn because it didn't fit the pattern of the other poems.

In high school I knew little about walls and fences and barriers, although they were there; I can look back and see how they surrounded me. Since those days, I've had some experience of walls, and there is an essential truth in Frost's beautiful opening line, "Something there is that doesn't love a wall."

We've seen it at Dayspring Farm, where an old stone wall, much like the one Frost wrote about, began to tumble. Now it's been wonderfully rebuilt by our good friend Bill Shane from New Hope House, but the heavy rains rush down the hill against it, and already I can see the need for spring mending time. Something wants that wall to fall into a pile of rocks.

It's not that walls are necessarily a bad thing. I rather like having the walls of my room. Living with thirty other people would be impossible for me if I couldn't escape to the solitude of my own space, defined by its four walls.

Something, though, doesn't love that kind of wall either. At the Open Door community, we are always in the process of plastering holes and cracks where a long, hard life has begun to wear those walls away. On a trip to South Florida to help my sister rebuild from hurricane damage, I was astounded to see many of the walls from my childhood blown down. I didn't recognize the house I grew up in; many of my friends were left homeless; and the old neighborhood was a pile of rubble, with houses and walls collapsed. We loved those walls that defined our homes, churches, schools, stores, and workplaces, but something there is that doesn't love a wall.

In the poem, the speaker tells of going out in the springtime to meet his neighbor and to rebuild the wall that separates their property. The heaving of the ground from heavy freezes has caused even boulders to spill. So with the wall between them, they walk down the line and put the stones back together. The neighbor has a favorite saying which he learned from his father (and probably his father learned it from his father, and so on): "Good fences make good neighbors." He likes it so much that he says it a couple of times.

For the seven years that I've lived at the Open Door, we've had an ongoing struggle to be good neighbors. During my first summer here, the neighbors in back of us began to complain of the noise and smell and sight of so many homeless people in the backyard. We agreed to put up a high wood fence to separate us. It is a beautiful fence and well constructed. And it works. The people who live in back don't see us, smell us, or hear us anymore. Good fences make good neighbors, I suppose, although I'm not sure you can call a person with whom you have no contact your neighbor.

In the poem, the speaker says of his neighbor that he won't go behind his father's saying. He doesn't seem interested in the history: Did a cow several generations ago get into their neighbor's garden? Was there a feud over property lines? When the history and meaning is forgotten, the fence really becomes nothing but a dividing wall between the two neighbors. You almost get the sense that the only time they have anything to do with each other is at spring mending time, when they rebuild the wall that divides them.

While the fence at the Open Door is a good one, it does keep us from being neighbors. They don't know what happens in our lives, and we don't know what happens in theirs. I doubt they know that on the morning of Sunday, November 15, 1992, a man died in their neighbor's yard. And I don't know what happened to them that day. Was a child born in their family? Did an old grandfather die in his bed?

On that fence, that dividing wall, there is now a memorial plaque to Robert Vernon Ford, who died on that Sunday morning in our backyard. That dividing wall is an appropriate place for a memorial to Bobby, because we must remember that the barriers that divide human beings from each other – by race, class, sex, age, and so on – cause death.

Bobby Ford was fifty-four years old when he died, and he left behind a large number of friends. I don't know much about Bobby Ford; there were barriers between us. He lived outside; I live inside. He was an older black man; I'm a younger white woman. I come from the privileged race and class – the oppressor; he was oppressed. I do know of his joyful, friendly presence that always reached across those barriers with a laugh, a grin, and a greeting. "Hello, Elizabeth!" he'd call from the benches in the backyard. "How're you doing today?" Sometimes I wished he'd be quiet, but Bobby was always present with a friendly word.

I cannot imagine what his life was like. Fifty-four is a dignified age, when a person should be able to look forward to slowing down for retirement. Instead Bobby was trapped in the rush of our filthy, rotten system. Two days before he died, he told me of another part-time job he'd found: some nowhere job, paying minimum wage. How could Bobby hope to get off the streets? About the only comfort a part-time, minimum-wage job offers is enough money to buy a bottle of vodka to drink away the miseries with your friends. It was cold and rainy in November. How can a fifty-four-year-old man keep any shred of dignity, much less a good and cheerful humor, when he has no home to go to day and night after day and night, stretching into years? No wonder his heart broke on November 15.

So with Bobby's friends and family we gathered at the fence on the evening of November 22 to remember him and to hang the plaque. After we sang, told stories, prayed, and read God's

Word, we moved close to the fence to watch as the plaque with Bobby's name and his birth and death dates was hung behind the bench where he spent many days and nights, and where he finally died.

Now spring mending time is here, but in a different way from Robert Frost's poem. Because of the resurrection, we can go behind the old saying; we don't have to rebuild the walls that separate us. The reconciliation, however, isn't easy or cheap. After all, breaking down the dividing walls cost Jesus his life. And while we were distracted by the barriers, Bobby Ford lost his life, too.

We have a price to pay to keep the walls down. The cow might accidentally come into the garden, so we'll have to walk her back to the neighbors and replant the lettuce. There might be confusion over who owns what part of the property. From time to time we might have to smell a bad odor. We will have to become invested in each other's lives. I'll know what happened to you on November 15, and you'll know what happened to me. And we will weep and gnash our teeth in frustration when Bobby Ford's friends go off and get drunk again. But we will love her and forgive him and help them to stay sober, because the walls that divided us are just a pile of rocks now. ♦

Charles E. Moore

MAINTAINING THE INTERNAL integrity of a community takes commitment and effort by its members. But a community centered in Christ will not just exist for itself. It will naturally want to share the life it experiences with others. It will reach out to people buffeted by waves of isolation and rejection who are longing for something new. In short, it will be an open community. But reaching out to others and including others in the life of the community both take time and discernment.

Every community has its limitations. A healthy community understands that it cannot save the world; not all who coming knocking on the front door can automatically be invited to stay. Out of love for them and for the community, it may sometimes be necessary to say no. That does not mean coldness of heart. One can say no while also offering help and taking time to listen.

Although welcoming the stranger is a virtue and a mission God has called us to, it should not become an ideal we blindly and legalistically follow. Not everything Jesus uttered was within earshot of the crowds; sometimes he spoke only to his closest followers. It takes prayerful discernment to determine how much to include others in the life of the community. It's often better to hold a person off from the start because of the community's limitations than to welcome him only to then ask him to leave. A thoughtless open-door policy will eventually tax the community beyond measure.

When a community welcomes people, especially those with deep needs, it's important that they have a basic understanding of what the community is about and what is expected of them. To function well, a community will have patterns, rhythms, practices, and rules that facilitate harmony and a spirit of working together. Newcomers need to understand this, even if they don't plan to stay for long, and even if they are offered more flexibility.

Our community house in Albany, New York, was only a couple of years old. After much prayer and discernment, the fifteen of us invited a pregnant woman we knew off the streets to live with us. We would support her as she carried her baby to term and learned to care for her newborn. She, in turn, would help out in the community and share our meals. But after the baby was born, it became clear she no longer wanted to stay. Although she still needed help, she started refusing our counsel and became more recluse. We, in turn, became increasingly irritated, missing the joy of sharing our community life with her. In the end, she found a distant relative to live with.

Community life and offering that life to others is a balancing act. To do this well, a community must maintain a strong center where members are truly cared for and nurtured, a committed core into which one can then gradually invite others. A living community full of love will indeed have its door open. But that door is open for a purpose: there is something real and alive within to offer others. ◆

Next Door

• • • • •

Charles E. Moore

AGREAT DEAL HAS BEEN WRITTEN about how the church must be "missional." For many Christians, the days when we tried to attract people to come to church are over. Jesus' incarnation shows us that we are to meet people where they are at: in the workplace, dance studio, pub, gym, or other such meeting place. Do justice, show mercy, take part in the warp and woof of the world, season the world with salt by penetrating and transforming it. Move into the neighborhood, perhaps with a few other like-minded Christians, and see where God is already at work. Contextualize and incarnate the gospel right where people are, not where you wish them to be. Let the rhythms and lifestyle patterns of your neighbors shape your communal life and worship. Be present.

This vision is laudable, and it touches upon something that is very important. It is certainly a needed corrective to the imperialist mode of traditional missionizing. Nevertheless, it is never enough, and on its own is bound to be short-lived.

The gospel is not just about being present in the world but about being the good news, demonstrating in concrete ways that in Christ a different kind of existence is possible. When the Spirit gives birth to communities in which people can see God's kingdom of justice, peace, and joy at work, they will be drawn into it.

Those who emphasize missional Christianity readily recognize the need for some kind of community. Without it, one's witness can fast dissipate into oblivion. Recognizing this danger, many believers are now banding together around a cause such as urban renewal, creation care, or prison reform. However, without the proper foundation, such causes can easily undermine a community.

To be sure, there is also the danger that tightly knit communities turn in on themselves and lose sight of the greatness of God's kingdom, becoming self-satisfied and self-absorbed, small-minded and hardhearted to the plight of others. But the answer is not to get consumed with some grand project, however noble it may be. Only if we first learn how to be Christ's body together can we have anything distinctive to show and give as a community.

Jean Paul Sartre once quipped: "Humanity I love; it's my neighbor I can't stand." It's easy to love an abstraction, to pursue an ideal, to start a worthy project. But when it comes to loving the person right next to us (or right next door), when it comes to the hard work of building up Christ's body "until we all reach unity in faith," being "joined and held together by every supporting ligament" in love (Eph. 4:11–16), that is a different matter.

In his book *Who Cares?*, David Schwartz describes an incident where a woman was about to jump off a bridge over the Susquehanna River. Behind her, busy traffic sped home. One man, however, saw what was happening from his nearby office window. Shaking himself into action, he grabbed the telephone and started to dial 911. Could the police or ambulance or crisis intervention team possibly make it there in time?

While dialing he saw a city bus crossing the bridge. The bus drove slowly along the right lane. As the bus neared the woman, the door opened. The driver, in one continuous motion, stopped, leaned out of the open door, grabbed the woman's arm from behind, and pulled her backward into the bus.

The man in the office was left wondering: "That bus driver didn't flag down a police officer. He hadn't dialed 911. He simply grabbed the woman and saved her. But I dialed 911 instead. Why? Why didn't I just dash across the street and do the same?"

In a complex and often impersonal world, we have come to rely on systems and institutions to perform simple deeds which used to happen spontaneously, informally, and personally. We have lost the art of personally caring for each other. Long ago I came across an article entitled, "Mankind is not my neighbor." The title was enough to make me throw it aside. But as I read and pondered its central point, I had to concur: God's love is very specific, very small. The Good Samaritan was good because he got his own hands dirty.

The particularity of God's love is vividly described in Jesus' parable of the sheep and the goats (Matt. 25:31–46). This parable is often quoted, especially by those committed to works of mercy and hospitality: whenever you feed the hungry, give water to the thirsty, welcome the stranger, clothe the naked, and visit the sick or those in prison, Jesus says, you've done it to him. These are surely some of the most challenging words Jesus uttered. But are they fully understood? What often gets left out in quoting this parable is Jesus' reference to "the least of these brothers of mine." This is not just a poetic turn of phrase. Most of us presume that Jesus simply saw all the hungry and thirsty as his brothers and sisters. But is that all he meant? Elsewhere in Matthew we read, "And if anyone gives a cup of cold water to one of these little ones because he is my disciple, I tell you the truth, he will certainly not lose his reward" (10:42).

God's universal love and his great mercy for the world are ultimately known and revealed in the particularity of human beings loving each other as brothers and sisters. This is why Jesus gave us his body – both on the cross and in the church. The church is not an abstraction or an institution or a service provider. It is far more holy than that. Its works of mercy flow out of a daily life that bears witness to mercy.

Surely God loves the poor, but his love is most vividly and radically demonstrated when his own followers, his brothers and sisters, band together and actually serve one another. When we avoid or bypass one another, the "least of these brothers of mine," in the name of serving the oppressed, when we have no "family of faith" to which we belong and where daily, practical deeds of love are expressed, we are at risk of failing to minister to the needs of Christ himself. Of course we should love the disadvantaged and advocate for justice and bring healing to blighted neighborhoods "over there," but let's not forget what it means to give one another a drink of water here and now.

Taking care of "the least of these" means that together, as Christ's body, we ensure that in the community each person's basic needs are met and that no one is left alone to fend for herself. In this way, at least among us, rich and poor cease to exist. The "worries" of daily life – getting food on the table, paying the bills, getting the shopping and laundry and cleaning done, caring for children, being needed and listened to – are carried together. If we cannot do this among ourselves, then what do we have to bring to the broken world?

Dorothy Day observed that programs, institutions, master plans, models, policies, and the like "betray the demand of loving one's neighbor. In fact, we prefer mechanisms of justice precisely so as to not have to engage in the ongoing struggle to love." True community – where relationships that are bound together in Christ and for Christ and humble deeds are an everyday reality – prepares us and propels us to do these same kinds of deeds for whomever we meet, wherever we find ourselves. This is our mission: to demonstrate how steady, simple, faithful relationships based on mutual service are the most powerful, healing force there is in the world. This is the gift we bring to the world. And it is this gift the world so desperately needs. ◆

48

Interruptions

• • • • •

Emmanuel Katongole and Chris Rice

A T T H E C O N C L U S I O N of a week of meetings at
the Lausanne Forum on World Evangelization in
Pattaya, Thailand, in 2004, each of the thirty or so
issue groups had an opportunity to give a five-minute report to
the general assembly of their recommendations for the future
of Christian mission. Our issue group on reconciliation was
number twenty-two in a series of presentations. The night
before, someone in our group had an idea: instead of a five-
minute report, we would do a foot washing to communicate
what our group was all about. So when the time for our report
came, we set up on the convention floor twelve people with
basins and towels. Then as two people narrated what happened
in our group during the week, the twelve people washed each
other's feet: a Catholic priest, an Orthodox priest, and an
Evangelical pastor; an Israeli and a Palestinian; a black, a white,
and an Asian American; Hutu and Tutsi; male and female.

At the end of the presentation, the polite silence of the convention hall was interrupted by a standing ovation. But then it was time for another group to present its five-minute report to the assembly. The show had to go on. Looking back, however, we think that interruption of one report after another offered us a glimpse of what the church is called to be: a community on its knees, washing feet across divides.

Of course, we have to acknowledge that the actual reality we live in is much different. We live in a world of war, conflict, and genocide inspired by racial, tribal, and religious identities. More often than not, the church self-segregates neatly along these dividing lines. Even within the same denomination or congregation, various divisions often fuel battles and animosities. This is the church we know. Without a glimpse of something new like we saw at Pattaya, we might assume that the divisions of race, tribe, and nation are not only inevitable but even normal.

Unless the church is able to be the space where people who share different cultures and histories can receive their common gift and invitation to the same journey, then the church herself becomes just one more actor in the history of division and conflict. Instead of healing the tensions and brokenness of the world, the church can become an epicenter that radiates and intensifies these divisions.

More than a space carved out for dialogue, the church is called to be a people who share a story and a journey. When we met in Pattaya with representatives of people groups from around the world, the first few days were filled with many awkward moments and silences. There did not seem to be a lot that Hutu and Tutsi, Palestinian and Israeli, Americans and Albanians, Evangelical and Orthodox had in common. But as we prayed with and for one another, sang and worshiped together, read and reflected on scripture, listened to each other's stories of pain and hope, a sense of communion – of being fellow travelers – began to emerge. . . .

The scene of a divided church on its knees, washing one another's feet, pointed to a communion beyond race, tribe, nation, and denomination. The primary task of the church in reconciliation is not to mediate but to point beyond the conflict. New creation directs us beyond radical divisions to an alternative way of living together.

This is the very nature and essence of the church: to exist as the sign of a reality beyond itself. It is not that the church is the new reality. The church's mission is to gesture to this reality beyond us. The promise of a new life is what gives the church its uniqueness as well as its challenge – namely, to be an imperfect yet compelling demonstration plot of the new creation we announce.

The church's freshness always breaks through in the form of an interruption. What made the foot washing at Pattaya such a powerful sign was the fact that it was an interruption to the smooth, methodical, predictable, and well-organized program of the convention. The foot washing did not really fit in with the five-minute report each group was expected to give. It disrupted this flow. But as a result, people felt a fresh wind of the Spirit.

We worry that some might find in our description a beautiful but very quaint view of the church as a community, satisfied with bearing witness to her story but not in conversation with other players or actors. This is not what we are advocating. . . .

We proclaim a future that is not seen. This is why our interruptions are not limited to a time of conflict but are just as needed during the so-called peaceful times. For the church to be capable of interruption, we must exist as a community that is willing to adjust itself to the constant interruption of the stranger. The church is not only an interrupting community: we are ourselves always interrupted . . .

There is a story told by all the evangelists (with varying details), which we need to retell in order to capture its full breadth:

> Now one of the Pharisees was requesting [Jesus] to dine with him, and he entered the Pharisee's house and reclined at the table. And there was a woman in the city who was a sinner; and when she learned that he was reclining at the table in the Pharisee's house, she brought an alabaster vial of perfume, and standing behind him at his feet, weeping, she began to wet his feet with her tears, and kept wiping them with the hair of her head, and kissing his feet and anointing them with the perfume. Now when the Pharisee who had invited him saw this, he said to himself, "If this man were a prophet he would know who and what sort of person this woman is who is touching him, that she is a sinner." (Luke 7:36–39)

This story speaks right to the nature and mission of the church. It confirms that the church is an interrupted gathering of a beloved community. The dinner party is interrupted by the unwelcome presence of a stranger. In fact, it is through this interruption that the beloved community is called to see more clearly that we are not a lifestyle enclave. The community of Jesus is not a spiritual gated community or a ghetto of moral righteousness. Instead the stranger constantly interrupts our life. Hospitality, openness, and an ongoing engagement with the stranger are hallmarks of our life together.

Through this interruption our community is able to recover the extravagant love and service that our existence is about. It helps us remember that our life together is always about the very concrete and mundane realities of service – acts as concrete as the tears, jar, oil, hair, and feet of this interrupting woman's prophetic witness. We may get excited about committee meetings and programs to end homelessness in our city, but the alternative to homelessness we are called to embody requires the daily work of homemaking. In cooking dinner and making beds with love, men and women alike live the gospel that this woman proclaims with her actions.

We also learn from this story that there is something urgent about the church's ministry that we too often forget. We need the interruption and gift of the stranger to be drawn back into this urgency. Whereas Luke's version of the story does not specify the time when this event takes place, all the other evangelists are careful to note that it was right before the Passover. Seen from this angle, it becomes obvious that the action of the woman at Simon's house is an anticipation of the wider story of the Passion. This interruption happens in the midst of a violent story about the battering of Jesus' body.

In the history of the church, St. Francis's ability to read the signs of his time stands out as an example of the way attention to the wider story enables us to interrupt the powers that be. Looking back at history, we can see that Francis's movement of friars who begged on behalf of the poor coincided with the rise of a money economy and the new merchant class in Europe. Francis interrupted the new economy with a reminder of God's providence. He was able to do this, however, only because he struggled honestly with the question of how to live the gospel faithfully as the son of a cloth merchant. Attending to the question of discipleship in the concrete reality of his own context, Francis started a movement that would transform Christendom.

The anointing at Bethany reminds the beloved community of the wider story in which we always find ourselves. In relation to the story of the Passion, the anointing at Bethany points us to the gifts of forgiveness, hospitality, service, and extravagant care. Only by being a community open to interruption is the church capable of bearing these gifts and thus offering a freshness that goes beyond skills and techniques to a whole way of life, grounded in a story and vision of a beyond. ◆

Hospitality

• • • • •

Christine D. Pohl

A NUMBER OF YEARS AGO I was part of a church that decided to make hospitality central to its identity and life. We welcomed hundreds of refugees and many local poor and homeless people into our lives and worship. We shared homes, church, finances, meals, and energy. We attempted to respond to every person's need. It was an incredibly fruitful and blessed time. Within only a few years, however, the church itself had collapsed under the weight of ministry, the leaders worn out from unrelenting numbers of needy strangers, the parishioners wary of any further commitments.

We were unwilling to close the door, to tell anyone there was no room. Deeply troubled by the inhospitality of many Christians during the Holocaust, we were determined to welcome the refugees and strangers of our own day. Under the pressure of needs all around us, we were not careful to nourish our own lives, or to put guidelines in place that made sure workers had adequate rest and renewal. Eventually, we were only able to move from crisis to crisis, and gradually the quality of hospitality weakened. . . .

Communities struggle with boundaries and they struggle without them. All households and communities have some boundaries, although some are more explicit about them than others. Some communities, as a matter of principle, work with minimal boundaries while others establish a significant number of guidelines for both hosts and guests. Boundaries can be literal doors and walls, but they can also be rules, policies, or mission statements. They are shaped in relation to space, resources, relationships, roles, commitments, and identity.

A closed door is the most tangible kind of boundary, but boundary issues are worked out at various levels. Some communities by their rural or isolated location deal with boundaries before people get to the door; strangers must somehow know about the place and make a significant effort to find it. Other communities welcome strangers only through referrals; in that way they make advance choices about which strangers, how many, and when they will receive them. Some communities live in the midst of need and must make decisions every time a person comes to the door.

Boundaries are troublesome in the context of hospitality for a number of reasons. By definition, hospitality is gracious and generous. Limiting hospitality seems to undermine what is fundamental to the practice. But boundaries are also a problem because so many of them are hidden. While we are likely to notice the most obvious ones – for example, turning someone away or saying there is no room – we are unlikely to notice how even our own occupations, neighborhoods, and churches can, in themselves, create boundaries that shut out most strangers, especially needy ones.

Because Christian hospitality reflects divine hospitality, when it fails it is especially devastating. Claims to have run out of resources or to have "no more room" are particularly problematic when we reflect on the abundance of God's household. There is a certain moral horror associated with turning persons away; when refugees are excluded and left in danger, or when homeless persons are left outside on freezing nights, it is rarely morally sufficient to say that there was not enough room.

The wideness of God's mercy and the generosity of God's welcome must frame our thinking about limits and boundaries. God's kindness continually challenges us to reconsider our commitments. Jesus and the stranger stand outside, asking our communities to enlarge their borders and to share their resources. As we welcome the poor, the stranger, or the marginal person, they help us to remember that each of us is an alien and a stranger, welcomed only by God's generous invitation. The practice of hospitality challenges the boundaries of a community while it simultaneously depends on that community's identity to make a space that nourishes life.

Sometimes welcome must be limited and distinctions made, however, if only for the sake of other guests or members already within the community. The amount of space available and the physical and emotional capacity of the hosts and guests impose certain limits. . . .

At three o'clock one morning I woke to the sound of pouring rain. I was staying in the guest room of one of the communities of hospitality. Just outside my window I could hear a chorus of coughing. Because the city had become exceedingly harsh in how it dealt with homeless people, about thirty men and women found refuge in the yard of this community every night. They must have been cold and getting wetter by the minute. An overwhelming combination of sadness and horror engulfed me – I looked around at my large and sparsely furnished room and realized that the only thing between thirty cold, wet people and a dry room was a locked front door. . . .

These people – outside the door, coughing and wet – these people had names and faces. They were known to the people inside the house. They came into the house for meals during the day. How could we leave them outside when there were still corners of open space inside? Of course I have lots of space in my own home, but I had never before felt so awkward about keeping it for myself. At home, during an ordinary day, I do not encounter any homeless people, and no one ever camps in my backyard because they have no other shelter.

The next day I spoke with one of the women who had lived and worked in the community for eleven years. I asked her how she survived, knowing that the house could not take in everyone, knowing that although they provided a home for many people, some people were always left outside. How did she make peace with it and keep going? She responded that you never make peace with it, but you do what you can.

In offering hospitality, practitioners live between the vision of God's kingdom in which there is enough, even abundance, and the hard realities of human life in which doors are closed and locked, and some needy people are turned away or left outside. A door – open or closed – is one of the most powerful images of hospitality. Responses of "Yes, of course we have room – please, come in" and "No, there's no room tonight" may be daily fare for hosts and guests, but these phrases also distill difficult questions about boundaries, scarce resources, and a place within community.

We rarely see the consequences of lifestyles that have little room for strangers. Most of the time we do not live close enough to the needs of strangers, much less to our limits, to have no choice but to close the door on a particular person. We do not encounter the same soaked person the next morning, or know that the one who is coughing at breakfast slept in the rain the past night. And although we might feel some dismay at leaving someone outside or hungry, our lives are sufficiently insulated that we do not feel such pain very often.

If we are genuinely concerned about the needs of strangers, offering hospitality requires courage. It involves not only a willingness to take some risks in welcoming others, but it also requires the kind of courage that lives close to our limits, continually pressing against the possible, yet always aware of the incompleteness and the inadequacy of our own responses. At the same time, living so close to the edge of sufficient resources increases our dependence on, and our awareness of, God's interventions and provision.

Can we say yes to everyone who comes to us? If we limit our hospitality do we risk turning Jesus away? If we say yes to everyone, how will we keep what we offer from becoming diluted, more and more inadequate and impersonal? If we welcome a very troubled person, how will the people we have already welcomed into our lives be affected? Do we have a special responsibility to them? Do we have to be careful about our own needs – will our strength be sufficient for the tasks, no matter how much we take on? If we burn out in six months, what then?

Edith Schaeffer of L'Abri Fellowship captures some of the tension with which many of us live when she writes that "because there are more people than we have time or strength to see personally and care for, it is imperative to remember that it is not sinful to be finite and limited." When hospitality is not practiced widely in the larger society, or when resources are not distributed fairly or adequately, personal hospitality cannot respond to every need. It can, however, meet some needs; it can be a living demonstration of what is possible when people care. ◆

Kathleen Norris

IN MY EXPERIENCE visiting monasteries, it is extremely rare for a guest, even one who commits gaffes in choir or elsewhere, to be made to feel unwelcome, let alone like someone who is contaminating the monastic purity of the place. I do sometimes run across spit-and-polish novices, still clinging to romantic notions of the life, who are desperately keen on determining exactly what is monastic and what is not. They are often ill at ease with guests, as if worried by the distractions we bring with us, the worldliness that hovers over us like a cloud. I have come to see this slight resistance to the guest as a healthy thing, a necessary part of a Benedictine's formation in hospitality. Benedict knew that this tension would be there; I believe this is why he so emphatically states in his Rule that "all guests who present themselves are to be welcomed as Christ." This leaves the novice little room for maneuvering around the practice of hospitality. And no chance at all to simply ignore the guests who come.

Like most serious and rewarding human endeavors, Benedictine hospitality is a process, and it takes time for people to figure out how best to incarnate it. As with so many other aspects of monastic formation, it is the elderly who provide the models. Not long ago I heard a novice speak of a nun with Alzheimer's in her community, who every day insists on being placed in her wheelchair at the entrance to the monastery's nursing home wing so that she can greet everyone who comes. "She is no longer certain what she is welcoming people to," the younger woman explained, "but hospitality is so deeply ingrained in her that it has become her whole life." Better an old fool welcoming people at the door with her whole heart and soul, Benedict might agree, than a distracted, cold, or officious monk or nun with faculties intact.

A story about hospitality that I treasure comes from a writing workshop that I used to teach every summer at a monastery. Each year as I read the evaluations I found that no matter what they thought of me as a teacher, the students deeply appreciated the hospitable atmosphere. More than once the comment sheets were crammed with praise for the monks, with nary a mention of my classroom work.

I found that I always had to answer general questions on the first night: Why are some called brothers – aren't they all priests? Will they allow anyone to attend their worship? Why do they go to church so often? One year on the second day of class a shy, soft-spoken student told the group that she had gone to the abbey visitor center to ask some more questions. But the monk had been short with her, saying, finally, "I don't have time for this; we're trying to run a monastery here!" She felt bad and wondered if she should go apologize for having bothered him. I responded by saying that what she had experienced was an aberration, and she might simply let it ride for the time being. As I expected, the monk, a man recently professed, soon tracked her down and apologized profusely. All in all, it was a useful exchange. The guest discovered that monks are human; and the monk came to his senses regarding Benedict's Rule on the reception of guests.

Leave us alone, willya? We're trying to run a monastery! Surely that sentiment is an ever-present temptation to Benedictine men and women. In my experience, however, it rarely surfaces. Benedictines often tell me they receive so much from their guests that they could never repay it, and many guests feel the same way about the hospitality they receive. Benedict knew that hospitality could be life-saving for both monk and guest. I believe that he wanted Benedictine women and men to be so deeply grounded in hospitality that it would color everything they do and say.

And in his Rule he indicated an acute awareness of the dangers of implosion in the monastic life if it sought insularity against "the world." He instructs Benedictines not to turn their backs on the world, even as they seek to detach themselves from worldly values. This seems to me the core of Benedictine hospitality. To reject the world is to reject other people. And to reject other people is to reject Christ himself. ◆

50

Connections

· · · · ·

David Janzen

C HRISTIAN INTENTIONAL communities have
been seized by a gospel vision so radical that they
are countercultural within mainstream Christianity
itself. They do not accept the authority of those who counsel
assimilation back into the mainstream. But we should also be
wary of any group so full of the truth that they need no one
else. Communities that go it alone are likely to fail, while those
that band together greatly increase their chances of sustaining
growth or reaching maturity.

The early Christian movement was highly networked among
its newly sprouted communities around the Mediterranean
Sea. To get a taste of this vital collaboration of friends and
coworkers, read the last chapter of Paul's Letter to the Church
in Rome. Here we get a quick tour of families, house churches,
and mission partners. Paul greets no less than twenty-nine

friends, relatives, coworkers, and acquaintances. These greetings, moreover, are extended by eight of Paul's companions in
the gospel, including the scribe taking dictation, who sneaks
into the Bible by adding, "I, Tertius, who wrote down this
letter, greet you in the Lord." I am amazed that Paul knows so
many "sisters and brothers" in a city he has not yet visited.

The reasons for Christian communities to connect with each
other are many and similar to the reasons why individuals join
local communities – for fellowship and support in their calling,
to grow in discipleship of Jesus by drinking from a larger pool
of wisdom and good judgment, for mentoring and leadership
development, for emergency care in times of crisis, and because
it is energizing to make friends with others of like mind.

When our Kansas community, New Creation Fellowship,
was just finding its way, we welcomed visits from members
of Reba Place. We found immense encouragement in these
connections and would visit Reba Place in return. Many of the
issues that we faced in community they had already struggled
with – whether it was renovating bedrooms to fit in more
people, discerning spiritual gifts, or mourning departures.
These community visits made us wiser and gave us confidence
in ways that would never have happened by ourselves. Our
leaders began regular phone consultations with their mentors
in other communities. In this way, we avoided some major
blunders. This way of coming alongside imparted wisdom and
confidence without hierarchical or formal structures. Looking
back, I would conclude that all the how-to books about
community are not worth as much as good mentor relationships and a pattern of visits that build friendships between
communities.

To enter into a partnership with other communities signals
that a community is taking seriously its identity and future,

that living together is not just a phase but a divine calling and way of life for the long haul.

Forging connections with other communities takes time and creativity. Communities can come together for a variety of reasons: visits and tours hosted by communities in turn, retreats on themes of common interest, learning from out-of-town guests with more community experience, celebrating important events such as weddings and baptisms, working on projects together, having roundtable conversations, or sharing skills.

As they share hospitality, pray for one another, and gather for special events, trust and deeper connections grow between communities. Christ's body is built up. Without these connections new communities and even established ones risk becoming self-absorbed.

This raises the question of how intentional communities might relate to the broader church. For those committed to intentionally sharing life with others, church is not simply a place to go to. Discipleship happens as we serve, love, correct, and forgive each other in daily interactions where we cannot hide our true selves from one another. It is actually about learning to love one another as Christ loved us.

Of course, conventional churches are places where self-giving love occurs. Christian communities attempting to put this love into daily, material practice can easily look down on the kind of Christianity expressed in the practice of "going to church" weekly, comparing the more radical life of intentional community to the wider church and taking pride in the difference. But true Christian community can never make one feel holier than anyone else. Community is a gift, not a badge of honor.

The question of the relationship between Christian community and the wider church is a complex one. There is no one right model. The model that most resembles the New Testament churches is a communal one. The social template on which these early churches grew was their experience of the Jewish synagogue, a grassroots community base for a people in exile that could be formed wherever a minimum of ten families wanted to assemble. The synagogue was at the same time a center for worship, a place of study, a hub for all kinds of gatherings including decision-making about ethical issues, and a locus of mutual aid. The synagogue was not under any outside authority but was relationally connected to other such groups by frequent visits, traveling scholars, a common scripture, and a shared salvation history performed in seasons of celebration. The early church built on this communal foundation wherever the Holy Spirit created a spiritual family of Jews and Gentiles united in following Jesus.

There is simplicity in this arrangement because the daily rhythm of community life does not need to be coordinated with another church body. It also weaves community and being the church together, demonstrating that in Christ a radically new social reality is genuinely possible. But it has its challenges, especially for new emerging communities which need to cover the essentials of being Christ's body, which includes teaching, baptisms, marriages, mission, and pastoral care in times of crisis. The synagogue minimum of ten families is realistic about the range of gifts needed for healthy church life.

Some communities and churches may find that a more dialogical relationship is most fruitful. The high commitment of sharing daily life attracts people who want to belong to the fellowship but do not yet feel called or ready to make all the changes and sacrifices involved in sharing all things in common. There are also congregations in which a more committed community core naturally emerges that is distinct from the congregation at large. In such cases, something like a missionary order within a larger congregation forms, which does not insist that all members of the church must participate fully. This allows for more natural interchange, but it also faces the challenge of figuring out where one's priority lies – with the church or with the community.

There are other communities whose members participate in different congregations. Such arrangements make an ecumenical witness but also pose a challenge to an integrated community life because experiences of church are not shared and participation in them creates tugs in different directions with schedules and commitments that do not always mesh. In this case, the interrelation of community and church risks becoming too thin on either end. On the flip side, however, the interaction between a particular community and the various local churches can help other Christians see what everyday life in Christ with others is like.

Among these different possibilities it remains an important priority to be connected with other believers. A vital community life is never found by sequestering oneself into communities that revolve around themselves. A community filled with God's Spirit will naturally seek deeper connections with the larger body of Christ. The unity and community they share among themselves, deep as it is, is but a microcosm of the greater unity which Christ prayed for: "Father, may they all be brought to complete unity to let the world know that you sent me and have loved them even as you have loved me" (John 17:23). ◆

51

Wounds

• • • • •

Catherine de Hueck Doherty

TODAY, across a confused world, people seek Christ!
They seek the reality of Christ, or, to put it another
way, they seek the real Christ, the Christ of the
Gospels, the one they have read about but cannot seem to find.

In this seeking people ask one another, "How do you find
Christ? Where is he? Where can I find him?" Who, then, is this
Christ that they seek? Why does he seem to be so illusive, so
unreal, so difficult to meet? It seems to me that the answer to
these questions is exceedingly simple: We meet Christ in a real
Christian.

What a strange and seemingly simplistic answer! Yet it is
the true answer, and I don't think there is another. People have
to be shown. The time of mere talking is over.

After his resurrection, Christ showed his disciples his
wounds and they believed. These wounds were visible signs of
Christ's love for them and for all of us. No one needed to say

anything, least of all Christ. Thomas the Doubter was the only one who spoke.

Today, it seems to me, we must likewise show the wounds of Christ to people, for then they will believe. This is what people are seeking today: someone who will show them the wounds of Christ so that they may touch him and be reassured.

But we must go further. Christ prepared breakfast on the beach for his friends. We, too, by our service, must show how much we love our brothers and sisters, all those who are seeking the Lord.

But even all this – to show the wounds, to prepare meals – is not enough. One must open one's heart with a lance by taking that lance in one's own hands. We must accept all human beings as they are, without wanting to change or to manipulate them. It is a benediction and a joy in itself that they come to us.

People will not know God unless we, their neighbors, their brothers and sisters, show Christ to them in the tremendous love that Christ has for them. This is the acceptable time, so that people may once again say what was said of the early Christians, "See how these Christians love one another – and us!"

Yes, we must open the doors of our hearts. We must open the doors of our homes. We must accept people as they are. We must serve them, and we must show them the wounds of our love. . . .

No, words are not enough. But a loving glance, a wound, a breakfast cooked for a friend, a welcome through an open door into an open heart, these will do it. It is only then, when my brother and my sister have been filled with my supper, when they have beheld my wounds of love for them, when they have experienced a totality of acceptance, that they will be open to the glad news. ◆

Ed Loring

A FRIEND TOLD ME about a friend of his in Florida who owns a very fine sailing boat that he keeps anchored at a marina. One day he discovered that a homeless man was sleeping in his boat. He initially let the event pass, but soon realized the homeless man was now living in his boat. The owner responded with gifts of food and blankets and then visited the man. Not long afterward, he gave the man a bucket and long-handled window washer and asked him to wash windows at his business in return for a room at a hotel. If you give a man a fish he gets hungry again; if you teach him how to fish he can eat forever. The act was loving and kind, generous and caring. The homeless man took his new tools, thanked the boat owner, and began work. Shortly thereafter, the boat owner checked on the man's progress, but the man had disappeared, never to be seen again.

This story illustrates vividly and with pathos the consequences of not listening to the poor and hungry in our midst. Love, the harsh and dreadful love in action, teaches us to listen rather than to speak. We need to receive a description of the hell of homelessness and the poison of prison rather than prescribe programs and desires for the lives of powerless people. We must repent from the arrogance of power and walk humbly with our God in loving servanthood.

The boat owner and I don't know why the homeless man, who stowed away each night in the bottom of a boat, disappeared. But let us use our imagination a moment. Perhaps he was afraid of heights and could not work washing windows. Maybe his eyes were dim or his teeth pained him. As is true with most homeless people, his feet perhaps were raw and his toes twisted from frostbite years before. He may have been a lazy, no-good bum who loved being hungry, sleeping in a damp boat, and having no friends. He could have been an alcoholic or drug addict who sold the bucket and blade for a few hours of relief from poverty, racism, disgust, and bodily pain. We do not know. But we do know this: he was a human being, a homeless man, created in the image of God and loved by Jesus.

When we listen to the poor we drop the ideology that what one needs is a job. Rather we reduce the distance and stand and listen, as my wife Murphy Davis says, with "ears trained by scripture," and respond with the simple and hospitable question, "How may I be helpful?" That question rooted in love and openness re-creates the poor and makes them a subject of their own lives rather than an object of our programs. "How may I be helpful?" gives respect but demands engagement. The question of love and relationship gives empowerment and demands servanthood. The question is gospel: it is good news to the poor!

The boat owner was loving and did more than most of us. But he failed to meet the homeless man in his humanity and personhood. Perhaps the man would have said, "I need a bus ticket to Chicago, where my brother lives." We do not know. We must change our agenda with the homeless poor. We must listen, for most want to work but are far from ready for employment. We have commercialized our relationships, and we see the unemployed as people for whom a job will solve their personal and social problems. But the issues are far deeper and wider than that, and it is time for us to recognize these truths as well. . . .

We need each other. "How may I be helpful?" is a question that incarnates the love of God and that will change our lives, as well as bring to an end homelessness, hunger, and prisons as we know them in this land.

There are biblical and theological reasons for listening to the poor with ears trained by the scriptures. As we learn from the cry of the poor – respecting the pain, anguish, and hell and hearing the truths of racism, sexism, and class violence as well as the faith, courage, hope, and majesty of the suffering endurance – we hear the voice of God. In the cry of the poor we hear the cry of Jesus Christ himself. We are called to conversion, to a new life in solidarity and love with those same folk who followed Jesus and sat at table and ate with him, to the disgust of the Pharisees. . . .

"How may I be helpful?" is not only the key to new life and a door to a shared struggle for peace and justice; the question is also the distinguishing mark of public discourse among prophetic people of faith. The difference between social work – programs for the poor designed by professionals for clients – and biblical servanthood for liberation and justice is love, a love that is accepting and that even welcomes suffering. Dr. Martin Luther King Jr. teaches us well and often that sacrificial love is the resource for redemption in our personal lives and social struggles for justice. The suffering that accomplishes the "listen question" to the homeless and prisoner is the suffering of solidarity. God does it every night and day for you and me! The suffering is part of the grace of "standing with." There is a suffering sacrificial love in accepting the consequence of life with, among, and on behalf of the oppressed and prisoner.

Together, hand holding hand, we confess that we will not hide in comfort zones. We will not avoid the pain and suffering. We will not allow suburbia and segregation to shape our loves and lives, nor our idea of justice. We shall reduce the distance, pick up our cross, and ask, "How may I be helpful?" ◆

Mercy

◆ ◆ ◆ ◆ ◆

Dorothy Day

THE SPIRITUAL WORKS OF MERCY are to admonish the sinner, to instruct the ignorant, to counsel the doubtful, to comfort the sorrowful, to bear wrongs patiently, to forgive all injuries, and to pray for the living and the dead.

The corporal works of mercy are to feed the hungry, to give drink to the thirsty, to clothe the naked, to ransom the captive, to harbor the harborless, to visit the sick, and to bury the dead.

When Peter Maurin talked about the necessity of practicing the works of mercy, he meant all of them. He envisioned houses of hospitality in poor parishes in every city of the country, where these precepts of our Lord could be put into effect. He pointed out that we have turned to the state through home relief, social legislation, and social security, that we no longer practice personal responsibility, but are repeating the words of the first murderer, "Am I my brother's keeper?"

The works of mercy are a wonderful stimulus to our growth in faith as well as love. Our faith is taxed to the utmost and so grows through this strain put upon it. It is pruned again and again, and springs up bearing much fruit. For anyone starting to live literally the words of the fathers of the church – "The bread you retain belongs to the hungry, the dress you lock up is the property of the naked"; "What is superfluous for one's need is to be regarded as plunder if one retains it for one's self" – there is always a trial ahead. "Our faith, more precious than gold, must be tried as though by fire."

Here is a letter we received today: "I took a gentleman seemingly in need of spiritual and temporal guidance into my home on a Sunday afternoon. I let him have a nap on my bed, went through the want ads with him, made coffee and sandwiches for him, and when he left, I found my wallet had gone also."

I can only say that the saints would only bow their heads, and not try to understand or judge. . . . These things happened for our testing. We are sowing the seed of love, and we are not living in the harvest time. We must love to the point of folly, and we are indeed fools, as our Lord himself was who died for such a one as this. We lay down our lives, too, when we have performed so painfully thankless acts, for our correspondent is poor in this world's goods. It is agony to go through such bitter experiences, because we all want to love, we desire with a great longing to love our fellow human beings, and our hearts are often crushed at such rejections. But, as a Carmelite nun said to me last week, "It is the crushed heart which is the soft heart, the tender heart."

◆ ◆ ◆ ◆ ◆

ST. FRANCIS was "the little poor man" and none was more joyful than he; yet Francis began with tears, with fear and trembling, hiding in a cave from his irate father. He had expropriated some of his father's goods (which he considered his rightful inheritance) in order to repair a church and rectory where he meant to live. It was only later that he came to love Lady Poverty. He took it little by little; it seemed to grow on him. Perhaps kissing the leper was the great step that freed him not only from fastidiousness and a fear of disease but from attachment to worldly goods as well.

Sometimes it takes but one step. We would like to think it is always so. And yet the older I get, the more I see that life is made up of many steps, and they are very small affairs, not giant strides. I have "kissed a leper," not once but twice – consciously – and I cannot say I am much the better for it.

The first time was early one morning on the steps of Precious Blood Church. A woman with cancer of the face was begging (beggars are allowed only in the slums) and when I gave her money (no sacrifice on my part but merely passing on alms which someone had given me) she tried to kiss my hand. The only thing I could do was kiss her dirty old face with the gaping hole in it where an eye and a nose had been. It sounds like a heroic deed but it was not. One gets used to ugliness so quickly. What we avert our eyes from one day is easily borne the next when we have learned a little more about love. Nurses know this, and so do mothers.

Another time I was refusing a bed to a drunken prostitute with a huge, toothless, rouged mouth, a nightmare of a mouth. She had been raising a disturbance in the [community] house. I kept remembering how Saint Therese said that when you had to refuse anyone anything, you could at least do it so that the person went away a bit happier. I had to deny her a bed but when that woman asked me to kiss her, I did, and it was a loathsome thing, the way she did it. It was scarcely a mark of normal human affection.

We suffer these things and they fade from memory. But daily, hourly, to give up our own possessions and especially to subordinate our own impulses and wishes to others – these are hard, hard things; and I don't think they ever get any easier.

◆ ◆ ◆ ◆ ◆

WE HAVE REPEATED so many times that those who have two coats should follow the early church fathers who said, "The coat that hangs in your closet belongs to the poor." And those who have a ten-room house can well share it with those who have none. How many large houses could be made into several apartments to take in others? Much hospitality could be given to relieve the grave suffering today. But people are afraid. They do not know where it will end. They have all gone far enough in generosity to know that an ordeal is ahead, that the person taken in will most likely turn into "the friend of the family." No use starting something that you cannot finish, they say. Once bitten is twice shy. We have all had our experiences of ingratitude, of nursing a viper in our bosom, as the saying goes. So we forget about the necessity of pruning, in the natural order, to attain much fruit. We don't want to pay the cost of love. We do not want to exercise our capacity to love.

There are many stories one could tell about Catholic Worker life, but it is always better to wait until years have passed so that they become more impersonal, less apt to be identified with this one or that.

There is a story, however, about a reader of the paper, and this happened long enough ago so that we can tell it. Our friend adopted a young girl and educated her, and the young girl proved to be a great joy and comfort. Now she has entered a contemplative order to spend her life in prayer and work. The same reader then took in another young woman, who brought home a fatherless baby, and when that was forgiven her, went out and brought in still another, and there was apt to be a third. Our friend wrote and begged us for advice and help as to what to do. Was she contributing to the delinquency of this girl by forgiving seventy times seven, and was she perhaps going to have seventy times seven children to take care of?

It is good to think of the prophet Hosea, whom I have mentioned before in writing on love. He was commanded by God to take a harlot to wife, and she had many children by other men. He was a dignified, respected teacher of his people, and he was shamed and humiliated by the wife of his bosom. Yet he was to go down in history as the type of the love of God for his adulterous people.

Love must be tried and tested and proved. It must be tried as though by fire. And fire burns.

We may be living in a desert when it comes to such perceptions now, and that desert may stretch out before us for years. But a thousand years are as one day in the sight of God, and soon we will know as we are known. Until then we will have glimpses of community in play, in suffering, in serving, and we will begin to train for that community. ◆

• • • • •

Discussion Guide

PART I

A Call to Community

- When the world looks upon the church today, what "style of life" does it see?

- Is there anything in this chapter that strikes you as new or provocative? What?

- What do you think about Blumhardt's statement: "Anything that is going to last must have a much deeper foundation than some kind of spiritual experience"? What is he driving at?

Related Scripture: Matthew 7:15–29; 1 Timothy 5:3–16

- What do you think about Lohfink's claim that most Christians' lives would be relatively unaffected if they stopped going to church?

- Why, do you think, does faith lead to a "more and more intensive communion"?

- Modern households are very different from New Testament–era ones. Has this affected how we understand church today?

Related Scripture: Colossians 3:1–4:1

- How are the metaphors of "body" and "family" similar? How are they different?

- Miller prefers the metaphor of family. Do you agree with him?

- Hellerman's piece highlights the central role the church played in the lives of the first Christians. What do you think about this? Should the church play such an influential role?

Related Scripture: Romans 12:1–16; 1 Corinthians 12:12–31; Mark 10:28–31; 1 Timothy 5:1–25

- ◆ Kraus understands Pentecost as part of the gospel story, the drama of redemption. Is it a culmination? A beginning? Or both?

- ◆ Why is Pentecost so important, according to Kraus? How does it relate to the topic of community?

- ◆ What new understanding of the Holy Spirit have you gained after reading Kraus's piece?

Related Scripture: Acts 2; Ephesians 3:7–13

- ◆ If "everything has been created free in common," as Stadler argues, can private property be justified?

- ◆ How might private property be a hinderance to forming community?

- ◆ What arguments are used against the "communism" of the early church in Acts 2 and 4?

- ◆ Is Luke's description of the early church meant as a norm for all Christians, or just an inspiring example?

Related Scripture: Acts 4:32–5:16; 11:27–30; 1 John 3:16–18

- ◆ In what way is the church an extension of Christ's incarnation?

- ◆ How might Bonhoeffer's understanding of the church affect the way we are the church together today?

- ◆ What do you think of Bonhoeffer's example of Philemon and Onesimus? What implications might this example have for our own social lives as Christ's followers?

Related Scripture: Matthew 28:16–20; Acts 9:1–6; Philemon

- In your opinion, are there old wineskins the church needs to discard in order to receive a new work of God's spirit?

- In what ways should the church manifest a distinct life of its own, in contrast to the broader culture?

- What potential dangers might there be in thinking of the church as countercultural?

Related Scripture: Matthew 5:13–16; 1 Peter 2:4–12; Ephesians 5:1–16

- What common threads do you see in this chapter?

- What other communities or communal movements are you aware of, either in the past or in the present?

- What strikes you most after reading this chapter?

Related Scripture: Acts 2:17–21; 38–39; John 17:20–21

PART II

Forming Community

- What concrete steps could you take in order to experience more community with others?

- What do you find most challenging in this chapter?

Related Scripture: Colossians 3:12–17; Galatians 6:1–10

- Why must human fellowship be rooted in divine fellowship?

- Living in community is one thing, experiencing deep fellowship another. What is the difference?

- What factors hinder us from sharing ourselves with one another?

Related Scripture: 1 Thessalonians 2; 2 Corinthians 6:11–13; 7:2–16

- Bonhoeffer says a community can break down if it has sprung from a "wish dream." What does he mean? Have you ever experienced or witnessed such a breakdown?

- Is all "visionary dreaming" bad? Is pursuing ideals always dangerous?

- Why is thankfulness so important when it comes to building community?

Related Scripture: 1 Corinthians 13:1–7; 1 Timothy 1

- Katz says "disillusionment is a grace from God." What does he mean by this?

- O'Connor says living in community can bring out problems you didn't even know you had. Why is that?

- When are you tempted to withdraw from others? Why?

Related Scripture: Proverbs 27:17; Galatians 6:1–10

- Arnold mentions a number of obstacles to community. What are they? Can you think of any others?

- Which of these obstacles can you relate to the most?

- Why is "the dismantling of our own power" so important when it comes to life in community?

Related Scripture: Romans 12:3–5; 14:14–15:6;
1 Corinthians 1:4–17; 3:1–22; 2 Corinthians 12:1–10

- Which of the "poisons" described in this chapter do you struggle with most?

- Can you think of other "poisons" that can kill a community?

- Does our time belong to us? Are there other things we claim that might not be ours?

Related Scripture: Philippians 2:1–18; Acts 8:9–25;
1 Corinthians 1:10–17

- Why is listening to one another so difficult? What does it mean to listen well?

- How have you experienced the gift of being listened to? How does listening foster healing?

- How might words "function more as walls than as gates"?

Related Scripture: Proverbs 17:28; 18:2, 3; 20:5; Philippians
2:19–30; James 1:19

- Gish suggests that we are not fully in community "unless all is committed and shared." What do you think about this? Is community all or nothing, or can one get there by degrees?

- Is it ever possible to totally give up self-interest?

- "Dying to self" is often misconstrued. What does it actually mean to die to oneself?

Related Scripture: Mark 10:17–31; Luke 9:23–27; 14:25–35; Hebrews 10:32–39

- There is "community," and then there is "Christian community." What's the difference?

- What does it mean to have Christ as the center of community? Why is this so important? From your experience, what happens when Christ is not at the center?

- Bonhoeffer makes a clear distinction between "human love" and "spiritual love." What's the difference? Why does it matter?

- Why is the cross, in particular, so important in community life?

Related Scripture: Matthew 16:13–20; 18:19–20; Philippians 3:7–21; 1 John 2:3–8

- Christian community may be a biblical teaching, but why is God's call, and the certainty of God's call, so important?

- If community is based on God's call, does this mean it is not for everyone?

- How does one know or discern God's calling?

- Why do you think Arnold says that when we see our particular tasks as something special we will go astray?

Related Scripture: 1 Corinthians 1:26—2:5

- Why is making lifelong promises such a foreign concept in our culture?

- What things keep you from making lifelong promises? How has the reality of infidelity in our culture affected your life?

- What might be some of the blessings of making and keeping lifelong promises, especially as it relates to sharing life with others in community?

Related Scripture: Judges 11:29–40; Ecclesiastes 5:4–7

Life in Community

- ◆ There are some very deep thoughts about love in this chapter. Which one strikes you most?

- ◆ At the end of the day, community with others matters only if love is being built up. In your experience, what keeps genuine love alive?

- ◆ In your own community or fellowship, are there ways love has grown cold? How so? What can help to reignite your love for one another?

Related Scripture: Galatians 5:6; 1 Corinthians 13; 1 Thessalonians 1:2–10; Revelation 2:1–7

- ◆ Powers says community offers people opportunities to learn how to work rightly. How can we ensure this happens?

- ◆ Arnold says working with others is the best way to test our faith. Have you experienced this?

- ◆ What does Alexander mean when he says that you should clean the toilets and not "worry much about using your other gifts"?

Related Scripture: John 13:1–17; Matthew 25:31–46

- What do you think of Alexander's view of vocation?

- For many of us, our self-worth is tied to the kind of work we do. Does this square with the call of discipleship?

- Does your current work conflict with your true vocation as a disciple of Jesus?

Related Scripture: Ephesians 4:1–6; Acts 20:32–35; 1 Thessalonians 2:7–12; 2 Thessalonians 3:6–13

- What are some things that make it difficult for people to truly accept one another?

- Are there ways in which you have not felt accepted?

- How do you tend to deal with members of the church who cause you pain?

- Does accepting others as they are mean we have to ignore those things in them that need to change?

Related Scripture: Romans 14:1—15:7

- Irritations are a fact of life, but how we deal with them can make or break a community. What advice in this chapter did you find most helpful?

- Why do irritations so easily grow out of proportion?

- Does "not judging" another person mean we are never to talk to them about a problem they may have?

Related Scripture: Ephesians 4:2–3, 25–27; Hebrews 3:13; 12:14–15; James 4:11–12; 1 Peter 4:8

- How can differences be a blessing? When might they cease to be a blessing?

- Is diversity an obstacle to finding unity in community? Or is sameness a bigger danger?

- Do you agree with Chittister that we need people who think differently?

- In a healthy, Christ-centered community, how important is diversity?

Related Scripture: Galatians 3:26–28; 1 Corinthians 12:14–26

- How do you tend to deal with conflict in your life? How does your church community deal with it?

- What advice in this chapter do you find most helpful?

- In what ways can conflict actually be an opportunity?

- What happens when conflict is not dealt with well?

Related Scripture: Matthew 18:15–20; Galatians 2:11–14

- What does the word "unity" mean to you? How is it different from uniformity?

- Jesus could have prayed for many things, but at the end of his life he prayed for unity among his disciples (John 17:20–23). Why, do you think, was unity so important to him?

- How can we become united "heart and soul" with one another? What does it take? What things undermine unity?

Related Scripture: Matthew 6:23–26; Philippians 2:1–12

- O'Connor claims that "true dialogue is difficult for everyone." What does "true dialogue" entail? Why is it so difficult?

- In your church community, is dialogue encouraged or discouraged?

- Why do we fear disagreement? How might disagreement be a good thing?

- In the end, what is the point of dialogue? What goal are we trying to achieve?

Related Scripture: Acts 15

- Many people today are uncomfortable with leadership. Why is that?

- What happens when a community lacks leadership?

- Leadership is one of the gifts Christ gave to the church. What does this gift involve?

- From reading this chapter, what have you learned about authority?

Related Scripture: Matthew 23:8–12; Luke 22:24–30; 1 Timothy 3; 1 Peter 5:1–7

- Why does the word "submission" have such negative connotations today? What does this tell us about our culture or the way the world operates?

- What does true submission entail? Can you think of biblical examples?

- How does the discipline of submission actually free or empower us?

- Is community possible without submission?

Related Scripture: Ephesians 5:21; Hebrews 13:7–21

- This chapter contains two honest reflections about money and possessions. Is there anything in particular you can relate to?
- Life in community means sharing, and at some level this includes money. How important is sharing money in community?
- Jesus warns against mammon and "the deceitfulness of wealth." How might pooling money and possessions be a protection against these destructive powers?

Related Scripture: 1 Timothy 5 and 6; 2 Corinthians 8:1–15

- What is your experience when it comes to children in community?
- Why is it difficult for families to live in community? What can communities do to better accommodate the needs of families?
- Moore writes that "what is good for children is good for the community." Has this been true in your experience?

Related Scripture: Matthew 18:1–14

- Single people and married couples have unique needs and unique contributions to make in community. What are they?
- In what ways do married couples and singles need each other?
- Since people living in community are not exempt from sexual temptation, boundaries are needed. What might those boundaries be?

Related Scripture: 1 Corinthians 7

- How is solitude, as described in this chapter, more than just being alone?
- People often think community and solitude are mutually exclusive. Why is this a mistake?
- What would you say to someone who says: "Community is not for me – I'm the kind of person who needs a lot of space"?
- How and when do you make time for solitude in your own life?

Related Scripture: Mark 1:35–39; Luke 10:38–41

- What does it mean to be transparent?
- Is there a risk of being too transparent in community? What needs to happen for transparency to be healthy and safe?
- If confession is a blessing, why is it so hard to confess our sins to one another?

Related Scripture: 1 John 1; 2 Corinthians 6:11–13

- Before reading this chapter, what did you think about church discipline?
- How has this chapter helped you understand what church discipline is and why it is important?
- Have you experienced a member having to leave your community or church? Could that relationship have been restored through repentance, church discipline, and forgiveness?

Related Scripture: 1 Corinthians 5:1–13; 2 Corinthians 2:5–11

- Why is it sometimes so hard to forgive each other?

- What insights in this chapter have helped you understanding the value of forgiveness?

- What do you think about the advice Thomas à Kempis gave to his monks?

Related Scripture: Matthew 6:14–15; 18:21–35; Luke 17:1–10; Ephesians 4:32

- In what way is the "common table" more than a piece of furniture?

- Why is regularly sharing meals so important for community life?

- In what ways might sharing meals be an act of resistance against the forces that dominate people's lives today?

Related Scripture: Matthew 9:9–13; 14:13–21; Acts 2:46

- Why is celebrating and feasting important? Besides those mentioned in this chapter, can you think of other reasons?

- Why stop for tea? Do you?

- Is celebrating the same thing as partying? What's the difference?

- From your experience, what makes for a good celebration?

Related Scripture: Psalm 150; John 2:1–11

PART IV

Beyond the Community

- ◆ Ehrenpreis asserts that Christian community is the best way to put love for the poor into practice. What does this mean?

- ◆ What does Perkins mean by a "quiet revolution"?

- ◆ Of the three Rs that Perkins outlines, which do you think is the hardest to practice?

- ◆ What do you think about Perkins's view of "structural change"? Is it realistic?

Related Scripture: Matthew 5:13–16; 13:1–43;
1 Thessalonians 4:1–12

- ◆ What does Peterson mean by sectarianism and why is it so bad?

- ◆ How can we as Christians combat the natural tendency to congregate with people like us?

- ◆ Trueblood says the church must always be finding new ways to transcend itself. What does he mean? How might we do that?

Related Scripture: 1 Corinthians 5:9–11; 14:22–25;
2 Corinthians 6:14–18

- ◆ Are walls or fences always bad? Why or why not?

- ◆ In reaching out to others, a community is always at risk of losing itself. How so?

- ◆ What questions do you have after reading this chapter?

Related Scripture: James 2:1–13; 2 John 7–11

- ◆ What is Moore's main caution about communities that are formed around a mission?

- ◆ Why does he suggest that "mankind is not my neighbor"? Do you agree?

- ◆ Have you ever experienced a community pulled apart by some good cause or mission?

Related Scripture: John 13:34–35; Romans 15:23–29; Galatians 6:9–10

- ◆ The authors of this chapter assert that the "church's freshness always breaks through in the form of an interruption." What do they mean by this?

- ◆ What kind of interruptions do you resist or resent?

- ◆ What's so good about the "gift of the stranger"?

Related Scripture: Galatians 3:26–28; Acts 10 and 11

- ◆ Why is hospitality so important for a community?

- ◆ What prevents us from extending hospitality to others?

- ◆ Pohl says that "sometimes welcome must be limited and distinctions made." How does this square with the ideal of unconditional love and God's great mercy?

♦ Pohl ends with some tough questions. Discuss them. Are there other questions you might add?

Related Scripture: Hebrews 13:1–3

50. Connections **331**

♦ Why do communities need to be connected with other communities?

♦ The relationship between "community" and the "church" is a complex one. Of the models Janzen mentions, which one do you tend to favor? Why?

♦ What do you find most helpful from this chapter?

Related Scripture: Romans 15:23—16:27; 1 Corinthians 16; 2 Corinthians 8:1–15

51. Wounds **336**

♦ What does Doherty mean when she says we must show the wounds of Christ to people? Why is this so important?

♦ How might Loring's piece illuminate or complement Doherty's thoughts?

♦ Why is Loring's question, "How may I be helpful?" so important?

Related Scripture: Luke 10:25–37

52. Mercy **342**

♦ Is it possible to have a living community without performing works of mercy?

♦ Have you ever "kissed a leper"? Did it change you?

♦ Day says, "Love must be tried and tested and proved . . . as though by fire." Having read this book, are you ready to get closer to the fire?

Related Scripture: Matthew 11:25–30; Luke 3:11; 7:36–50

Further Reading

The Community of the King, Howard A. Snyder
Biblical insights on the church as the community of God's people
and his agent in reconciling all things.

The Community of the Spirit, C. Norman Kraus
This concise theology of Christian community connects salvation
and reconciliation with the body of God's people.

Discipleship, J. Heinrich Arnold
A pastor's insights on following Jesus in the daily grind of community living.

Follow Me, Ivan J. Kauffman
A history of monastic and lay communities throughout Christian
history including both Catholic and Evangelical traditions.

God's Revolution, Eberhard Arnold
Short selections on the themes of community, living in accordance
with God's justice, and the presence of God's kingdom.

Homage to a Broken Man, Peter Mommsen
This biography of J. Heinrich Arnold tells the story of a community
that lost its focus on Jesus and how through struggle, repentance,
and forgiveness the tracks were reset.

The Intentional Community Handbook, David Janzen
The nitty-gritty of what it takes to live in intentional community.
Janzen weaves together real-life stories with biblical reflection.

Jesus and Community, Gerhard Lohfink
This in-depth study on the church as a contrast community draws
on the Old and New Testaments and early Christian writings.

A Joyful Pilgrimage, Emmy Arnold
A lively, firsthand account of the beginnings of the Bruderhof
community.

Life Together, Dietrich Bonhoeffer
Bonhoeffer explains the role prayer, confession, the Word, solitude,
and ministry play in Christian community.

Living in Christian Community, Arthur G. Gish
Gish provides both biblical insights and practical advice on living in community from an Anabaptist perspective.

The Mark of a Christian, Francis A. Schaeffer
An exposition of Jesus' commandment to love one another. Schaeffer reminds the reader that love, and the unity it attests to, is the final apologetic for the truth of the gospel.

Paul's Idea of Community, Robert J. Banks
A non-technical look at how the first Christians gathered in small household communities and what this means for the church today.

A Peculiar People, Rodney Clapp
The church is not a religious institution but a distinct community whose alternative way of life subverts the dominant powers and practices of this age.

The People Called, Paul D. Hanson
This major work of biblical theology demonstrates how community is the overriding vision of God's plan of redemption.

Pilgrims of a Common Life, Trevor Saxby
A sourcebook that traces the practice of Christian community of goods from the early church to today.

Why We Live in Community, Eberhard Arnold
A call to community by the founder of the Bruderhof, with a reflective response by Thomas Merton.

Sources and Acknowledgements

Plough sincerely thanks each of the authors who contributed to this book, and the publishers and estates that allowed us to include the work of writers who are no longer living. All selections, except those that are in the public domain, are reprinted with the express permission of the author, publisher, or agent in question. Quotations from scripture follow the translation preferences of the individual writers and translators.

PART I: A Call to Community

1. **The Great Idea:** Fyodor Dostoyevsky, *The Brothers Karamazov,* trans. Constance Garnett (New York: Macmillan, 1912).

2. **Blessed Community:** Rufus Jones, *Rufus Jones: Essential Writings,* ed. Kerry Walters (Maryknoll, NY: Orbis Books, 2001), 111–115, 120–122.

3. **Style of Life:** Christoph Friedrich Blumhardt, *Action in Waiting* (Rifton, NY: Plough Publishing House, 2012), 139–144.

4. **Embodiment:** Gerhard Lohfink, *Does God Need the Church? Toward a Theology of the People of God,* trans. Linda M. Maloney (Collegeville, MN: The Liturgical Press, 1999), 261–264. Copyright © 1999 by Order of Saint Benedict. Reprinted with permission.

5. **Brothers, Sisters:** Hal Miller, "Church as Family," *Voices in the Wilderness,* reprinted at http:// www.home-church.org. Joseph H. Hellerman, "A Family Affair," *Christianity Today,* May 2010, 43–46.

6. **Pentecost:** C. Norman Kraus, *The Community of the Spirit* (Grand Rapids, MI: Wm. B. Eerdmans, 1974), 9–16, 24–25. Used by permission of Wipf and Stock Publishers, www.wipfandstock.com.

7. **Christian Communism:** Ulrich Stadler "Cherished Instructions," ca. 1537, in *Anabaptism in Outline,* ed. Walter Klaassen (Walden, NY: Plough Publishing House, 2019), 107–108. José P. Miranda, *Communism in the Bible* (Maryknoll, NY: Orbis Books, 1987), 7–11. Helmut Gollwitzer, *Vortrupp des Lebens* (München: Chr. Kaiser Verlag, 1975), trans. Marjorie Hindley.

8. **A Visible Reality:** Dietrich Bonhoeffer, *The Cost of Discipleship,* trans. Reginald H. Fuller (London: SCM Press, 1959), 212, 223–232. From *The Cost of Discipleship* by Dietrich Bonhoeffer, translated from the German by R.H. Fuller, with revisions by Irmgard Booth. Copyright © 1959 by SCM Press Ltd. Reprinted with the permission of Scribner, a division of Simon & Schuster, Inc. All rights reserved.

9. **Counterculture:** Howard A. Snyder, *Liberating the Church: The Ecology of Church and Kingdom* (Downers Grove, IL: InterVarsity Press, 1983), 118–126, abridged for this collection.

10. **The Way:** Alden Bass, written for this collection.

PART II: Forming Community

11. **A Vision:** George MacDonald, *Thomas Wingfold, Curate* (New York: G. Routledge and Sons, 1876).

12. **Life's Task:** Eberhard Arnold, transcript, October 8, 1933 (Bruderhof Historical Archive EA 163) and Eberhard Arnold, transcript, March 18, 1932 (Bruderhof Historical Archive EA 4), translated from the German and abridged for this collection.

13. **It Takes Work:** Charles E. Moore, written for this collection.

14. **Communion:** Thomas R. Kelly, *A Testament of Devotion* (New York: Harper and Brothers, 1941), 82–83, 86–87. Arthur G. Gish, *Living in Christian Community* (Scottdale, PA: Herald Press, 1979), 65–68. Charles E. Moore, written for this collection.

15. **Idealism:** Dietrich Bonhoeffer, *Life Together,* trans. John W. Doberstein (New York: Harper and Row, 1954), 26–30. English translation copyright © 1954 by Harper & Brothers, copyright renewed 1982 by Helen S. Doberstein. Reprinted by permission of HarperCollins Publishers.

16. **Illusions:** Arthur Katz, *True Fellowship: Church as Community* (Bemidji, MN: Burning Bush Press, 2009), 10–12. Elizabeth O'Connor, *Journey Inward, Journey Outward* (New York: Harper and Row, 1968), 25–27, 54–55 . Copyright © 1968 by Elizabeth O'Connor. Reprinted by permission of HarperCollins Publishers.

17. **Obstacles:** Eberhard Arnold, transcript, August 9, 1933 (Bruderhof Historical Archive EA 139) trans. Kathleen Hasenberg. Eberhard Arnold, transcript, July 26, 1933 (Bruderhof Historical Archive EA 125), previously published in English as "A Personal Word by Eberhard Arnold Spoken on the Occasion of His Fiftieth Birthday," in *Eberhard Arnold: A Testimony to Church Community from His Life and Writings* (Rifton, NY: Plough Publishing House, 1973), 29–33.

18. **Poisons:** C. S. Lewis, *The Screwtape Letters* (New York: Macmillan, 1982), 95–99. Copyright © 1942 C. S. Lewis Pte. Ltd. Extract reprinted by permission. Basilea Schlink, "Being Annoyed" in *You Will Never Be the Same,* (Minneapolis, MN: Dimension Books, 1972), 124–126.

19. **Listening:** Henri J. M. Nouwen, *Compassion: A Reflection on the Christian Life* (London: Darton, Longman and Todd, 2008), 79–80.

Henri J. M. Nouwen, *Making All Things New: An Invitation to the Spiritual Life* (San Francisco: Harper and Row, 1981), 83–88. Dietrich Bonhoeffer, *Life Together*, trans. John W. Doberstein (New York: Harper and Row, 1954), 97–99.

20. **Surrender:** Arthur G. Gish, *Living in Christian Community* (Scottdale, PA: Herald Press, 1979), 46–56.

21. **The Center:** Dietrich Bonhoeffer, *Life Together,* trans. John W. Doberstein (New York: Harper and Row, 1954), 21, 25–26, 32–37. Friedrich Wilhelm Foerster, *Christ and the Human Life* (New York: Philosophical Library, 1953), 323–324.

22. **God's Call:** Henri J. M. Nouwen, *Reaching Out: The Three Movements of the Spiritual Life* (Garden City, NY: Doubleday, 1986), 153–155. Copyright © 1975 by Henri J. M. Nouwen. Copyright renewed 2003 by Sue Mosteller, Executor of the Estate of Henri J. M. Nouwen. Used by permission of Doubleday, an imprint of Knopf Doubleday Publishing Group, a division of Penguin Random House LLC. All rights reserved. Henri J. M. Nouwen, *Compassion: A Reflection on the Christian Life* (London: Darton, Longman, and Todd, 2008), 81–82, 84. Eberhard Arnold, "Why We Live in Community," *Plough Quarterly* no. 18, Autumn 2018, 77–78. Andreas Ehrenpreis, *Brotherly Community: The Highest Command of Love* (Walden, NY: Plough Publishing House, 2016), 13–15.

23. **Promises:** Jonathan Wilson-Hartgrove, *The Awakening of Hope: Why We Practice a Common Faith* (Grand Rapids, MI: Zondervan, 2012), 67–71, 82–86. Copyright © 2012 by Jonathan Wilson-Hartgrove. Used by Permission of Zondervan, www.zondervan.com. Nicholas Ludwig von Zinzendorf, *A Collection of Sermons from Zinzendorf's Pennsylvania Journey, 1741–42,* trans. Julie Tomberlin Weber (Bethlehem, PA: Interprovincial Board of Communication Moravian Church in North America, 2001), 16–17.

PART III: Life in Community

24. **Love:** Thomas Merton, *No Man Is an Island* (New York: Harcourt Brace Jovanovich, 1978), 3–7, 9–10, 166–167, 169–170. Copyright © 1955 by The Abbey of Our Lady of Gethsemani and renewed 1983 by the Trustees of the Merton Legacy Trust. Reprinted by permission of Houghton Mifflin Harcourt Publishing Company. All rights reserved. Søren Kierkegaard, *Provocations,* ed. Charles E. Moore (Farmington, PA: Plough Publishing House, 1999), 110–113.

25. **Deeds:** Mother Teresa, *No Greater Love* (Novato, CA: New World Library, 2002), 22–23, 26–27, 30, 68–69. Thomas E. Powers, *24*

Magazine Vol. 5, No. 4, Winter 1975–76, 8. Eberhard Arnold, *Eberhard Arnold: Writings Selected* (Maryknoll NY: Orbis Books, 2000), 80. Eberhard Arnold, *Foundations and Orders of Sannerz and the Rhon Bruderhof, 1920–1929* (Rifton, NY: Plough Publishing House, 1976), 15, 23. John F. Alexander, *Being Church: Reflections on How to Live as the People of God.* (Eugene, OR: Cascade Books, 2012), 185. Used by permission of Wipf and Stock Publishers, www.wipfandstock.com

26. **Vocation:** John F. Alexander, *Being Church: Reflections on How to Live as the People of God.* (Eugene, OR: Cascade Books, 2012), 70–82.

27. **Acceptance:** Jürgen Moltmann, *The Open Church: Invitation to a Messianic Lifestyle* (London: SCM Press Ltd, 1978), 27–33. Copyright © 2012 SCM Press Ltd. Used by permission of Hymns Ancient & Modern Ltd. All rights reserved. Adele J. Gonzalez, *The Spirituality of Community* (Maryknoll, NY: Orbis Books, 2009), 88–90.

28. **Irritations:** Anthony de Mello, *The Way to Love: Meditations for Life* (New York: Image, 2012), 85–88. Copyright © 1991 by Gujarat Sahitya Prakash of Anand, India. Used by permission of Doubleday, an imprint of the Knopf Doubleday Publishing Group, a division of Penguin Random House LLC. All rights reserved. Roy Hession, *The Calvary Road* (London: Christian Literature Crusade, 1950), 21–22. Thomas à Kempis, *The Imitation of Christ: A New Reading of the 1441 Latin Autograph Manuscript,* ed. and trans. William C. Creasy (Macon, GA: Mercer University Press, 2015), 16–17. Eberhard Arnold, August 1925 (Bruderhof Historical Archive EA 25/13), previously published in English in *God's Revolution: Justice, Community, and the Coming Kingdom* (Farmington, PA: Plough Publishing House, 1997), 113–114.

29. **Differences:** Joan Chittister and Rowan Williams, *Uncommon Gratitude: Alleluia for All That Is* (Collegeville, MN: Liturgical Press, 2010), 31–44. Copyright © 2010 by Order of Saint Benedict. Reprinted with permission. Henri J. M. Nouwen, Donald P. McNeill, and Douglas A. Morrison, *Compassion: A Reflection on the Christian Life* (London: Darton, Longman and Todd, 2008), 77–78. Copyright © 1982 by Donald P. McNeill, Douglas A. Morrison, and Henri J. M. Nouwen. Used by permission of Doubleday, an imprint of Knopf Doubleday Publishing Group, a division of Penguin Random House LLC. All rights reserved.

30. **Conflict:** David Janzen, *The Intentional Christian Community Handbook* (Brewster, MA: Paraclete Press, 2013), 111–117. Copyright © 2013 by David Janzen. Used by permission of Paraclete Press, www.paracletepress.com. Sister Penelope Lawson *This Is Life: A Book for the Busy* (London, SCM Press, 1960), 109–112. Hans Denck, "Concerning

the Love of God," 1526, in *Anabaptism in Outline,* ed. Walter Klaasen (Walden, NY: Plough Publishing House, 2019), 216. Amy Carmichael, in Frank Houghton, *Amy Carmichael of Dohnavur* (Fort Washington, PA: Christian Literature Crusade, 1979), 219, 349–50.

31. **Unity:** Peter Riedemann, *Love Is Like Fire: The Confession of an Anabaptist Prisoner* (Walden, NY: Plough Publishing House, 2016), 65–67. Chiara Lubich, *Essential Writings: Spirituality, Dialogue, Culture* (New York: New City Press, 2007), 102, 80–81. Stephen B. Clark, ed., *Patterns of Christian Community: A Statement of Community Order* (Ann Arbor, MI: Servant Books, 1984), 65–74.

32. **Dialogue:** Elizabeth O'Connor, *The New Community* (New York: Harper & Row, 1976), 102–105. Reprinted by The Potter's House Press, 2015. C. Christopher Smith, *How the Body of Christ Talks* (Grand Rapids, MI: Brazos Press, 2019), 48–49, 90–91. Used by permission of Brazos Press, a division of Baker Publishing Group.

33. **Leadership:** J. Heinrich Arnold, *Discipleship: Living for Christ in the Daily Grind* (Walden, NY: Plough Publishing, 2014), 106–116.

34. **Submission:** Richard J. Foster, *Celebration of Discipline* (New York, NY: Harper San Francisco, 1988), 111–114. Copyright © 1978 by Richard J. Foster. Reprinted by permission of HarperCollins Publishers and of Hodder and Stoughton Ltd. John F. Alexander, *Being Church: Reflections on How to Live as the People of God.* (Eugene, OR: Cascade Books, 2012), 229–232.

35. **Money:** Jodi Garbison, "An Uncommon Purse," in *Cherith Brook Catholic Worker,* Lent 2011, 4. Jenny and Justin Duckworth, *Against the Tide, Toward the Kingdom* (Eugene, OR: Cascade Books, 2011), 63–66. Used by permission of Wipf and Stock Publishers, www.wipfandstock. com.

36. **Children:** Charles E. Moore, written for this collection.

37. **Family Values:** Andy Crouch, "Extended-Family Values: Why Married and Single People Need Each Other," *re:generation quarterly,* Summer 1997.

38. **Solitude:** Henri J.M. Nouwen, *Clowning in Rome: Reflections on Solitude, Celibacy, Prayer, and Contemplation* (Garden City, NY: Doubleday, 1979) 13–16. Copyright © 1979 by Henri J. M. Nouwen. Revised edition copyright © 2000 by the Estate of Henri J. M. Nouwen. Used by permission of Doubleday, an imprint of Knopf Doubleday Publishing Group, a division of Penguin Random House LLC. All rights reserved. Eberhard Arnold, transcript, July 30, 1933 (Bruderhof

Historical Archive EA 124), previously published in English as "The Creative Pause," *The Plough,* November 1984, 7–8.

39. **Transparency:** Roy Hession, *The Calvary Road* (London: Christian Literature Crusade, 1950), 11–16. Dietrich Bonhoeffer, *Life Together,* trans. John W. Doberstein (New York: Harper and Row, 1954), 111–112.

40. **Repentance:** St. Benedict of Nursia, *The Rule of Saint Benedict: A Contemporary Paraphrase,* paraphrase by Jonathan Wilson-Hartgrove (Brewster, MA: Paraclete Press, 2012), 51–52. Copyright © 2012 Jonathan Wilson-Hartgrove. Used by permission of Paraclete Press, www.paracletepress.com. Johann Christoph Arnold, *Seventy Times Seven: The Power of Forgiveness* (Farmington, PA: Plough Publishing House, 1997), 146–151. J. Heinrich Arnold, *Discipleship: Living for Christ in the Daily Grind* (Rifton, NY: Plough Publishing House, 2011), 134–140.

41. **Forgiveness:** Johann Christoph Arnold, adapted from *Seventy Times Seven: The Power of Forgiveness* (Farmington, PA: Plough Publishing House, 1997), 14–30 and *Seeking Peace: Notes and Conversations along the Way* (Farmington, PA: Plough Publishing House, 1998), 102–106.

42. **At Table:** Leonardo Boff, "Table Fellowship: Rebuilding Humanity," trans. Anne Fullerton, April 18, 2008, http://www.leonardoboff.com. Dietrich Bonhoeffer, *Life Together,* trans. John W. Doberstein (New York: Harper and Row, 1954), 67–69.

43. **Celebration:** Richard J. Foster, *Celebration of Discipline* (New York, NY: Harper San Francisco, 1988), 190–191, 196–198. Juan Mateos, *Beyond Conventional Christianity* (Manila: East Asian Pastoral Institute, 1974), 256–257, 264–265, 311–313. Jeremiah Barker, "Feasting at Teatime," *Plough Quarterly* No. 36, Summer 2023, 10–11.

PART IV: Beyond the Community

44. **Revolution:** Andreas Ehrenpreis, *Brotherly Community: The Highest Command of Love* (Walden, NY: Plough Publishing House, 2016), 25–28, 49–50. John Perkins, *A Quiet Revolution: The Christian Response to Human Need, a Strategy for Today* (Waco, TX: Word Books, 1976), 213–216.

45. **Comfort Zones:** Eugene H. Peterson, *Christ Plays in Ten Thousand Places: A Conversation in Spiritual Theology* (Grand Rapids, MI: Wm. B. Eerdmans, 2005), 239–242, 244. Copyright © 2005 Wm. B. Eerdmans Publishing Co. Reprinted by permission of the publisher; all rights reserved. Elton Trueblood, *The Company of the Committed* (New York: Harper & Brothers, 1961), 68–69.

46. **Good Fences:** Elizabeth Dede, "Something There Is That Doesn't Love a Wall" in *A Work of Hospitality: The Open Door Reader, 1982–2002*, ed. Peter R. Gathje, (Atlanta: The Open Door Community, 2002), 328–331. Charles E. Moore, written for this collection.

47. **Next Door:** Charles E. Moore, written for this collection.

48. **Interruptions:** Emmanuel Katongole and Chris Rice, *Reconciling All Things: A Christian Vision for Justice, Peace and Healing* (Downers Grove, IL: InterVarsity Press, 2008), 110–117.

49. **Hospitality:** Christine D. Pohl, *Making Room: Recovering Hospitality as a Christian Tradition* (Grand Rapids, MI: Wm. B. Eerdmans, 1999), 127–132. Copyright © 1999 Wm. B. Eerdmans Publishing Co. Reprinted by permission of the publisher; all rights reserved. Kathleen Norris, *Amazing Grace: A Vocabulary of Faith* (New York: Riverhead Books, 1998), 264–266. Excerpt(s) from *Amazing Grace* by Kathleen Norris, copyright © 1998 by Kathleen Norris. Used by permission of Riverhead, an imprint of Penguin Publishing Group, a division of Penguin Random House LLC. All rights reserved.

50. **Connections:** David Janzen, adapted from *The Intentional Christian Community Handbook* (Brewster, MA: Paraclete Press, 2013), 173–189.

51. **Wounds:** Catherine de Hueck Doherty, *The Gospel without Compromise* (Notre Dame, IN: Ave Maria Press, 1976), 88–91. Ed Loring, *I Hear Hope Banging at My Back Door: Writings from Hospitality* (Atlanta: The Open Door Community, 2000), 67–70.

52. **Mercy:** Dorothy Day, *Dorothy Day: Selected Writings,* ed. Robert Ellsberg (Maryknoll, NY: Orbis Books, 2005), 98–99, 109–110, 227–228. Copyright © 1983, 1992, 2005 by Robert Ellsberg and Tamar Hennessey.

Index of Authors

If you liked *Called to Community*
you should have the companion volume . . .

Following the Call
Living the Sermon on the Mount Together

400 pages, softcover,
5.5 x 8 $18.00

**Eberhard Arnold • Wendell Berry • Dorothy Day
Meister Eckhart • Søren Kierkegaard • C. S. Lewis
Richard Rohr • Dorothy L. Sayers • Mother Teresa
Leo Tolstoy • N. T. Wright • and others**

I strongly recommend
this book for study,
reflection, and
prayerful living.

Richard J. Foster,
author of *Celebration
of Discipline*

Edited by Charles E. Moore

Jesus' most famous teaching, the Sermon on the Mount,
possesses an irresistible quality. Who hasn't felt stirred and
unsettled after reading these words, which get to the root of the
human condition?

This follow-up to *Called to Community* taps an even broader
array of sources, bringing together prophetic voices from every
era and a range of traditions to consider the repercussions of
these essential words.

More than a commentary or devotional, this book is designed
to be read together with others, to inspire communities of faith
to discuss what it might look like to put Jesus' teachings into
practice today.

**Fifty-two readings
to spark discussion
on putting Jesus'
most central
teaching into
practice.**

"**As I read this collection,** I tried to imagine the authors of the various
reflections in conversation. What would Leo Tolstoy say to Karl Barth, or
Francis of Assisi to Wendell Berry? The more I read, though, the more I
started to imagine all of them in one place – listening to Jesus give the
Sermon on the Mount. And, before long, I found myself blending into
the crowd with them, hearing these strange, arresting, upending words
of life. This book will prompt you to surprise, to delight, to melancholy,
to argument, and, at every turn, will lead you back to Jesus."
Russell Moore, *Christianity Today*

Other Titles from Plough

Why We Live in Community
Eberhard Arnold and Thomas Merton
Everyone's talking about community these days. Arnold and Merton suggest it
can be lived, too.

Salt and Light: Living the Sermon on the Mount
Eberhard Arnold
Thoughts on the "hard teachings" of Jesus and their applicability today

God's Revolution: Justice, Community, and the Coming Kingdom
Eberhard Arnold
Topically arranged excerpts from talks and writings on the church, family, govern-
ment, world suffering, and more

Watch for the Light: Readings for Advent and Christmas
Dietrich Bonhoeffer, Annie Dillard, Thomas Merton, C. S. Lewis, and others
Selections from some of the world's greatest spiritual writers provide inspiration
for the most widely celebrated holiday of the year.

Bread and Wine: Readings for Lent and Easter
**Wendell Berry, Dorothy Sayers, Henri J. M. Nouwen, G. K. Chesterton,
and others**
"Has there ever been a more hard-hitting, beautifully written, theologically inclusive
anthology of writings for Lent and Easter? It's doubtful." —*Publishers Weekly*

Plough Publishing House
845-572-3455 · info@plough.com · **www.plough.com**

151 Bowne Drive, PO Box 398, Walden, NY 12586, USA
Robertsbridge, East Sussex TN32 5DR, UK
4188 Gwydir Highway, Elsmore, NSW 2360, Australia